DEVON & CO
AIRFIELDS
SECOND WORLD WAR

Graham Smith

COUNTRYSIDE BOOKS
NEWBURY, BERKSHIRE

COUNTRYSIDE BOOKS
3 Catherine Road
Newbury, Berkshire

To view our complete range of books,
please visit us at
www.countrysidebooks.co.uk

ISBN 1 85306 632 X

The cover painting is from an original by
Colin Doggett and shows
a Liberator GRV1 of No. 224 squadron attacking
a U-boat off the French Atlantic Coast.

Designed by Mon Mohan

Produced through MRM Associates Ltd., Reading
Printed by Woolnough Bookbinding Ltd., Irthlingborough

CONTENTS

DEVON & CORNWALL'S WORLD WAR II AIRFIELDS

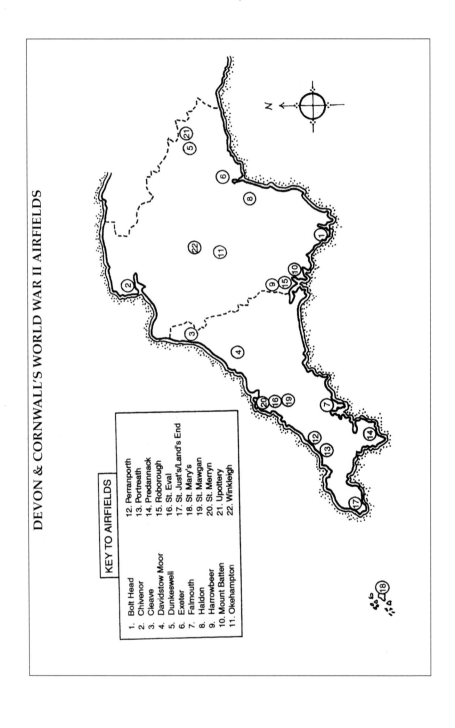

KEY TO AIRFIELDS

1. Bolt Head
2. Chivenor
3. Cleave
4. Davidstow Moor
5. Dunkeswell
6. Exeter
7. Falmouth
8. Haldon
9. Harrowbeer
10. Mount Batten
11. Okehampton
12. Perranporth
13. Portreath
14. Predannack
15. Roborough
16. St. Eval
17. St. Just's/Land's End
18. St. Mary's
19. St. Mawgan
20. St. Merryn
21. Upottery
22. Winkleigh

CONTENTS

I

SETTING
THE SCENE

On 23rd July 1910, as dusk was approaching, thousands of spectators watched spellbound as Claude Grahame-White in his Henry Farman biplane took off from Poniou Meadow just to the east of Penzance; bad weather had delayed an earlier departure. The fragile biplane flew low over Penzance and away in the direction of Newlyn before turning east to pass over Mount's Bay. Some fifteen minutes later when the aeroplane returned to the large field, Grahame-White had accomplished a flight of about six miles. Thus on this summer evening aviation in the South-West was born, just a fraction less than a year after Louis Bleriot's epic flight across the English Channel.

Grahame-White was perhaps the country's foremost aviator, especially since the Hon. Charles S. Rolls had been tragically killed in a flying accident at an aviation meeting at Southborne only eleven days earlier. Grahame-White had also attended this meeting and it was reported that he received over £1,300 from passenger fees and prizes; earlier in April he had been the first airman to fly at night, whilst engaged in an air race from Manchester to London. The reason for his presence in Cornwall was his audacious boast that he would fly over the combined three Fleets, then sheltering in Mount's Bay awaiting a Royal review, and drop an 'imaginary' bomb on the flagship, HMS *Dreadnought*. This quite fearless and talented airman was utterly convinced of a glorious future for aeroplanes, but more especially he

The Henry Farman biplane.

Claude Grahame-White, then perhaps the country's foremost aviator.

fully realised their capabilities for military purposes. Grahame-White considered that his well-publicised flight would be a practical and dramatic demonstration to the Government and military chiefs of the aeroplane's potential as a new weapon of war. Later in the year

Grahame-White would open an aeroplane factory and aerodrome at Hendon, which was grandly styled 'London Aerodrome', where thousands would throng to experience their first taste of flying. Fortunately he lived long enough to see his passionate and abiding faith in powered flight completely vindicated; he died in 1959 aged 80 years.

Twelve months later, in July 1911, a small grassed field at Exeter was used by the competitors in the *Daily Mail* Round Britain Race. This newspaper, under its founder Viscount Northcliffe, had been and would continue to be in the vanguard of support and financial sponsorship for aviation. In June 1912 another celebrated pioneer aviator, Henri Salmet, brought his Bleriot monoplane to Bude, Launceston and Newquay; he was also sponsored by the *Daily Mail*. The following year Grahame-White gave exhibition flights at Torquay, and in September yet another famous airman, Gustav Hamel, flying a Bleriot aeroplane visited Padstow, Portreath and Penzance. During this visit Hamel achieved his ambition to be the first airman to fly to Land's End, but sadly he was lost over the English Channel during May 1914. One month earlier Salmet had returned to the South-West, again financed by the *Daily Mail*. This time he was flying his new Bleriot two-seater, which enabled him to carry a passenger; it could also be adapted into a float-plane.

Since Grahame-White's flight over Mount's Bay, military aviation had made quite remarkable progress. The Royal Flying Corps was constituted by Royal Warrant on 13th April 1912 and formed one month later with a Naval Wing, Military Wing, Central Flying School and a factory for building aeroplanes. Two years later, on 1st July 1914, the Naval Wing became known as the Royal Naval Air Service (RNAS), and gradually the links between the two air services were severed. It would be the RNAS that established a strong aviation presence in the South-West during the latter years of the First World War.

During early 1915 the threat of enemy U-boats became very real – in March four vessels had been sunk near the Scilly Isles – and in an attempt to combat this new menace the Admiralty established a number of airship stations around the coasts, of which five were sited in the South-West, at Mullion, Bude, Laira (near Plymouth), Merryfield (Maryfield) and St Mary's, with an airship mooring post at RNAS Padstow. One of the major airship stations was situated at Mullion on the Lizard Peninsula. This 320 acre site was commissioned in June 1916 and had been provided with a massive airship shed, 300 feet long, 100

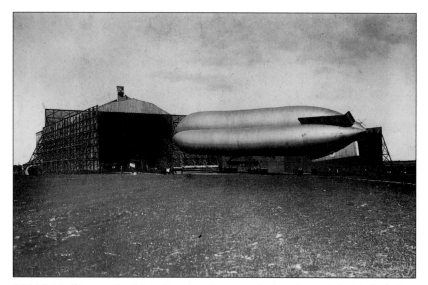

RNAS Mullion on the Lizard peninsula, commissioned as an airship base in 1916. (RAF Museum)

feet wide and 70 feet high, with a second smaller one erected about a year later. Since 1915 the Admiralty had placed their faith in the 'SS' (Submarine Scout) non-rigid airships to seek out the U-boats; Coastal Class and, later, the smaller 'SSZ' or Zero airships operated from these stations, in fact the Zeros were assembled at Mullion. The airships were commonly known as Blimps and as one intrepid Naval airman later recalled, 'To fly a ship on a nice day was a really delightful experience. One felt that the air was entirely one's own . . .'. However, there were a number of accidents, indeed the first Coastal Class airship due for Mullion – 'C.8' – crashed into the sea off Start Point in May 1916, killing three of the four man crew. In March 1917 'C.22' was lost but her four airmen were rescued, and in April 1918 'SSZ.15', which also operated from Mullion, was lost at sea.

Besides these airship stations there were a number of aeroplane and seaplane stations in the area, used by Flights of anti-submarine aircraft operating inshore coastal patrols. The Flights operated from Mullion, Newlyn, Falmouth, Padstow, Prawle Point, St Mary's, Tresco, Torquay, Westward Ho and Cattewater (Plymouth). They were mainly equipped with Short 184 seaplanes, Curtiss H12 Large America flying boats, and de Havilland DH 6 patrol aircraft. The DH 6 was not particularly

9

inspiring either in appearance or apparently to fly, as it was variously called 'The Crab', 'The Clutching Hand' or 'The Flying Coffin!'; perhaps not surprisingly there were several instances of crashes. All these airship, seaplane and aeroplane stations operated under No 9 (Operations) Group, South-West Area, which had its headquarters at Mount Wise, Devonport.

With the formation of the Royal Air Force on 1st April 1918, the Royal Naval Air Service and the Royal Flying Corps were amalgamated. Most of the patrol Flights were upgraded to RAF squadrons, one of which, No 234, operating from Tresco, would return to serve in Cornwall during the Second World War. In August No 71 (Operations) Wing was created at Penzance, with another Wing – No 72 – controlled from Cattewater. After the Armistice in November 1918 few of these stations survived very long; the last airship flight left Mullion in January 1919, and aeroplane operations there ceased two months later. The sheltered haven of Cattewater, Plymouth, which had opened as a RNAS seaplane base in February 1917, survived until 1922 when it was placed on a Care and Maintenance basis. Briefly during August 1922 the Seaplane Development Flight used the facilities at St Mary's, and brought its large flying boats – a couple of Singapore F.2As and a Short Cromarty – for trials.

In May 1919 Plymouth was the scene of an aviation event of some historical moment and importance – the arrival of the first aircraft to successfully cross the Atlantic. Three American Navy-Curtiss NC flying boats – 1, 3 and 4 – commanded by Commander John H. Towers, US Navy, left Trepassy Bay, Newfoundland on 16th May, their first intended stop being Horta in the Azores. However, only NC-4 under the command of Lieutenant-Commander A.C. Read arrived at Horta, the others were forced down onto the sea. NC-1 sank but its crew was rescued, whereas NC-3 with Commander Towers as pilot, taxied the remaining 200 miles to the Azores, but was unable to continue the flight. NC-4 left the Azores alone, flying via Lisbon and Ferrol del Caudillo in Spain, and it eventually arrived at Plymouth on 31st May, being escorted into the harbour by RAF Felixstowe flying boats. The total distance flown was 3,925 miles in just over 57 hours' flying time. Lieutenant-Commander Read and his crew returned in triumph to the United States and NC-4 remains on display in the National Air & Space Museum in Washington. Because of this successful flight the world seemed suddenly a little smaller, an impression that was emphasised a fortnight later by Alcock and Brown's epic non-stop flight across the

Curtiss NC-4 Flying Boat at Plymouth, May 1919. (Smithsonian Institution)

Atlantic in a landplane – a Vickers Vimy bomber.

It was on 1st May 1919 that civil flying returned to the country after the war, with the publication of the Air Navigation Regulations which were intended to impose controls on commercial aviation. With the rapid and almost unseemly rundown of the RAF in the immediate heady years of peacetime Britain, there was a plethora of ex-Service aircraft available for purchase by private individuals. Perhaps the most ubiquitous aircraft of the 1920s was the Avro 504 or the 'Immortal 504' as it became known, one of, if not *the* truly classic training aircraft of all time. Many companies throughout the country bought Avro 504s and offered 'joy rides' to the public, who were more than eager to discover for themselves the excitement of this new form of transport.

One of the first companies into this field of aviation was the Berkshire Aviation Company, which had been formed in May 1919, and it brought its Avro 504s to the South-West in February 1924 offering the public 'joy rides' from rudimentary fields outside a number of towns and villages. It is interesting to note that Alan Cobham, who was so influential in popularising flying during the inter-war years, had been a founder member of the company but had left in 1920 to become involved in aerial photography. By May of the same year Cornwall had its own 'joy riding' company when Captain Percy Phillips, DFC, an ex-RFC pilot, set up the Cornwall Aviation Company Ltd at St Austell, which had

11

originally operated from a field at nearby Rocky Parc. The company would offer pleasure flights in 504s, as well as develop the business of flying banner advertisements, which was such a feature of these post-war years, but operated mainly outside the area.

Commercial aviation in its true sense was born on 25th August 1919 with the first flight of paying passengers from London to Paris. Nevertheless, during the 1920s there were relatively few recognised aerodromes in the country as such. The majority of the flying – both private and commercial – was conducted from rudimentary fields, often with the minimum of facilities for either airman or aircraft. Devon and Cornwall were certainly no exception to this rule. For instance Chelson Meadow, a racecourse just east of the river Plym at Plymouth, which had been used for flying prior to the First World War, was now being used again; in 1923 Alan Cobham flew a trial flight from there to London carrying passengers and mail. He was then working as a pilot (although the term 'driver' was more commonly used!) for the newly formed de Havilland Aeroplane Hire Service, which advertised 'An aeroplane to take you anywhere for 2/- [10p] a mile'! In the same year a polo field at Roborough, just to the north-east of Plymouth, was also being used for flying, and by 1929 the Plymouth Aero Club would be based there. In the same year Haldon, near Teignmouth, was the venue of a public flying meeting, which was held at a field close to the golf course. Also in 1929 (August) the golf course at St Mary's in the Isles of Scilly was used for the first time for private aircraft.

Just a year earlier, on 1st October, RAF Cattewater reopened after considerable and prolonged construction work had been completed at the old First World War site, as well as on extra land that had been purchased, to make it into a large permanent Service station. In 1929 the name of the station was changed to Mount Batten and it quickly developed into a major RAF marine station. During the pre-war years Mount Batten would house all of the Service's main flying boats – Supermarine Southamptons, Walruses and Stranraers, Saro Londons, Short Singapores, Blackburn Irises and Perths and finally Short Sunderlands – as well as a number of smaller seaplanes and floatplanes, such as Hawker Ospreys, Fairey IIIFs and Swordfish.

It was during the early 1930s that flying really caught the public's imagination and interest, its popularity seemed to know no bounds. The first Empire Air Day was celebrated in May 1934 when RAF and civil aerodromes were opened to the public to view new aircraft and be treated to air displays. They attracted large and enthusiastic crowds, as

12

did the various Air Races, especially the prestigious King's Cup. Much of this popularity was due to the drive and enthusiasm of Sir Alan Cobham, KBE, AFC (he had been knighted in 1926) and his so-called Air or Flying Circus, which was billed as the 'World's Greatest Air Pageant'. It toured the length and breadth of the country with Sir Alan's avowed intention of making Great Britain 'air minded'. In August 1932, his 'Circus' was at Teignmouth, Wadebridge, Camelford, Camborne, Penzance, Plymouth, Okehampton and Bude. In the following three years a number of other towns in Devon and Cornwall were visited. The final appearance of his 'Ferry Show' took place at Sidmouth on 24th August 1935, whereas two days later his 'Astra Show' completed an engagement at Penzance. On these National Aviation Days, as they were known, thousands of spectators were treated to aerobatic displays, stunt and 'crazy' flying, wing-walking and parachuting; also it was estimated that well over one million people throughout the country had experienced the joy of flying for the first time.

Despite the public's obvious fascination with flying there were under 3,500 licensed pilots in the country in 1934, of whom only 6% were women, notwithstanding the well-publicised flying exploits of the Duchess of Bedford, Lady Bailey, Amy Johnson and Jean Batten. Furthermore there were only some 1,170 aircraft registered in the country, and according to the *Progress of Civil Aviation* published in

Sir Alan Cobham's 'Flying Circus' in the early 1930s. (Flight Refuelling Ltd via Colin Cruddas)

13

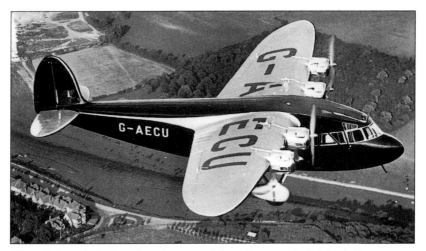

Short Scion: A similar aircraft operated from Barnstaple & North Devon Airport from 1935.

1935, there were just 90 aerodromes or landing grounds operating in the previous year, of which 21 were municipal. In 1930 Roborough had been taken over by the Plymouth Corporation, and an airfield close to Barnstaple used in the summer of 1932 by a local flying club would later become known as the North Devon Airport with services to Lundy Island, using Short Scions, as well as routes further west. Haldon was being used by the Great Western Railway for an air service from Cardiff to Plymouth in April 1933, and four years later it would host a Devon Air Day. Over the next few years a number of new aerodromes appeared; Lundy Island, Denbury (Torbay), Trebelzue (Newquay), Dawlish, Ilfracombe, St Just's (Land's End), St Merryn, and Exeter (the second municipal 'airport' in Devon, which opened in May 1937) operating a variety of passenger services, mainly to encourage the summer tourist trade. Shortly before the outbreak of the Second World War a new airfield was opened at St Mary's, which would be one of a number of civil airfields (St Just's) to remain open throughout the war. Nevertheless, in 1939, it was stated that there were just 105 aerodromes that were licensed as 'permanent'.

Although there were several flying clubs and schools in the two counties, the cost of flying was high and thus was still a rather exclusive pastime; the average flying instruction fees were in the region of 30 shillings (£1.50) per hour, putting it well beyond the aspirations of the general public. However, in 1938 the Civil Air Guard was launched by the Government, with the intention of bringing flying instruction within the reach of the average man and woman and creating a reserve of trained pilots. For about £10 a member of the Civil Air Guard could receive one year's flying instruction, the commitment was an undertaking to accept service in any capacity with aviation in a state of war emergency. The response was quite amazing; over 34,000 applied in the first two weeks, of whom about 4,000 were enrolled. By July 1939 well over 3,000 had gained their pilot's licence by this method, and many ultimately served in the RAF or the Air Auxiliary Transport during the war. Certainly pilot training under the Civil Air Guard scheme took place at both North Devon Airport at Barnstaple and Exeter.

At the outbreak of war the Air Navigation (Restricted in Time of War) Order was promulgated: all club and private flying ceased, most of the aerodromes were closed and many were requisitioned by either the Air Ministry or the Admiralty. Mount Batten was the only operational Service station in the two counties, although Cleave was being used as a basic landing ground from early 1939 and St Eval opened in late 1939. The next few years would see a rapid and dramatic change. The Royal Air Force along with units of the Fleet Air Arm, the United States Army Air Force and the United States Navy would operate from a number of the pre-war civil and private airfields along with thirteen new wartime airfields. Virtually all the famous (and some less familiar) Allied aircraft of the Second World War operated from these airfields with notable success, and yet less than thirty years had elapsed since Grahame-White's brief flight.

The Royal Air Force

At the outbreak of the Second World War the Royal Air Force was by far the junior Armed Service. It had been in existence for barely twenty-one years, and its progress thus far had been less than easy. In its early years the Service had been compelled to fight doggedly to retain its independence, and then when its survival was ensured, it suffered from a woeful lack of public funds to develop and expand, although for most of these so-called 'peacetime' years, its airmen had been in action in some corner of the world.

The RAF in the early 1930s, although small, was nevertheless very professional, highly motivated and technically well trained both in the air and on the ground. This was largely due to the legacy of Viscount Trenchard, Chief of the Air Staff from 1919 to 1929, and who was known as 'The Father of the RAF', a title he abhored! Trenchard had established the Officer Cadet College at Cranwell, a Staff College for senior officers at Andover, as well as the Apprentices School at Halton. He had also introduced the short service commission scheme for pilots with four years on the active list followed by six years on the reserve. During his period of tenure the Auxiliary Air Force and University Air squadrons had been inaugurated and the Officers' Engineering School at Henlow produced a constant stream of highly skilled aeronautical engineers for the Service, most notably Sir Frank Whittle. Perhaps the really radical change to be introduced after Trenchard's departure was the formation of the RAF Volunteer Reserve in April 1937, which began to take men of non-commissioned rank for pilot training; hitherto virtually all pilots had been officers in the General Duties branch. RAFVR airmen would

Air Marshal Trenchard, the Chief of the Air Staff, inspects the first aircraft apprentices to pass out of Halton, 17th December 1924. (RAF Museum)

16

make an invaluable contribution to the operational squadrons.

In 1935 the RAF was still essentially a biplane Force, but by 1939 this situation had radically changed due largely to the massive expansion of the Service in the late thirties. It was now predominantly equipped with monoplanes with most of the famous wartime aircraft either in service or well along the design and development stages. Numerically there was also a considerable difference, from about 3,000 aircraft (including reserves) in 1935 to some 10,000, of which about one fifth could be considered front-line, although amongst this number were some aircraft that proved to be of dubious operational value and no match for the Luftwaffe, most notably the Fairey Battle.

The Service had been comprehensively reorganised ready to fight an air war. In July 1936 the old 'Air Defence of Great Britain', which had been created in 1925, was dissolved, and in its place four separate and functional Commands were formed, each with a precise and specific role – Bomber, Fighter, Coastal and Training – to be followed later by several other Commands. This was the basic structure under which the Royal Air Force waged its bitter and costly war. The only real major change was the formation of Tactical Air Forces during 1943.

It was this Service, some 175,000 strong, that would face the might of the Luftwaffe, then considered to be the most powerful air force in the world. However, few realised just how quickly these airmen would be faced with their sternest test or indeed the major contribution they would ultimately make in the difficult years ahead. On the first day of the war, HM King George VI sent a personal message to all members of the Service: '[In] the campaign which we now have been compelled to undertake you will have to assume responsibilities far greater than those which your Service had to shoulder in the last War. One of the gravest will be the safeguarding of these Islands from the menace of the air. I can assure all ranks of the Air Force of my supreme confidence in their skill and courage and in their ability to meet whatever calls may be made upon them.' The RAF went into action just after noon on Sunday 3rd September 1939 and almost six years later 70,253 aircrew had been killed or were missing in action with another 22,924 wounded and over 13,100 taken prisoners of war; furthermore, 9,671 ground crew were killed and 4,490 made prisoners of war. No fewer than thirty Victoria Crosses were awarded to its airmen. The junior Service had paid a high price for its share in the final victory.

Coastal Command

For much of the Second World War Coastal Command was ill-equipped for the important roles it was called upon to play, and of these none was more vital and critical than its long and bitter U-boat offensive. In November 1940 A. V. Alexander, the First Lord of the Admiralty, called it the 'Cinderella of the RAF', an apt description as it would remain the smallest of the three operational Commands throughout the war.

In 1937 the Command's Air Officer Commanding-in-Chief Air Marshal Sir Frederick W. Bowhill, KCB, CMG, DSO, had been clearly instructed as to the primary functions of his Command – reconnaissance in home waters, close co-operation with the Royal Navy, and counter offensive action in defence of seaborne trade. Both the Admiralty and the Air Ministry underrated the importance of air cover for shipping convoys, as well as the potential of anti-shipping and anti-submarine strike aircraft; with the result that the development of suitable aircraft for both roles had been very tardy. Furthermore the Royal Navy was confident that its vessels equipped with Asdic (a kind of 'underwater radar') would be able to locate enemy submarines, and that its ships, along with carrier-borne aircraft, were quite capable of dealing with German surface vessels. In its wisdom the Admiralty also considered that the greatest threat to Allied shipping would come from surface raiders rather than submarines. The tragic losses of the passenger liner *Athenia* along with HMS *Courageous* and *Royal Oak* to U-boats early in the war, demonstrated that the lessons of the First World War had not been heeded. In January 1939, the Air Staff allocated the task of bombing the German Fleet in ports and at sea to Bomber Command, hence Coastal Command was virtually left with a purely reconnaissance role.

Coastal Command entered the war with just nineteen squadrons to cover the whole coastline of the United Kingdom – just under three hundred aircraft – of which about 60% were fully operational with trained crews. Its main reconnaissance aircraft was the Avro Anson, which had entered the Service in 1936 and although admirable in many respects was severely limited as a combat aircraft. Its planned replacement, the Lockheed Hudson, had only recently entered the Service, in one operational squadron and another re-equipping. The Hudson became a great asset to the Command, providing its backbone

Avro Anson over the Fleet in 1939.

The Lockheed Hudson became a great asset to Coastal Command.

for several years; ten squadrons were operating in February 1942. It was a Hudson of No 269 squadron that captured *U-570* on 27th August 1941 – the Command's first unaided U-boat success. Its strike force, if indeed it could be so described, comprised just two squadrons of torpedo bombers equipped with the obsolete Vickers Vildebeest biplanes, that dated back to the late 1920s. However, there were five squadrons of flying boats, three equipped with Short Sunderlands, which would become the stalwart of the Command in its battle against U-boats.

Three new aircraft planned in the pre-war years, came into operation in 1940. Two were dismal failures. The Blackburn Botha was seriously under-powered and was withdrawn after barely six months' service. The Saro Lerwick flying boat, planned as a substitute for the Sunderland in order that Shorts could concentrate their production on the new Stirling bomber, was considered dangerously unstable both on the water and in the air, and the project was abandoned after only twenty-one had been built. This meant that two squadrons were compelled to retain their biplanes, the London and Stranraer flying boats, until Shorts were able to renew their Sunderland production, and the Consolidated Catalinas became available from America. The only really successful aircraft was the Bristol Beaufort, which operated successfully as a torpedo bomber in the early years of the war. Sadly missing in the Command's armoury was the possession of a long-range land-aircraft, and it was forced to survive on 'crumbs' grudgingly wrested from Bomber Command; first Armstrong Whitworth Whitleys, then the doughty Vickers Wellingtons, and later Handley Page Halifaxes, until the arrival in quantity of its long-range saviour – the Consolidated Liberator.

Despite appearing a rather antiquated force, the Command was quickly into action. On 5th September 1939 an Anson of No 208 squadron was credited with the first strike against a U-boat, though the

Bristol Beaufort I: A most successful torpedo bomber.

20

crew's claim for a 'killing' was rejected for the lack of conclusive evidence. Thirteen days later Sunderlands of Nos 204 and 288 squadrons achieved the first air-sea rescue of the war, picking up 34 crew members of the *Kensington Court* torpedoed west of the Scillies. The Command claimed another notable 'first' on 8th October 1939 when Hudsons of No 224 squadron shot down the RAF's first enemy aircraft of the war – a Dornier 18 flying boat.

By the end of January 1940, fifteen of the Command's aircraft were equipped with ASV (Air-to-Surface Vessel) Mk 1 radar sets, and on the 30th of the month a Sunderland of No 228 squadron sighted and attacked a damaged U-boat, *U-55*. This first U-boat 'kill' was shared by the Command and the Royal Navy. Less than two months later (11th March) a Blenheim of Bomber Command became the first aircraft to sink a U-boat, *U-31*, unaided by surface vessels. It was during early 1940 that Air Chief Marshal 'Ginger' Bowhill, unimpressed with Bomber Command's attempts to attack German ships at sea, decided to go onto the offensive with Hudson 'Battle Flights'. They were placed on constant stand-by for immediate action should a positive sighting of enemy shipping be reported. They also became involved in the ill-fated Norwegian campaign of May.

As the official pamphlet *Coastal Command* (published in 1943) noted, 'Coastal Command's task was made heavier by the occupation of Norway, Holland and France, which gave Hitler many advanced bases for the invasion of Britain and for his campaign against our Atlantic life-lines'. Despite Bowhill's scant resources his Command went onto the offensive, mounting bombing attacks on German coastal targets by Hudsons and Beauforts, while oil installations in occupied Holland were attacked at night. During the air fighting over Dunkirk in late May, Hudsons especially provided escorts for the convoys of small vessels crossing the Channel, and with the threat of invasion during the Battle of Britain, the Command conducted strikes against the likely invasion ports, with Boulogne coming in for special treatment. During the Battle, Coastal Command lost one hundred and thirty aircraft, along with two hundred and eighty airmen.

Nevertheless, the Command was rapidly developing an anti-submarine offensive in its own right, with well over 50% of its aircraft engaged on U-boat patrols; even obsolete Fairey Battles were engaged in the operations – further evidence of the paucity of the Command's resources. In August Hitler ordered 'a total blockade of Britain', which meant that the 'Battle of the Atlantic' had begun in earnest. It would be

Focke-Wulf 200-Condor – known as the 'Scourge of the Atlantic'.

a prolonged and costly battle that was waged by the Command's crews right up to the final days of the war. As Winston Churchill later wrote, 'The only thing that ever frightened me during the war was the U-boat threat. The Battle of the Atlantic was the dominating factor all through the war.' During the last six months of 1940 the average monthly loss of Allied shipping was some 425,000 tons, although not all as a result of U-boat action. By the end of 1940 over 1,280 ships had been sunk, about 45% of them by U-boats. German U-boat losses were thirty-three, only two being destroyed by aircraft alone.

During the autumn of 1940 a new and disturbing factor in the Battle of the Atlantic became evident, the threat of the Focke-Wulf 200Cs or Condors, known as the 'scourge of the Atlantic'. This four-engined aircraft had first flown as a civil airliner in July 1937, and had been successfully converted into a most effective long-range maritime bomber with an operational range in excess of 2,200 miles and an endurance of 14 hours. The Condor was well armed and could carry four 500 pound bombs, and their close co-operation with U-boats became a menacing feature of the Atlantic sea war. In fact on 26th February 1941, Condors sank seven ships and damaged four more from one single convoy.

From mid-1940 the Command mounted regular and extensive sea-area patrols from dawn to dusk and at night when conditions were favourable. It was its proud claim that the Command never called off operations; many were conducted in quite atrocious weather conditions and often in very hostile circumstances – as can be judged by the four Victoria Crosses awarded to its airmen. One Coastal Command pilot later recalled: 'Regular, monotonous hours of flying over unbounded sea watching water with little to relieve the sheer drudgery. A constant need for alertness and concentration was required . . . 99% boredom interrupted by 1% heart-thumping action' – really the epitome of the Command's official motto, 'Constant Endeavour'.

In November 1940, there was a serious debate at the highest levels as to whether the Command should be handed over to the Royal Navy to be run as a separate Naval Air Service along with the Fleet Air Arm. The final outcome was that it remained firmly in the RAF, although the operational control of the U-boat war still resided with the Admiralty. The dispute did at least have a positive result, the approval of fifteen additional squadrons by June 1941, and the immediate formation of No 221 squadron with Wellington ICs equipped with the improved ASV Mk.II equipment.

In March 1941 Bristol Beaufighters first entered operations with Coastal Command as a long-range fighter and they would become very effective in the anti-shipping strike role. The previous month a new Group, No 19, was formed with its headquarters at Mount Wise, Plymouth; it held the operational control of the vital south-west approaches, and the Bay of Biscay, where the French Atlantic ports housed and supplied the U-boats. The Bay, about 300 miles by 120 miles, was really *the* battleground of the U-boat offensive, as the majority of U-boats had to sail out and return to their supply bases. As Air Marshal Sir John Slessor, KCB, DSO, MC, the Command's AOC-in-C during 1943/4 later wrote, '[It] was the one place where we could be absolutely certain that there would be U-boats to be found and killed.'

The long-range capabilities of the Command were increased in March 1941 by the first appearance of the Catalina flying boats. In June the first squadron of Liberators was formed but it did not become operational until September. Also two squadrons were based in Iceland, as the convoys from America were taking a more northerly route in an attempt to avoid the U-boats. Then in mid-April the operational control of Coastal Command was taken over by the Admiralty. This effectively meant that the Royal Navy laid down the operational tasks and their priority and the AOC-in-C through his Group Commanders was responsible for carrying them out. The close liaison between Coastal Command and the Royal Navy throughout the war was considered to be 'an example of inter-Service co-operation at its best.' In May the

Consolidated Liberator: The Command's long-range saviour. (via J. Richards)

Command's aircraft played a significant role in hunting and tracking the German battleship, *Bismarck*.

The close co-operation with the Royal Navy owes much to the standards set by Air Chief Marshal Bowhill. He had joined the Navy in 1904, later trained as a pilot and joined the RNAS; he would command one of its first aircraft carriers. Bowhill had a total appreciation of the Navy's needs and it was said that 'he had seawater in his veins'! In June 1941 he left to take over the newly formed Ferry Command, and was replaced by Air Marshal Sir Philip B. Joubert de la Ferte, KCB, CMG, DSO, who had been Bowhill's immediate predecessor in 1937. Joubert was a radio/radar expert, and was fully conversant with the maritime uses of radar. Under his keen support and enthusiasm the Command's Operational Research Unit grew and developed, tasked with the scientific examination of all aspects of the Command's work, but especially its offensive against U-boats.

Although the Air Marshal returned to the Command as it was beginning to increase in strength, now comprising thirty-five squadrons plus two Fleet Air Arm squadrons on loan, he could still only call upon about three hundred operational aircraft on a daily basis. The paucity of long-range aircraft remained its greatest weakness. The Command's top priority continued to be the U-boat offensive, but the other tasks laid to its aircrews were a constant watch for German warships, attacks on ports and German coastal shipping, reconnaissance for the Navy, minelaying, and the ongoing battle against enemy maritime aircraft and fighters. From August the Command was required to provide support for the Arctic convoys, and in the same month it was given the control of all the Air-Sea Rescue operations; another additional role to add to those of the Photographic Reconnaissance and Meteorological Units, which had been placed under Coastal Command in June 1940 and March 1941 respectively.

During the summer of 1941 there was a marked reduction in the losses of Allied shipping, and towards the end of the year, it was intimated that the Battle of the Atlantic had been won. Even the Admiralty vouchsafed the view that 'the U-boats' primary object seems, at least temporarily, to be no longer the destruction of enemy shipping'. This temporary respite was largely due to bad weather and the diversion of submarines to the Mediterranean rather than the Command's valiant efforts; and it proved to be a 'false dawn'. By December over 500,000 tons of shipping had been sunk, and this figure increased steadily and very alarmingly during 1942 when the number of U-boats known to be operating in the Atlantic rose from 101 in February to 204 by December, prowling in what became known as 'wolf packs'. The Battle of the Atlantic was now at its most critical stage, and according to Churchill was 'a terrible event in a very bad time'. The Government's Code and Cypher School at Bletchley Park had achieved a partial breaking of the German Naval code, and in May 1941 received a U-boat Enigma machine, which would ultimately lead to greater pre-knowledge of U-boat operations. Nevertheless, during 1942 and the early months of 1943 Coastal Command was stretched to its very limits.

Despite all the herculean efforts of the Command the Battle of the Atlantic was apparently being lost. The U-boat packs were effectively exploiting the so-called 'Atlantic Gap', an area of sea some hundreds of miles wide in the northern Atlantic, where the convoys were out of the range of air cover. Air Marshal Joubert warned that if the shipping

Beaufighter TFX of No 455 squadron. (RAF Museum)

25

Short Sunderland: The stalwart of Coastal Command.

losses continued at such a rate, the country would not survive another year. To compound its problems, anti-shipping operations were proving to be very costly, forty-three aircraft were lost in May alone. The effort to build up its Beaufighter force was a slow and painful business. Joubert had great difficulty in persuading the Air Ministry that the Beaufighter was the ideal anti-shipping aircraft; although it must be said that Fighter Command's night-fighter force had the priority of Beaufighter production, as it faced the Luftwaffe's 'Baedeker' raids during the summer of 1942. Joubert was utterly convinced of the potential of Beaufighter strike wings, but the first would not become effective until the following year; the first 'Torbeaus' – torpedo carrying Beaufighters – entered the fray later in the year. The Command's slim resources were further stretched by Operation Torch – the Allied landings in North Africa – when it was required to provide air cover for the convoys of troops and supplies.

In spite of the Command's struggles and problems, it was not quite all doom and gloom during 1942. Hampdens were now being used as torpedo bombers, albeit that they dated from 1936 and were Bomber Command's 'cast offs'! More Whitley and Wellington squadrons were transferred from that Command, and later in the year two Boeing Flying Fortress squadrons became operational along with two extra squadrons of Sunderlands and Liberators. The first 'Leigh Light' aircraft became

26

operational in May from Chivenor, and two months later the first U-boat (*U-502*) 'kill' using this light was made. The Command's aircraft were now armed with Torpex filled depth-charges, a more effective explosive, and also provided with a greatly improved firing pistol. At the end of the year ASV Mk.III, a version of Bomber Command's H2S centrimetric radar, able to locate a convoy at some forty miles distance and detect a submerged U-boat from twelve miles, became available; although within a year the enemy had developed a warning receiver, Naxos-U, to replace their Metox used against the earlier ASV equipment.

On 5th February 1943 Air Marshal Sir Philip Joubert left the Command and he was replaced by Air Marshal Sir John C. Slessor, CB, DSO, MC, KCB, who had recently attended the Conference of Allied Chiefs of State in Casablanca, where it had been boldly stated that, 'the defeat of the U-boat must remain a first charge on the resources of the United Nations.' Slessor's arrival at Command Headquarters in Northwood proved to be most propitious. He was considered to be 'the rising star of the RAF', perhaps a belated acknowledgement of the important role Coastal Command was playing in the European air war. Slessor proved to be a most able and popular commander, and a fine leader. He was perhaps fortunate in taking over the Command when all the hard work and development under Bowhill and Joubert were beginning to bear fruit. Certainly Slessor inherited a greatly strengthened force, comprising eighteen anti-submarine squadrons, twelve flying boat squadrons and thirteen squadrons of anti-shipping aircraft and long-range fighters. Included were units of the USAAF and US Navy operating under No 19 Group's control.

By the end of the summer of 1943 it could be said with some conviction that the Battle of the Atlantic had finally been won. From May to the end of August 118 U-boats in total had been destroyed, a loss rate which Grand Admiral Karl Döenitz, their overall commander since the outbreak of the war, considered 'an intolerable level'! Of this total Coastal Command units had accounted for 41, over half of them destroyed in the Bay of Biscay. But these operations had proved to be costly, with 80 aircraft lost to enemy action, bad weather or accidents. Air Chief Marshal Sir Charles Portal, the Chief of the Air Staff, sent a congratulatory message to Coastal Command, which was printed in the Command's *Review*. This was a unique monthly publication, issued to every squadron, which gave a comprehensive and valuable insight into the day-to-day work of the Command. Sir Charles expressed his 'admiration and warmest thanks for your achievements in the anti-U-boat war during the month ended [May]. The brilliant success achieved in this vital field is the well deserved result of tireless perseverance and devotion to duty.'

Nevertheless, U-boats continued to be a menace. During the preparations for D-Day Coastal Command units were heavily engaged in Operation Cork ensuring that neither U-boats nor German surface vessels attacked the armada of vessels gathered for the invasion of Europe. In fact twenty-five U-boats were sunk by Coastal Command during May and June 1944. From then onwards U-boat activity was at a rather low ebb. In 1945 the Command destroyed nineteen bringing its total to two hundred and seven, including those sunk by USAAF and US Navy units and those shared with Naval vessels; almost one third of the total destroyed during the war.

Perhaps the major feature of Coastal Command in the final eighteen months of the war was the anti-shipping operations of its Beaufighter Strike Wings. The first had been formed at North Coates in November 1942 but did not become effective until the early months of 1943 and by the summer the fearsome TFX Beaufighter had made its first appearance, specially developed for strike operations equipped with rocket projectiles. During 1944 especially these Strike Wings became a most effective force and operated from several bases around the coasts.

A surfaced U-boat flies the black surrender flag, May 1945. Coastal Command's war is at an end. (via S. Cox)

Some of the squadrons were later equipped with Mosquitos and they operated up to 4th May 1945. During the war Coastal Command sunk over three hundred and sixty vessels with another one hundred and thirty-four damaged, but for the loss of over eight hundred and fifty aircraft.

Coastal Command had aircraft on patrol throughout the whole twenty-four hours on most days of the war, but its operations went largely unpublicised and unrecognised. Without doubt its airmen played a major and decisive part in winning the Battle of the Atlantic, one of the momentous victories of the Second World War. As Sir John Slessor wrote in *The Central Blue* (1956), 'the crews of Coastal Command certainly did not get their meed of public recognition at the time, nor have they since'. The Command lost 1,511 aircraft in action and another 1,770 due to fatal crashes on return. In the process 5,866 airmen were killed in action with another 2,340 lost in accidents or due to other causes. Their contribution to the final victory can be seen as equal to those of Bomber and Fighter Commands.

Fighter Command

The Battle of Britain was perhaps the most critical air battle of the Second World War, when during those few summer months of 1940 its young pilots – The Few – held the fate of the nation in their hands. Their narrow victory owed much to the foresight, planning and resolution of their first Air Officer Commanding-in-Chief, Air Marshal Sir Hugh C. T. Dowding, KCB, CMG. He was, perhaps, an unusual choice to command a young and rather extrovert band of airmen. Dowding was aged 54 years and getting close to retirement, a rather aloof and private person with a sharp and abrupt manner. Nevertheless, he was a fine strategist of air warfare with a cool judgement, and a most able administrator with complete confidence in his subordinate commanders.

When Dowding arrived at Bentley Priory, Stanmore in July 1936 to set up the headquarters of the new Command, he was dismayed at the woeful inadequacies of his force, which had suffered from the overriding concept that 'the bomber will always get through' and thus money spent on fighter defence was 'wasted'. It comprised just nine fighter stations in the country with fifteen squadrons, all equipped with biplanes. By August 1939, his Command had expanded to thirty-seven

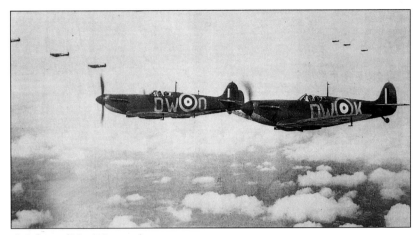

Spitfires of No 610 squadron.

squadrons, most equipped with Hawker Hurricanes and Supermarine Spitfires – both outstanding fighters. Nevertheless it still fell far short of the fifty-two squadrons that Dowding considered the minimum necessary to provide an adequate defence of the country.

Dowding had put in place a most effective ground control and communications system that survived the heat of battle. The first line of defence were the RDF (Radio Direction Finding) or 'Chain Home' stations that were sited along the coasts. It was his bold decision to establish the first twenty stations, and by July 1940 fifty-six RDF stations were operational. Friendly aircraft were recognised by an IFF (Identification, Friend or Foe) device. The information from these stations was passed directly to the Command's Filter Room where it was assessed for accuracy. The Chain Home stations in the South-West were sited at Carnarton, Drytree, Ramehead, West Prawle, and Hawstor.

Once the enemy aircraft had passed over the coast, the Observer Corps ('Royal' from April 1941) tracked the progress of the enemy formations, and passed their sightings directly to Command headquarters. Other information came from the Government Code & Cypher School at Bletchley Park, gleaned from Ultra decrypts, and from the 'Y' Service – 'Home Defence Units' sited along the coasts with operators listening to German R/T conversations; one was situated at Street in Somerset. In addition the Command established a close liaison with the Army's Anti-Aircraft Command, its headquarters sited in the

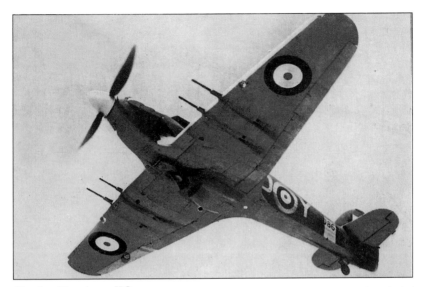

Hawker Hurricane IIC.

grounds of Bentley Priory. The RAF Balloon Barrage squadrons, along with some 4,000 searchlights, completed an excellent Home Defence System that proved vital in the coming Battle.

Dowding soon had his slim resources reduced by the transfer of Hurricane squadrons to serve in France, and this depletion of his force became more serious from 10th May 1940 with the German invasion of the Low Countries. In a matter of days the equivalent of ten squadrons were sent to France and with a demand for even more; also two squadrons and most of their pilots were lost in the Norwegian campaign. Dowding considered that France was 'a lost cause', the defence of Britain was his major task. Eventually his strong and dogged resistance to any further reduction of his fighters prevailed, when it was announced on 19th May, 'no more squadrons will leave this country whatever the need of France.'

It was the air battles over France that brought his pilots their first real taste of fighter combat. The action was most heated and costly on both sides; over 450 aircraft (mostly Hurricanes) were lost during this period, but with fighter production exceeding that number per month, it was the loss of some 300 experienced pilots that gave Dowding the greatest concern. As the last fighter squadron (No 501) left France on 18th June, Winston Churchill famously predicted, 'What General Weygand called the Battle of France is over. I expect that the Battle of Britain is about to begin.'

The Command's depleted squadrons were re-equipped and by 5th July its effective strength stood at fifty-one squadrons, mainly with either Hurricanes or Spitfires. New pilots were hastily 'found' by reducing the length of training courses, but also many were now filtering in from Europe and the Commonwealth, and they would make a vital contribution, although 80% of the Battle of Britain pilots were British. Dowding devised a system of moving hard-pressed squadrons out of the front-line to allow his experienced pilots a short respite from the stress of almost continual combat; this also enabled replacement pilots to be trained. His care and concern for his 'fighter boys' became legendary, and Winston Churchill dubbed them 'Dowding's chicks'!

In July, Fighter Command was divided into four Fighter Groups based on geographical divisions. No 11 covered London and the South-East, and it would bear the heaviest brunt of the Battle. No 12 operated from airfields in East Anglia with No 13 defending the North of England and Scotland. No 10 was tasked with the defence of the West Country and South Wales. Each was divided into a number of Sectors with a Sector station controlling one or more satellite airfields.

No 10 Group had its headquarters at Rudloe Manor, Box in Wiltshire, and comprised Sector stations at Middle Wallop, St Eval, Filton and Pembrey (altered slightly during the course of the Battle). In Devon and Cornwall there were three fighter stations at Exeter, Roborough and St Eval. The Group's commander was Air Vice-Marshal Sir C. J. Quintin Brand, KBE, DSO, MC, DFC, who had served in the RFC, and had commanded one of the first night-fighting squadrons, when he was known as 'Flossie' by his pilots! Brand had the distinction of destroying a Gotha bomber in the last German raid on England in the First World War. He had been knighted for his pioneering flight to South Africa in 1920. Brand would remain in charge of the Group until July 1941 before retiring from the Service two years later.

Despite the hectic air combats of early July when twenty-three RAF airmen were killed or wounded, it was later decided that the Battle of Britain officially started on 10th July and finished on 31st October 1940. Those were the dates authorised for the award of the 'Battle of Britain Clasp' to all airmen (just under 3,000) flying at least one operational sortie during this period. This was despite the fact that a RAF Order of the Day was promulgated on 8th August, 'The Battle of Britain is about to begin. Members of the Royal Air Force, the fate of generations lies in your hands'!

Air Vice-Marshal Sir C. J. Quintin Brand, KBE, DSO, MC, DFC, of No 10 Group.

The main Luftwaffe aircraft that the Few would face were the Heinkel 111s, twin-engined bombers, which were the backbone of the bomber force; the fearsome Stuka dive-bombers or Junkers 87s, later to be withdrawn because of heavy losses; and the versatile Junkers 88 – a strong, durable and manoeuvrable twin-engined fighter/bomber – probably the best in the world then. The Dornier 17 was the least effective Luftwaffe bomber with a far lighter bomb load but it could survive terrific damage. The Command's pilots were clearly instructed that 'the destruction of the enemy bombers is the main aim, and that action against fighters is only a means to an end.'

Of the two Luftwaffe fighters, it was the Messerschmitt 109E that earned the grudging respect of the RAF. On paper it was superior to the Hurricane, and to the Spitfire at higher altitudes, and without doubt it was a most formidable fighter; its only drawback was its somewhat limited range. The much-vaunted Messerschmitt 110C – the Zerstorer ('Destroyer') – was a twin-engined, two-seater fighter/bomber heavily armed with a much longer range but less manoeuvrable; it was completely outclassed by the RAF fighters. Both aircraft were produced by Bayerische Flugzeugwerke (Bf), but as the Luftwaffe's records showed both 'Bf' and 'Me', the latter will be used for ease of identification.

During the early weeks of the Battle the Luftwaffe attacked mainly Allied shipping convoys in the English Channel, ports and other coastal targets, largely with the intention of bringing the RAF fighters into action. On 1st August Adolf Hitler issued a directive (No 17), 'The Luftwaffe is to overpower the RAF with all its forces at its command and in the shortest possible time'. The defeat of the RAF in the air was considered an essential prerequisite for Operation *Seelöwe* (Sealion) – the invasion of Britain.

After two postponements, because of unfavourable weather, Reichsmarschall Hermann Göring planned his *Adlertag* or Eagle Day for 13th August. From then until early September the Luftwaffe launched a massive assault on fighter stations, RDF stations and aircraft factories. Between 24th August and 7th September there were thirty-three bombing attacks mostly directed at the airfields in No 11 Group. Air Vice-Marshal Keith Park, the Group's Commander, later maintained that, 'Had my fighter aerodromes been put out of action, the German Air Force would have won the Battle by 15th September'. But from 7th September the Luftwaffe changed tactics and proceeded to concentrate their bomber forces on daylight raids directed at London;

these operations continued well into the month. From then onwards came the night-raids against London and other provincial cities and ports. The day offensive now passed to waves of fighters and fighter/bombers operating at 30,000 feet and above, which created a different problem for Fighter Command.

In an air battle that waged almost continuously for 114 days, some days of fighting proved critical to the final outcome. On 8th and 11th August the RAF lost forty-five pilots and forty-nine aircraft whilst destroying fifty-two enemy aircraft, of which thirty-seven were fighters. Had the Command's pilot losses continued at such a rate Dowding would have had great difficulty manning the fighters that were being produced at over four hundred a month. However, 15th August would become known as 'The Hardest Day' and to the Luftwaffe as 'Black Thursday' when it lost seventy-six aircraft compared with the Command's losses of thirty-five and eleven pilots. The last eight days of August were probably the most critical period of the whole Battle. The RAF lost over one hundred and sixty aircraft in the air and on the ground with sixty-three pilots killed, against Luftwaffe losses of over two hundred and fifty aircraft and two hundred and ninety airmen.

On 15th September the Luftwaffe launched some 1,000 sorties over London and in the process lost sixty-one aircraft with another three damaged beyond repair (these figures were obtained from Luftwaffe records after the war). Fighter Command lost thirty-one fighters and sixteen pilots killed. It was a day of almost non-stop aerial combat and some of the 'dog fights' took place over the centre of London, long to be remembered by Londoners. The Air Ministry claimed '175 Raiders Shot Down', later increased to 185, and it was hailed as an historic victory giving a massive boost to the public's morale, subsequently to be celebrated as 'Battle of Britain Day'. Winston Churchill later wrote of the day's fighting, 'It was one of the decisive battles of the war, and like the Battle of Waterloo, it was on a Sunday.' Operation Sealion was postponed two days later, and finally abandoned on 12th October, at least as far as 1940 was concerned.

Nevertheless the raids continued with each side incurring heavy losses, and not before the middle of November could it safely be said that the Battle of Britain was really over. Surprisingly, only one Victoria Cross was awarded during the Battle, on 16th August to a Hurricane pilot, Flight Lieutenant J.B. Nicholson of No 249 squadron. It had been a hard and costly victory for Fighter Command, although by the end of

35

Beaufighter IF of No 604 squadron.

November its two chief architects – Dowding and Park – had been relieved of their posts in favour of Air Marshal W. Sholto Douglas, CB, MC, DFC and Air Vice-Marshal T. L. Leigh-Mallory, CB, DSO. At the time it seemed to be scant gratitude for their sterling and valiant efforts, but time has righted the balance and their somewhat tarnished reputations have been rightly fully restored.

Until the summer of 1941 the Command had the huge and difficult task of opposing the incessant nightly armadas of bombers, which stretched its meagre force of night-fighters. Bristol Blenheims had first trialled the rather rudimentary AI (Airborne Interception) radar sets, but in September they were joined by the powerfully armed Bristol Beaufighters, which became the salvation of the night-fighter force. They were assisted by Boulton & Paul Defiants, the unique turreted fighter that had been withdrawn from the Battle of Britain, and transformed into a useful night-fighter. Also a number of Hurricane squadrons were engaged on night-operations with some success.

In January 1941 Sir Archibald Sinclair, the Secretary of State for Air stated: 'Night-fighting is the most intense and important battle of those on which we are now engaged.' A greater number of Ground Control Interception stations became operational, but the night 'kills' were slow in coming – from just three victories in January to forty-eight in April, a figure that was doubled the following month. In January 1942 the first de Havilland Mosquito NF Mk.IIs began to enter the Service, and this remarkable and versatile aircraft would begin to tip the scales in favour of Fighter Command. During the summer of 1942 the Luftwaffe launched a series of heavy bombing raids on cathedral cities – the 'Baedeker' raids – when the night-fighters claimed over two hundred enemy aircraft destroyed. At long last the Air Ministry was able to

36

Mosquito NFII of No 157 squadron: the first to be equipped with this remarkable night-fighter.

report, 'the night-fighters are exacting a steady and mounting toll of enemy raiders . . . they have ensured that a heavy and sustained air offensive by the Luftwaffe is temporarily out of the question.'

During early 1941 Fighter Command had begun to take a more offensive role with a variety of operations that went under rather strange names – Circuses, Rhubarbs, Ramrods, Rodeos, Roadsteads and Rangers. These were a mixture of combined operations with light or medium bombers, individual or squadron fighter sweeps to attack airfields and transportation targets in France and the Low Countries, or anti-shipping strikes. Air Vice-Marshal Leigh-Mallory of No 11 Group with his faith in the effectiveness of large fighter formations, established Wings at his Sector airfields. However, it was not until 1942 when greater resources were available and the improved marks of Spitfires arrived, that these Wings became effective, if somewhat costly, strike forces. The Command, like Bomber, had become a cosmopolitan force with the addition of Polish, Czech, Belgian, French, Canadian, Australian, New Zealand and American squadrons.

The Spitfires were being refined and improved and with the provision of cannons becoming quite formidable ground attack aircraft, while the Hurricane gained a new lease of life as a formidable fighter/bomber. The new Spitfire marks were found wanting with the appearance of the improved Me 109Fs and the Focke Wulf 190s; the latter's all-round performance proved to be superior to the Spitfire Vs. These fighters would cause considerable problems for the Command until the Hawker Typhoon became more reliable and numerous, and

37

the Mark IX Spitfires appeared on the scene.

During 1942 the Command faced its biggest single task since the Battle of Britain, when in August most of its day-fighter squadrons were engaged in the ill-fated raid on Dieppe – Operation Jubilee. During the day (19th) the Command mounted almost 2,400 sorties and claimed over ninety enemy aircraft destroyed and two hundred probably severely damaged. It lost ninety aircraft in the process but the air offensive was hailed as a great victory because the Air Ministry was convinced that over one third of the Luftwaffe's force on the Western Front had been destroyed or damaged. After the war it was disclosed that the actual Luftwaffe losses were forty-eight destroyed and half that number damaged – in effect a major defeat for Fighter Command.

In November 1942 Air Marshal Sir Trafford Leigh-Mallory took over command when Fighter Command was at the zenith of its strength and power. In the following June the Force was double its size at the beginning of the war equipped with a massive phalanx of fighters – Hurricanes, Spitfires, Beaufighters, Typhoons, Mosquitos, and Mustangs. The new marks of Spitfires, especially, were proving themselves more than a match for the Luftwaffe fighters. Intruder raids and large fighter sweeps over France and the Low Countries had become the bread and butter of the squadrons, in addition to bomber escort duties for both Bomber Command and the USAAF's Eighth Air Force.

In the summer of 1943 as the Allied invasion of Europe was being planned, the days of a large Fighter Command were numbered; in November it lost almost two-thirds of its squadrons and its name, when the Second Tactical Air Force was formally established. This was effectively an amalgam of light bombers, fighters, fighter/bombers and transport aircraft specially designed to provide close tactical support for the Allied armies engaged in the invasion. The name 'Fighter Command' disappeared, in favour of 'The Air Defence of Great Britain' – a name that was redolent of the RAF of the early 1930s.

Leigh-Mallory was promoted to command the Allied Expeditionary Air Forces, and Air Marshal Sir Roderic M. Hill, KCB, MC, AFC, was appointed Commander of the ADGB; to remain at the helm for the rest of the war. Within two months the remaining squadrons of the ADGB were faced with a new German night-bombing offensive mainly directed at London. On 21st January 1944 the Luftwaffe launched Operation Steinbock in retaliation to Bomber Command's heavy raids on Berlin. By now the night-defence squadrons were far better prepared

Hawker Typhoon IB.

and equipped. In the first raid twenty-five enemy aircraft were destroyed out of a total attacking force of over two hundred and twenty. As the 'Little' or 'Baby' blitz, as it became known, progressed the Luftwaffe suffered increasingly heavy losses, mainly to Mosquito night-fighters. The bombing offensive drew to a conclusion towards the end of May when over three hundred enemy aircraft had been destroyed or damaged, amounting to 60% of the Luftwaffe's total bomber force.

In the run-up to Operation Overlord – the invasion of Europe – the ADGB squadrons flew well over eighteen thousand sorties, claiming over one hundred and ten enemy aircraft for the loss of forty-six fighters. During D-Day itself its fighters were fully engaged on beach-head and shipping support, as well as a number of offensive sweeps. But within weeks the fighter pilots would become engaged in another kind of Battle of Britain, this time pitting their skills against the unmanned *Vergeltunswaffe* or Revenge weapons – the V1 and later V2 rockets. From 13th June, when the first V1 rocket landed, until the end of March 1944, Fighter Command was credited with almost two thousand destroyed; the most successful fighter was the new Hawker Tempest, its pilots were credited with over six hundred victories.

On 15th October 1944 the Command regained its old and proud designation and was now deeply involved in escorting the massive daylight bombing operations. During March 1945 there were some night-intruder raids over eastern England with the object of attacking airfields as the bombers returned from operations. In the Luftwaffe's final incursion over England on 20th March, a Junkers 188 was shot down by a Mosquito NF Mk.XXX, and the final operation mounted by the Command in Europe came on 9th May when fighter squadrons provided air cover for the landing on Guernsey.

Like their colleagues in Bomber and Coastal Commands, the airmen of Fighter Command had fought a long and bitter war, and lost 3,690 airmen with 1,215 severely wounded and another 601 taken prisoner of war. Many of these brave airmen lie buried in the country churchyards close to their wartime airfields, although many more had no known graves and are remembered in the impressive RAF memorial at Runnymede. However, it is for their valiant efforts and brave sacrifices during the Battle of Britain, that they should never be forgotten. As one Battle of Britain pilot later recalled, 'High summer, 1940 . . . a time to be alive and British. Above all, perhaps, it was a time to have been a fighter pilot in the Royal Air Force.'

The Fleet Air Arm

Although the origins of Naval aviation can be traced back to March 1911 when the first four Naval officers arrived at Eastchurch on the Isle of Sheppey to be trained as pilots, the Fleet Air Arm *per se* dates from 1st April 1924 when it was formally acknowledged as an integral part of the RAF under the administrative control of the Air Ministry. The FAA barely comprised eighty aircraft in a dozen Flights, quite a marked difference to the 3,000 aircraft and 55,000 officers and men of the RNAS in April 1918, when it had been absorbed into the newly formed RAF.

During the 1920s there was a protracted and, at times, acrimonious dispute between the Air Ministry and the Admiralty concerning the operational control of the FAA, especially conducted by the two Chiefs, Earl Beatty and Viscount Trenchard. This 'storm in a tea-cup', as it has been described by one historian, was finally resolved in July 1937 by Sir Thomas Inskip, the Minister of the Co-ordination of Imperial Defence, who recommended that the FAA be transferred to the control of the Admiralty within the next two years; it became known as the Inskip Award. The Air Staff considered this political decision as 'disastrous . . . a body blow' to the rapidly expanding RAF.

On 24th May 1939 the Admiralty formally took control of the FAA, although the RAF would continue to be responsible for the flying training of its pilots. It had long been accepted that Naval pilots were a different breed from their RAF counterparts. In *The War in the Air* (Vol I of the Official History of the RAF) published in 1922, Sir Walter Raleigh wrote: 'When a sailor learns to fly, he remains a sailor, and the air for him is merely the roof of the sea.' Although the Air Staff had conceded back in 1924 that 70% of the FAA's pilots would comprise Naval or Royal Marine officers, the Navy was unable to supply enough volunteers to maintain this proportion; the FAA was never considered to be a bright avenue for promotion within the Navy! Henceforth its airmen would serve in the Air or (A) Branch of the Royal Navy.

During the inter-war years the FAA had suffered from a sad neglect of resources, perhaps even more so than the RAF. At the outbreak of war its actual strength was twenty squadrons (the squadron system had only been introduced in 1933) totalling three hundred and forty aircraft, all of which could be considered 'old fashioned'; about 65% were based on the aircraft carriers, and the rest were catapult seaplanes operating from battleships and cruisers. Its main Fleet aircraft were Fairey Swordfish and Blackburn Skua. The former was universally and affectionately known as the 'Stringbag'. This quite remarkable biplane had first appeared in 1935 and was now thought to be reaching the end of its natural life, but nevertheless it survived its replacement! The Swordfish's open cockpit offered rugged conditions for its crews, but this truly classic aircraft operated with great distinction and success throughout the war, as a torpedo bomber, anti-U-boat striker, minelayer, rocket projectile carrier and trainer in virtually every theatre of war. The Swordfish would be the last biplane to fly operationally. In direct contrast, the Skua was the FAA's first monoplane, entering the Service in late 1938 as the first monoplane able to operate from carriers, as well as being the Navy's first purpose-built dive bomber. The catapult squadrons were mainly equipped with Supermarine Walruses, Fairey Seafoxes and Blackburn Sharks, all biplanes, only adding to the image of the FAA as a rather tired and outmoded force.

The Royal Navy had eight aircraft carriers in commission in September 1939, with another seven on the stocks. The *Ark Royal*, then operating in home waters, was the most modern (1938) and the pride of the Fleet. The Admiralty had taken over eight RAF stations in May 1939, including Lee-on-Solent, which became the headquarters and barracks of the FAA ashore, styled as HMS *Daedalus*; but it was now

Swordfish Is of No 814 (FAA) squadron over HMS Ark Royal in 1939.

faced with the massive task of building a structure of training and supply facilities in a very short time, thus the majority of the FAA's shore bases in the country would be devoted to some aspect of advanced flying and fleet fighter training. However, for certain periods of the war FAA squadrons were granted 'lodger' facilities at many RAF airfields, mainly when operating under Coastal Command's control.

In the first month of the war the FAA achieved a notable first. On 25th September Lieutenant B.S. McEwen in a Skua of No 803 squadron from HMS *Ark Royal* shot down a Dornier 18 flying boat over the North Sea, the first German aircraft to be lost on operations. Then in April 1940 with the German invasion of Norway, FAA aircraft were in full action; on 10th April Skuas of Nos 800 and 803 squadrons from Hatson in the Orkneys attacked and sank the German cruiser *Königsburg* in Bergen Fjord. This was the first major warship to be sunk by air power alone; only one of the sixteen Skuas in the operation failed to return – a most impressive start to the FAA's anti-shipping operations. Three days later a Swordfish of No 700 squadron flown by Petty Officer F.C. Rice sunk *U-64*, the first of twenty-six U-boat 'kills' by FAA units, with Swordfish squadrons claiming the 'lion's share' – no fewer than twenty!

The value of the FAA's reconnaissance aircraft, known as 'the Eyes of the Fleet', was graphically demonstrated in the famous Naval action against the German pocket battleship, *Admiral Graf Spee* in December 1939, known as the Battle of the River Plate. A Seafox, crewed by Lieutenants E.D.G. Lewin and R.E.N. Kearney, was catapulted from the

Blackburn Skuas of No 803 (FAA) squadron.

cruiser HMS *Ajax* on 13th December and 'spotted' for the British squadron's guns – the first such occasion in World War II. Four days later the Seafox returned from its regular reconnaissance patrol with the news that 'the *Spee* has blown herself up'! Lieutenant Lewin was awarded the DSC for his actions, and Lieutenant Kearney was 'mentioned in despatches' – the FAA's first honours of the war.

In May 1940 the FAA was engaged in the air battle over France with its crews operating under Coastal Command providing air cover for the evacuation of Dunkirk; fifteen aircraft were lost in the fierce air fighting. During the Battle of Britain two FAA squadrons, Nos 804 and 808, were loaned to Fighter Command, and were used to defend Naval dockyards. The Admiralty temporarily transferred a number of pilots (twenty-two) to RAF fighter squadrons. Of the fifty-six FAA airmen that fought in the Battle, nine were killed, all whilst serving with RAF squadrons.

During 1940 several new fleet fighters entered the Service. The first was the Blackburn Roc, a direct development of the Skua, but equipped with a power-operated Boulton & Paul four-gun turret. The aircraft proved to have an inadequate combat performance, and although designed to operate from carriers it was solely confined to shore bases during its relatively short operational life. In June the first Fairey Fulmar, a two-seat fleet fighter became operational with No 808

43

Fairey Seafox.

squadron, and by 1942 they equipped fourteen squadrons. However, they were quickly superseded by Supermarine Seafires. It was in September that perhaps the most impressive early fleet fighter arrived at No 804 squadron to replace its Sea Gladiators – the Grumman Martlet I. This was the British version of the US Navy's F4F-3, a compact, 'tubby' aircraft that was described as 'a sweet machine to fly'; but it would be another twelve months before they served on carriers. On Christmas Day two Martlets of No 804 squadron became the first American aircraft to shoot down a German aircraft (Junkers 88) in the war. Also early in the year the so-called replacement for the Swordfish as a torpedo bomber came on the scene, the Fairey Albacore, another biplane. Although of sound design, its performance was not sufficiently advanced, and it was in fact survived by the Swordfish.

It can be said that the Fleet Air Arm 'came of age' whilst operating with the Mediterranean Fleet in late 1940. The first meritous action occurred on 22nd August when a small striking force of Swordfish destroyed four Italian warships (including a submarine) in Bomba Bay off the coast of Libya. Then on the night of 11th November 1940 twenty Swordfish of Nos 815 and 819 squadrons operating from HMS *Illustrious* attacked the Italian Fleet at anchor in Taranto harbour. The Swordfish, attacking in two waves, dived through a balloon barrage against fierce and heavy anti-aircraft fire. Eleven torpedoes dropped by the Swordfish crippled half of the Italian Fleet and this action was said to have changed the sea-war in the Mediterranean, all for the loss of two

Swordfish. Admiral Sir Andrew Cunningham, the Commander of the Mediterranean Fleet, noted, '[The action] shall be remembered for ever as having shown once and for all that in the Fleet Air Arm the Navy has a devastating weapon.' It was said that the Japanese planned their attack on Pearl Harbor along similar lines but of course on a larger scale. In the following March Swordfish, Albacores and Fulmars from HMS *Formidable* were heavily engaged in the Battle of Matapan, also in the Mediterranean; indeed, it would be in this theatre of war over the next few years that the FAA squadrons would see the most action, both from carriers and land bases.

During May 1941 the FAA's reconnaissance aircraft once again proved their worth and greatly assisted in the Navy's frantic hunt for the German battlecruiser *Bismarck* in the North Atlantic. On the 22nd a Martin Maryland of No 771 (FAA) squadron confirmed that the vessel, along with the *Prinz Eugen* had left Bergen. Two days later after the *Bismarck* had escaped from the attentions of the Home Fleet, it was sighted by Swordfish from HMS *Victorious*. A strike by nine Swordfish of No 824 squadron was made just after midnight in quite appalling weather conditions, and just one torpedo hit the vessel causing only slight damage. On the 26th the German battlecruiser was again spotted and fifteen doughty Swordfish from the *Ark Royal* managed to cripple its steering gear with three torpedo hits. The vessel was sunk by HMS *Dorsetshire* the following day.

During 1942 Sea Hurricanes equipped with arrestor hooks began to be used most effectively from aircraft carriers. In August whilst in defence of Malta convoys, Sea Hurricanes memorably engaged a strong force of German and Italian aircraft, and in three days of fierce air combat they shot down thirty-nine enemy aircraft and damaged many more for the loss of eight aircraft. It should be noted in passing that Hurricanes of No 46 (RAF) squadron had first landed on an aircraft carrier, *Glorious*, way back in May 1940 during the ill-fated Norwegian operation, despite the fact that none of the RAF pilots had any deck landing experience!

The Admiralty had also investigated the carrier use of Spitfires; trials were made aboard the *Illustrious* using Spitfire VBs fitted with arrestor hooks. The success of these test flights led to the conversion of a considerable number of Spitfire VBs into what became known as Seafire IBs, which were not, as yet, provided with folding wings. The first converted Seafires were introduced in June 1942, and ultimately purpose-built Seafire IIIs entered the FAA and would serve with

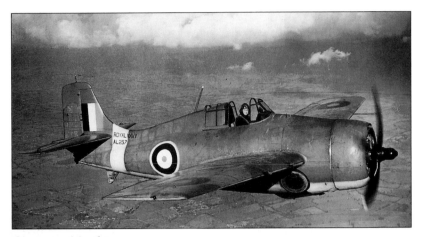

Grumman Martlet.

distinction until almost the end of the war, when they were replaced by Griffon-engined Seafire XVs.

It was the amazing Swordfish that continued to gain the acclaim. In February 1942, just six took part in the vain attempt to prevent the 'Channel Dash' of German warships from Brest through the English Channel to safer German ports. The flotilla of vessels – *Scharnhorst, Gneisenau* and *Prinz Eugen* – were first sighted in the late morning of the 12th. From Manston, Lieutenant Commander Eugene Esmonde, DSO, of No 825 squadron led six Swordfish on what proved to be a suicidal mission. The promised escort of some sixty Spitfires did not materialise, just ten managed to make the rendezvous. Esmonde led the first three Swordfish into a ferocious barrage from the German vessels. They were also attacked by a strong escort force of Me 109s and Fw 190s, and all three aircraft were shot down into the sea. The second three Swordfish made a similar attack with the same result. None of their torpedos hit the vessels, only five of the eighteen FAA airmen survived and were rescued by Naval vessels. Esmonde was awarded the Victoria Cross posthumously, the first FAA airman to be so honoured. He had been both a RAF and an Imperial Airways pilot before the war and had already survived the sinkings of the two aircraft carriers, as well as having taken part in the valiant Swordfish attack on the *Bismarck*, for which he had received the DSO. Vice-Admiral Ramsey, the Flag Officer, Dover, said of the Swordfish attack, 'In my opinion the gallant sortie of these six Swordfish constitutes one of the finest exhibitions of self-

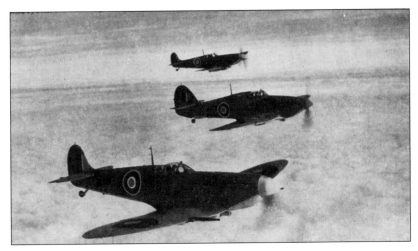

Two Seafires and a Sea Hurricane in the centre.

sacrifice and devotion to duty yet witnessed in this war.' This brave but valiant episode has passed into FAA history as 'the Gallant Sortie'. A Swordfish repainted to represent Esmonde's aircraft holds pride of place in the Fleet Air Arm Museum at Yeovilton.

In November 1942 FAA squadrons were fully involved in Operation Torch and many were also engaged in the subsequent Allied landings at Sicily, Salerno and the south of France. Whilst operating in home waters FAA torpedo bombers were active in the English Channel against enemy shipping. On 23rd May 1943 a Swordfish of No 819 squadron from the escort carrier, HMS *Archer*, piloted by Sub-Lieutenant H. Horrocks destroyed *U-752* with rocket projectiles, the first U-boat 'kill' with rockets and the seventh to be destroyed or shared by FAA aircraft in the previous twelve months. Indeed, by the end of the war Swordfish crews had sunk a greater tonnage of enemy shipping than any other type of Allied aircraft. The war record of the 'Stringbags' was probably unsurpassed by any other aircraft.

By 1944 the FAA was operating a number of new aircraft. The Fairey Barracuda torpedo bomber had entered the Service in January 1943; it was also known as the 'Beast of Burden' from the incredible variety of weapons and equipment it could carry. By 1944 there were twelve squadrons in operation, essentially replacing the Albacore rather than the Swordfish. Perhaps the FAA's most outstanding fleet fighter of the Second World War was the Vought Corsair; they began to filter into the

FAA during the summer of 1943, and over two thousand Corsairs of various marks served in a total of nineteen squadrons. Without doubt the Corsair was a truly classic Naval fighter. Another American aircraft to operate with the FAA was the Grumman Avenger, designed as a torpedo bomber but frequently used as a bomber. They mostly operated from carriers in the Pacific, but a few squadrons were engaged on anti-shipping strikes in the English Channel before and after D-Day. Fairey Aviation Company, which had long specialised in Naval aircraft, produced the Firefly, a two-seat reconnaissance fighter, that was introduced into the FAA in late 1943 and operated with the British Pacific Fleet during 1944/5. Fireflies would be still operating in the Korean War and they were not withdrawn from the Service until 1956.

In March 1944 the first landing of a twin-engined aircraft – Mosquito VI – on an aircraft carrier took place. In the following month carrier-borne aircraft, Fairey Barracudas, made a series of strikes against the German battleship *Tirpitz* then sheltering in Norwegian waters and scored fifteen direct hits with bombs. FAA operations against a variety of Norwegian targets would continue well into 1945; their final sorties were made shortly before VE Day.

The FAA made its contribution, albeit relatively small, to the massive air armada gathered for the invasion of Europe. Four FAA squadrons of Seafire IIIs and Spitfire Vs formed the 3rd Naval Fighter Wing at Lee-on-Solent as an Air Spotting Pool under the control of the Second Tactical Air Force, and five squadrons of Avengers operated from several fighter airfields. Whereas the indomitable and enduring Swordfish, now equipped with ASV Mk X, operated as an anti-shipping and anti-U-boat strike force under the control of Coastal Command from both Harrowbeer and Perranporth. Fighter support and protection was given by FAA aircraft operating from three escort carriers. These fighters were mainly Grumman Hellcats and Wildcats, which more usually operated in the Far East and the Pacific.

From 1944 most of the FAA action took place in the Pacific with the fleet and escort carriers of the British Pacific and East Indies Fleets. On 9th August 1945 Lieutenant Robert H. Gray, DSC, of the RCNVR, who was serving with No 1841 squadron on HMS *Formidable* destroyed a Japanese destroyer with a direct hit despite the fact that his Corsair was already engulfed in flames. The aircraft crashed into the sea off Honshu, the mainland island of Japan, and Gray was posthumously awarded the Victoria Cross, the second to a FAA airman (the same number as awarded to RNAS airmen in World War I). This was the last of thirty-two VCs awarded to Allied airmen. It is sad to relate that Gray had been flying operationally since 1941 and just a mere six days after his death Japan surrendered unconditionally.

The rise of Naval air power during the Second World War was nothing short of remarkable; by 1942 aircraft carriers had virtually replaced battleships as the principal fighting vessels of the Royal Navy – a revolution in Naval tactics. The Fleet Air Arm had grown from a meagre and antiquated air force into a large and modern strike force of some 1,300 aircraft with over 70,000 officers and men. It had fought with distinction in all theatres of war, and some 3,500 airmen had died. Those brave Naval airmen that have no known grave other than the sea are remembered on the Fleet Air Arm Memorial at Lee-on-Solent.

The Airfields

In 1939 there were two hundred and twenty aerodromes in the United Kingdom; the word derived from the Greek literally means 'aerial racecourse'. The Americanism 'airfield' did not come into general usage until the early years of the war. These aerodromes were almost equally split between Service and those publicly or privately owned. By 1945 the number of airfields had trebled, and they occupied some 360,000 acres of land, an area equivalent to about 40% of Cornwall. This prodigious increase was the result of an airfield construction programme conducted on a massive scale, which was probably the biggest and most ambitious building project ever completed in such a relatively short space of time.

Over £600 million was expended on construction and improvements to existing airfields during the war, which probably equates to £15 billion in today's values! Some 160 million square yards of concrete were laid down, said to be sufficient to build 'a 9,000 mile long 30 feet wide highway stretching from London to Peking'. When the programme had reached its peak in 1942, a third of the building industry – over 60,000 men – was devoted to the colossal operation, at a time when the country's manpower was stretched to its very limits and priority was accorded to their construction at the expense of clearing bomb damaged buildings. In 1942 on average one new airfield opened every three days.

In May 1934 the Air Ministry had set up an Aerodromes Board, headed by two retired senior RAF officers, given the task of selecting suitable aerodrome sites for the rapidly expanding Service. In the immediate pre-war years the Board had the luxury of being more selective in their choice of sites – relatively flat and well-drained land, free from both natural and man-made obstructions, and generally sited between fifty and six hundred feet above sea level to lessen the risk of flooding and the incidence of hill fog. The sites were invariably chosen to be set well away from large areas of population for obvious safety reasons, and the Board also worked to a remit of five miles or more distance between aerodromes.

However, with the outbreak of war and the immediate demand for airfields, the Aerodromes Board could ill-afford to be quite so selective, and it was forced to compromise on airfield locations, many of which fell short of their existing pre-war criteria. By 1940 the Board had located some 4,000 likely sites, though eventually only about 10% were actually developed into airfields. Of course the Air Ministry or the Admiralty had already requisitioned the one hundred or so civil and private aerodromes, but for a variety of reasons many were not considered suitable for operational use or further development into Service airfields. Nevertheless, Roborough, Haldon, Okehampton, St Mary's, Exeter and St Merryn were all used ultimately by military units, with the latter two becoming important RAF and FAA airfields respectively; although St Merryn was virtually a new airfield, as indeed was the North Devon Airport near Barnstaple, which was comprehensively developed into RAF Chivenor. The only new airfield site in the two counties to originate from the immediate pre-war 'Expansion' years was St Eval, where construction work commenced in 1938, and the airfield opened in October 1939.

The Board's normal selection procedure started with a long and laborious scrutiny of one inch Ordnance Survey maps, followed by an aerial assessment of the locality before a careful and accurate survey was made on foot, field by field, of any promising site, including an investigation into the nature of the subsoil. Once a location had been deemed suitable, the Air Ministry's Lands Branch undertook the legal acquisition of the necessary land, often in the region of about 600 acres. The regulations under the Emergency Powers (Defence) Act of 1939 virtually ensured instant possession by the Air Ministry, and although there was an appeals procedure in place, precious few were upheld. The most vociferous opposition came from the War Agricultural Committee, who were equally hard-pressed to use all available agricultural land for food production.

The site was now passed over to the Air Ministry's Directorate General of Works, familiarly known as 'Works and Bricks' or more disparagingly as 'Wonders and Blunders'! The Directorate was responsible for the maintenance, improvement and construction of Service airfields. It was the Directorate that arranged the contracts to the many famous civil engineering companies – Wimpey, Laing, McAlpine, French, Taylor Woodrow, and Richard Costain – that became greatly involved with the vast enterprise, as indeed did thousands of smaller sub-contractors, who were often local to the new airfield site. Also involved in airfield construction and improvements was the RAF Works Services (later to be renamed the Airfield Construction Service), which had been formed in March 1941, and one of its earliest projects in the area was Predannack on the Lizard. The Service would ultimately comprise of twenty squadrons (in the United Kingdom), with No 5012 ACS covering the South-West, and it undertook improvement work at St Eval, Chivenor, St Mawgan and Davidstow Moor.

Pre-war stations had been built to a particularly high standard, as they were intended to be permanent; indeed, many have withstood the test of time with several still operational. These 'Expansion' stations were specifically designed to blend into the local landscape. All the buildings were of brick and tile construction, the roadways, normally arranged to a set pattern, were laid in tarmacadam or concrete and a fair number of trees were planted to soften the aspect. Furthermore great care was taken to make the buildings aesthetically pleasing and they were imposing well-proportioned structures on neo-Georgian lines with impressive fronts and high porched entrances. These stations seemed to outwardly confirm the common belief in the 1930s that the RAF was 'the best flying club in the world'.

However, these rather grand and imposing stations were costly both in materials and time, and with the great urgency created by the demands of war the Works Directorate was forced to consider and develop far speedier and much more economical methods of construction. Therefore it ultimately produced hundreds of standard working drawings for airfield layouts, essential services, runways, hardstandings, buildings and hangars etc, with the result that the majority of wartime airfields were built to a fairly standard layout and pattern, with minor adjustments depending upon the local terrain. All were provided with comparable temporary technical buildings, workshops and offices, along with very similar living and communal

51

quarters and the same prominent landmarks, such as large black hangars, water towers and watch offices/control towers. Nevertheless, each airfield seemed to acquire a different and separate identity; as Richard Hough, a RAF fighter pilot and later famous biographer (who died in October 1999) recalled: 'I know of nothing more distinctive and memorable than a wartime airfield. To the outside world they may have all looked the same. To anyone who was going to live there for a while – and maybe die there – each stamped its nature indelibly on your mind . . .'

The first real construction work commenced with the provision of a concrete perimeter road which gave access to at least fifty dispersal points for parking aircraft, known as hardstandings. Back in February 1939 the Air Ministry decreed that all aircraft should be dispersed around the perimeter of airfields, in case of a surprise enemy aerial attack. The laying of the concrete or tarmacadam runways followed. The majority of pre-war Service aerodromes had been grass-surfaced, 'hard' or 'firm' runways were relatively late coming onto the scene. It was not until May 1939 that the decision was taken that all future bomber stations would be so constructed, and at the same time just eight 'priority' fighter airfields would also be supplied with 'firm' runways, although only two were completed by the outbreak of the war.

The prescribed lengths of the runways altered during 1940/1, but ultimately a standard specification was drawn up, which became known as a Class A Standard bomber station. The main runway measured 2,000 yards by 50 yards wide, with two subsidiaries, each 1,400 yards long but of the same width. The runways were to be laid as near to 60° to each other as possible, and they were invariably put down in the shape of a letter 'A'. Davidstow Moor, Dunkeswell and Upottery were Class A Standard airfields. Most wartime airfields were provided with three runways, although both Portreath and Predannack had an additional runway, whereas Winkleigh and Bolt Head, built as fighter stations had only two.

Perhaps the most distinctive and prominent landmarks on any airfields were the hangars; the name comes from the French word to describe 'a covered space for a carriage'! At pre-war stations these were large, substantial brick and steel structures, which dominated the aerodromes and the local landscape, whereas the wartime airfields were supplied with a variety of different types. All the wartime hangars had the same express purposes – mass produced and therefore relatively cheap and moreover they were quick and simple to erect. Most fighter stations were equipped with Blister hangars of varying sizes, known as 'Standard', 'Over' and 'Extra Over'. All were basically built of wooden arched ribs covered with curved corrugated iron sheeting. They did not require any flooring, and were flexible enough to be erected on uneven ground. The standard span was 45 feet and were either 25 or 45 feet long. Some 3,000 were produced by C. Miskins & Sons, and examples could be found at Bolt Head, Cleave, Exeter, Harrowbeer, Perranporth, Roborough, Portreath, Predannack, and Winkleigh.

A far larger and more substantial hangar was the Type 'T', developed by Tees-Side Bridge & Engineering Works in conjunction with the Air Ministry. They were of galvanised corrugated steel construction, and came in various sizes, but the most prevalent measured 240 feet in length, with an opening span of 113½ feet, and a height of 25 feet; these 'T2' hangars 'adorned' Davidstow Moor, Dunkeswell and Upottery. Another popular hangar was the Bellman, designed in 1936 by N. S. Bellman, a Directorate of Works' engineer. They were usually 175 feet long, 25 feet high with a span of almost 88 feet and could be found at Chivenor, Cleave, Harrowbeer, and Predannack.

Prior to 1939 air traffic control in the RAF was quite minimal; basically it was the duty of each pilot to log his flight with the duty station officer. But with wartime and the rapid expansion this all changed and one of the most vital airfield buildings was the watch

Construction work at a wartime airfield. (John Laing plc)

Aerial view of 'T2' hangar and hardstandings at Dunkeswell. (National Archives & Records)

office or control tower, as it later became known (another American term). The control tower is probably the one airfield building that evokes most nostalgic feelings and was second only in importance to the operations block. The building housed the air traffic control personnel and meteorological offices, and was fully equipped with telephone lines, radio and teleprinter apparatus and radar. It was the nerve centre of the airfield during operational flying. By late 1941 the building had become fairly standardised, known as Type 12779/41. It was a functional two-storey brick building rendered with concrete, and supplied with a railed balcony and railings on the flat roof. Some control towers were also provided with an exterior iron stairway. Several have survived and they appear rather gaunt set amongst the fields, notably at Davidstow Moor, Dunkeswell and Upottery.

Close to the control tower, and inscribed in two large white letters, about 10 feet in size, was the airfield's unique identification code. At night a mobile beacon unit, known as a 'pundit', flashed in red morse signals the airfield's code, hence why the identification letters were more commonly known as the 'Pundit Code'. Some of the codes were quite obvious, for instance 'UO' for Upottery or 'WK' for Winkleigh, but 'QB' for Harrowbeer or 'OH' for Bolt Head were not so recognizable.

Compared with pre-war stations, life on these wartime airfields could be quite rugged and rather less than comfortable, especially as some, in both Cornwall and Devon, were sited at fairly exposed locations. Most of the buildings were nothing more than pre-fabricated huts, some of timber and plasterboard, others of pre-cast concrete slabs, and there was never a shortage of the famous curved corrugated iron-sheeted Nissen huts, in a variety of lengths. The Nissen huts were the brainchild of Colonel Peter Nissen, who designed them for use in World War I when they were known as 'elephant' huts. They were still being used by the British forces in the Falklands conflict! Nissen huts invariably provided the living, messing and sleeping quarters of the airmen (and airwomen), and were normally grouped in a number of separate sites spread around the countryside, maybe a mile or so away from the operational side of the airfield and its technical site. These huts provided little in the way of comfort or warmth in the winter; nevertheless they are still fondly remembered by wartime airmen, but perhaps distance of time has lent enchantment to the memory!

Wartime airfields became closed communities, virtually self sufficient, providing the complex necessities of operational service, as well as catering for the needs of two thousand or more personnel. They were well provided with an intricate system of radio, telephone, radar,

The derelict control tower at Davidstow Moor.

and teleprinter services. The buildings were numerous and varied – an armoury, technical workshops, equipment and parachute stores, HF transmitter block, motor transport repair shops, briefing rooms, squadron and flight offices, instrument shops, photographic and meteorology sections, sick quarters, air raid shelters, fire and rescue sections, station headquarters and administration block, instructional rooms, operations block, guard room, standby set houses (for generators), *et al*. Many of these buildings were protected from blast by earth walls, with the operations block being the most substantial building, with blank and thick brick walls and a reinforced concrete flat roof. For the welfare of personnel there was usually a dental surgery, hairdresser, grocery store, cinema, NAAFI, gymnasium / concert hall and a church and / or chapel. For obvious safety reasons the bomb and ammunition stores were sited well away from the living and technical sites, in a series of narrow roadways protected by earthed boundary walls. The aviation fuel storage tanks were, if possible, installed underground, but if this was not possible they were surrounded by a brick wall and covered with earth.

The majority of wartime airfields have long since disappeared, most have been returned to agriculture. However, a certain number of airfield buildings and hangars have managed to survive the ravages of time, still adorning the countryside and being used for other industrial purposes. The wartime concrete appears to be more impervious to aging and wear, lengths of runways, perimeter roads and the odd hardstanding have endured and can still be discovered in and around

Some of the wartime concrete runways have survived – Upottery 1999.

the edges of fields, often the only links with a wartime past. This is my eighth book in the Airfields series, and during my research I have visited over 180 airfield sites around the country. I have found, quite remarkably, that each appears to have its own special atmosphere or ambience, despite the fact that so many were constructed to the same design. Certainly they are worth visiting as a vivid and poignant reminder of those stirring days of World War II. Most wartime airfields appear on Ordnance Survey Landranger maps which are generally available for reference in public libraries.

It is not the intention of these books to faithfully record all the squadrons that served at the airfields, but rather to describe the aircraft that flew from them and to reflect the nature of operations and brave actions conducted during the Second World War.

2

BOLT HEAD

This small and rather rudimentary Devon airfield was situated high on Bolt Tail headland, between Salcombe and Hope Cove, and adjacent to the Hope Cove GCI (Ground-Controlled Interception) station. Bolt Head had been brought into use in 1941 as a Forward Operating Base for fighter squadrons engaged in escorting medium bombers of No 2 Group, Bomber Command attacking targets in North-West France. In its early days it was little more than a grassed landing area with just a cluster of huts.

However, it was not fighters that first used the airfield but Lysanders of No 16 (Army Co-Operation) squadron, which arrived to give Army units their first experience of chemical warfare. The 'Lizzie', as it was familiarly known, had been designed by Westland Aircraft Ltd to an Air Ministry specification, A39/34, for a Army Co-Operation aircraft to replace the ageing Hector biplanes. The aircraft made its maiden flight at Boscombe Down in June 1936 and deliveries to the RAF began two years later to No 16 squadron. At the outbreak of war there were seven Lysander squadrons, four went over to France to serve with the British Expeditionary Force, where the aircraft's combat inadequacies were harshly exposed. The Lysander was particularly suited to small or improvised landing grounds, as it was able to land and take off on a very short run – about 240 yards.

The aircraft gained lasting wartime fame whilst used to land and pick up agents and 'passengers' in France on behalf of the SOE (Special Operations Executive). Over 1,600 Lysanders were produced and they

Westland Lysanders of No 16 (AC) squadron were the first aircraft to use the airfield.

also fulfilled another important wartime role, that of air-sea rescue, where they were used to spot ditched crews and pilots. Indeed, in the autumn of 1941 two Lysanders of No 276 (A/S/R) squadron, which had only recently been formed at Harrowbeer, began to operate from the airfield. Their first successful operation came in the afternoon of 18th December, locating the seven-man crew of a Halifax II of No 35 squadron, which had ditched about 60 miles from the English coast, after being severely damaged by flak over Brest – all were rescued.

It was now decided that the airfield could, if suitably improved, house at least one fighter squadron. During the winter of 1941/2 barrack huts were erected along with flight and administrative buildings. Fuel storage tanks were installed and a hard trackway was put down to the two Extended Blister hangars. The two grass runways were stabilised by laying down Sommerfeld tracking, which provided two runways, each 2,700 feet long, although these would be later extended to 4,200 and 3,680 feet respectively.

Sommerfeld tracking was 13 gauge, 3 inch mesh wire netting secured with metal pickets and further strengthened by flat steel bars. It had originated in the First World War, but during 1940 it was further developed by Kurt Sommerfeld, an Austrian engineer, and was used especially in the deserts of North Africa, where it acquired the name 'tin lino'! The tracking was easy to transport, lay and repair, and provided a robust and non-skid surface that could easily be camouflaged. It was most beneficial during the winter months when the tracking provided a reasonably secure and dry landing surface. It was increasingly used in this country as fighters became heavier, especially the American P-47s and RAF Typhoons.

Bolt Head now officially became a forward satellite airfield for Exeter in No 10 Group of Fighter Command. The first fighters to use the improved airfield were Spitfire VBs of No 317 'City of Wilno' squadron, part of the Polish Fighter Wing formed at Exeter in August 1941. The airfield, and the GCI station situated to the east, attracted the Luftwaffe's attention; on 7th March 1942 two Fw 190s, the scourge of coastal towns and airfields, made a surprise strafing attack, damaging a Spitfire that was just taking off. The Luftwaffe returned at the end of April and bombed the airfield without causing significant damage.

The Spitfire originated from an Air Ministry Specification F7/30 (later F37/34) to which R. J. Mitchell, the chief designer of Supermarine Aviation, responded with his first design of a revolutionary monoplane – F400. It was the successful marriage of Mitchell's airframe with a Rolls-Royce PV12 engine, later named Merlin, that ensured the aircraft's astounding success. It first flew on 6th March 1936, and was already known as the 'Spitfire', although Mitchell was not impressed. He is reported to have said, 'Sort of bloody name they *would* choose!' The aircraft entered the Service in August 1938, and the rest is history. Over 20,000 were produced in a bewildering array of marks and its last operational sortie was flown in June 1954. Douglas Bader considered it, 'the aeroplane of one's dreams.'

The Mark V was the most popular with over 6,400 being built, some 30% of the total production. It had first appeared in February 1941 and for the next eighteen months or so Spitfire Vs would be the mainstay of Fighter Command. There were three variants 'A' to 'C', depending on their armament of Browning machine guns and/or Hispano cannons, with the 'C' version able to carry one 500 or two 250 pound bombs. Each was powered by a Rolls-Royce Merlin 45 engine, giving a maximum speed in excess of 370 mph at 13,000 feet, and they were the first marks to be fitted with drop fuel tanks to increase their operational range. However, by the autumn of 1941 the Spitfire pilots found themselves at some disadvantage when faced with the Luftwaffe's new Fw 190s, which were about 20 mph faster at all altitudes, and could out-climb, out-dive and out-roll the Spitfire Vs.

The Polish pilots were mainly engaged in Rhubarbs and Mosquitos, basically small-scale harassing operations using cloud cover. One squadron commander maintained that these type of operations were well-suited to his pilots' temperament, as they 'seemed to recall the traditions of our country's cavalry'! On 15th March the squadron suffered a horrendous day. Twelve pilots had been detailed for a fighter sweep over Northern France, and on their return to Bolt Head the aircraft were short of fuel, adding to the problems of thick fog severely reducing visibility. Only two managed to land safely, the other ten were either force-landed or abandoned with five totally destroyed for the loss of one pilot killed and another three injured. In the following month the Polish Wing moved to Northolt and soon the airfield would be used by Spitfire VBs of No 310 squadron, the first to be formed (in July 1940) with Czechoslovakian refugees. It had moved from Perranporth to Exeter in May 1942 and was now commanded by Squadron Leader Frantisek Dolezal, DFC, who had flown with No 19 squadron during the Battle of Britain. The pilots would be engaged in a mixture of fighter sweeps, Rhubarbs, bomber escorts and convoy patrols.

In September the first Hawker Typhoons used the airfield. They belonged to No 257 squadron, which had only recently (July) been equipped with the new fighter. The Typhoon had been designed by Sidney Camm and was developed in 1937 from two prototypes. It had first flown in February 1940, and its subsequent development was hastened in order to counter the potent threat of the Fw 190s. The 'Tiffy', as it was affectionately called, was a large and brutish aircraft powered by a Napier Sabre I piston engine, and armed with twelve .303 machine guns, later replaced by four 20mm cannons. It entered the Service in September 1941 with No 56 squadron at Duxford, the same airfield that heralded the arrival of the Spitfire. However, serious problems dogged its early Service life, such as structural failures around the tail plane, cockpit leakages and a weak undercarriage. Additionally, its engine proved a little temperamental with poor performance at higher altitudes. Slowly all the problems were resolved, the original engine was replaced by the greatly improved Sabre IIA to C engines, and then its full potential as a fast low-level strike aircraft was realised. It became a superlative ground attack aircraft, a role in which it was quite devastating with the 2nd Tactical Air Force.

The 'Tiffy' pilots were busy working up to operational readiness; it was not the easiest aircraft to fly. They claimed their first success on 28th September – a Junkers 88. On 3rd November when Teignmouth was bombed by Fw 190s, the squadron's pilots managed to overtake four of them 30 miles west of Guernsey. Two were shot down and the others

Hawker Typhoon IB of No 257 squadron. (via J. Adams)

damaged. Early in the New Year the squadron moved to Warmwell.

On 26th September three squadrons, Nos 401 and 402 of the RCAF and No 133 (Eagle), used Bolt Head as an advanced base whilst engaged on escorting B-17s of the Eighth Air Force detailed to attack the Focke-Wulf plant at Morlaix U-boat pens at Brest. All three squadrons were equipped with Spitfire IXs, the 'stop-gap' mark hastily developed to combat Fw 190s. They were powered by the new Merlin 61 engines, giving a top speed in excess of 400 mph, and they proved to be more manoeuvrable than Fw 190s. The mark became so successful that over 5,700 were produced, second only to the mark Vs they replaced, and ultimately some sixty squadrons operated IXs.

The weather conditions for the Eighth Air Force's operation were quite atrocious, and the whole operation was a dismal failure; one of the American Bomb Groups was recalled, as was No 1 Fighter Group's P-38s. The day proved disastrous for No 133 squadron, one of three squadrons in Fighter Command manned by American volunteer pilots, then based at Great Sampford in Essex. Of the twelve Spitfires in action, four were shot down, with two pilots killed and two taken prisoner; one of these was the British acting Squadron Leader Gordon Bretell, who was involved in the famous 'Great Escape' and was one of the fifty POWs executed by the Gestapo. Four landed in France in error believing they were in Devon; one of the pilots managed to evade capture and escaped to Spain with the help of the French underground. Another aircraft managed to make it back to England but short of fuel, it crash-landed at Kingsbridge near to the airfield; the pilot escaped with minor injuries. The squadron had almost been wiped out, a tragic conclusion to its short time in Fighter Command. Three days later the squadron was disbanded to become the 336th Pursuit Squadron of the USAAF's 4th Fighter Group.

In late June 1943 the airfield received its first permanent squadron, No 610 (County of Chester), one of a number of Auxiliary Air Force squadrons that had been formed in 1936, and dubbed by Churchill 'the weekend fliers'! The squadron, operating Spitfire VBs, which were now rather out-moded, was engaged on fighter sweeps and convoy patrols; it also temporarily moved east to No 11 Group airfields to fly a variety of operations. The squadron left for Fairwood Common in December, although it would return briefly in the following May.

From March 1944 until early September several fighter squadrons used the airfield, some only briefly. Typhoon 1Bs of No 266 squadron arrived from Harrowbeer for five days, followed by Spitfire VBs of No 234 squadron, which had operated at St Eval during the Battle of Britain. When No 234 departed on 29th April more Spitfires landed; but these were a rare mark – XIIs. Powered by Rolls-Royce Griffon III or IV engines, they had clipped wings to provide increased speed at low altitudes and an even greater rate of roll with a strengthened fuselage. By reputation the XIIs had better handling qualities than all previous marks. Only two squadrons were equipped with them – Nos 41 and 91 – and it was the former that now arrived at Bolt Head.

This squadron was the first to operate XIIs in February 1943, and it was commanded by Squadron Leader Arthur A. Glen, DFC, who had joined the squadron in the summer of 1941. He was posted to No 126 squadron in Malta, where he brought his tally of victories to eight. In 1943 he rejoined the squadron claiming two Fw 190s in September, and was given command of the squadron in April. Their Spitfires had recently been modified for bombing and the pilots were fully engaged in practising bombing runs. No 41 remained at the airfield until after D-Day, except for a short spell of detachment in May.

No 610 squadron returned briefly in May with yet another Spitfire – XIVs – effectively the high-altitude version of the XIIs. They were capable of speeds well in excess of 400 mph, and would prove to be most successful against the V1 rockets or 'divers'. When No 41 squadron returned to Bolt Head, its pilots quickly became fully engaged on pre-D-Day operations. They flew dedicated patrols over the coastal areas to the west of Portsmouth, and on 5th June thirty-two

Spitfire XIIs of No 41 squadron.

sorties were flown to protect shipping crossing the English Channel. The pilots were in the air from dawn to dusk. On D-day itself twenty-five sorties were mounted, a mixture of shipping and A/S/R patrols, particularly around the Channel Islands. When the squadron left for West Malling in Kent on 19th June, it had lost three aircraft since D-Day.

The Spitfires were immediately replaced by Typhoon 1Bs of No 263 squadron, which as will be noted later had spent a peripatetic existence moving around a number of Devon and Cornwall airfields. The pilots were engaged in attacking a variety of coastal targets and shipping, including radar sites, during which it lost two aircraft (MN300 and MN477), the latter shot down on 24th June off St Malo.

Whilst all this urgent flurry of fighter activity was taking place, 'B' Flight of No 276 (A/S/R) squadron plied its trade from the airfield. It was equipped with six Spitfire LFVBs and six Supermarine Walrus IIs. The Spitfires normally operated in pairs mainly for their own protection. In late August the squadron moved to Querqueville (A.23), an advanced landing field in Normandy, being replaced by another A/S/R unit, No 275, which since April had been based at Warmwell. The squadron was also equipped with Spitfire VBs and Walrus IIs. The latter aircraft had virtually become the mainstay of A/S/R squadrons. This rather inelegant amphibian biplane had first flown in June 1933, then known as a Seagull V. It was designed by R.J. Mitchell of Spitfire

Auster IVs of No 652 (AOP) squadron at Bolt Head. (Museum of Army Flying)

Memorial stone at Bolt Head.

fame and was renamed Walrus in August 1935, entering the FAA in the following March. The Walrus II had a top speed of about 135 mph with a range of about 600 miles. It had a wooden hull with a railing around the forward fuselage to help survivors to climb aboard more easily. Some 740 Walruses were produced, being universally known as the 'Shagbat'. It was certainly a most welcoming sight to the hundreds of ditched crews and airmen. The squadron moved to Exeter in the autumn, leaving a small detachment at Bolt Head until the squadron was disbanded in February 1945.

Briefly over the D-Day period, No 652 (AOP) or Air Observation Post squadron moved into Bolt Head with its Taylorcraft Auster IVs, the direct military version of an American pre-war civilian sports aircraft. Being exceedingly light in construction, it was the manufacturer's proud boast that the tail section could be easily lifted by 'a young lady'! They were also blessed with the ability of a very short take off and landing run – just 150 yards; although they appeared fragile, the aircraft proved to be quite rugged, becoming indispensable for Army support duties. Early on 8th June the Austers left Bolt Head for an Advanced Landing Ground in Normandy. They were escorted across the Channel by a FAA Walrus and became the first British aircraft to be based in France after the invasion.

The last fighter squadron to operate from Bolt Head was No 611 (West Lancashire); it arrived on 17th July under the command of Squadron Leader William A. Douglas, DFC, Bar, appropriately an Auxiliary Air Force officer, who had previously commanded No 603 squadron. It was probably only right and proper that it would be Spitfires – IXs – that brought the airfield's wartime operations to a conclusion. By the end of August the last Spitfire had left for Bradwell Bay, and other than the detachment of A/S/R aircraft and the odd emergency landing Bolt Head's wartime activities had ceased. The airfield was placed under Care and Maintenance in April 1945.

Most of this small wartime airfield has long since disappeared under farming, although the National Trust does own some of the land, known as The Warren, where a fine stone memorial plaque stands at the intersection of what were the two runways. The old airfield and the memorial can be reached by taking the road from Marlborough to Soar, branching left to pass the old Coastguard cottages, where it is situated in the car park just beyond the cottages.

3
CHIVENOR

The churchyard at Heanton Punchardon affords a splendid panoramic view of this large Devon airfield, situated along the estuary of the Taw, which for over half a century had been an important RAF station. It owes its existence to the small grassed airfield, known as the Barnstaple and North Devon Airport, which was requisitioned by the Air Ministry at the outbreak of the Second World War. Even the Short Scions that had been used on the daily service to Lundy Island were brought into military use – on Army Co-operation duties in conjunction with searchlight batteries. Also an area of the original aerodrome was occupied by a Unit of the Civilian Repair Organisation set up by Lord Nuffield to co-ordinate the repair, rebuild and conversion of operational aircraft; from June 1940, Tiger Moths were repaired there.

With the Air Ministry's desperate need in 1940 to find suitable airfield sites, the prime location of this aerodrome made it ripe for further development. Some 500 acres of land adjacent and to the west of the original airfield were purchased by the Air Ministry, encompassing Marsh and Chivenor farms – hence its subsequent name. In May 1940 the building contract was awarded to George Wimpey & Co Ltd, and blessed with fine early summer weather the construction work continued apace. By the middle of June the first of the three projected 3,000 foot runways had been laid, as well as four Bellman and four Hinaidi hangars erected. They were rather uniquely sited in two parallel rows. The latter dated from the 1920s and although similar in design and size to the Bellman, it was clearly identified by its high pitched roof. Relatively few Hinaidi hangars were to be found at wartime airfields.

On 25th October 1940 RAF Chivenor opened although further building work was still in progress, and would not be completed until the following January. The new airfield had been allocated to No 17 (Training) Group of Coastal Command, then under the command of Air Commodore T. E. B. Howe, CBE, AFC, and a month later No 3 (Coastal) Operational Training Unit was formed there. Like the other two Commands, Coastal was faced with a major logistical problem of providing operational training for the large influx of crews leaving the flying training schools. Up until early 1940 front-line squadrons had been mainly responsible for the operational training of new crews, and this rather informal system had been quite satisfactory in peacetime. However, with the sheer number of new crews, plus the fact that all of the Command's meagre squadrons were considerably overstretched operationally, it became imperative that a number of OTUs should be established. The Command's first OTU had been formed in April, and the course, originally scheduled to last four weeks, had been extended to two months, because of the increasingly complex roles that General Reconnaissance (GR) crews now had to undertake.

The Unit was originally supplied with Ansons and Beauforts. The latter aircraft had been designed during 1935/6 as a torpedo/GR bomber intended for service in the Far East. Coastal Command was already scheduled to be equipped with another new torpedo bomber, the Botha. However, because of the conspicuous failure of the Botha as an operational aircraft, the Type 152 Beaufort was substituted, and it became the Command's standard torpedo-bomber until 1943.

However, the development of the Beaufort was not without problems. Production of seventy-eight was authorised in August 1936 straight 'off the drawing board', a fairly unusual occurrence in pre-war days, and yet the first prototype did not fly until 15th October 1938. This was partly on account of problems with its newly developed Bristol Taurus engines, which would continue to dog the aircraft after its introduction into the Service in December 1939 with No 22 squadron. The Beaufort I had a top speed of 235 mph with an operational range of 1,600 miles and was armed with four .303 machine guns, up to 1,500 pounds of bombs or one 1,605 pound torpedo; it required a crew of four.

During its first twelve months or so Chivenor was almost solely devoted to flying training of some description. Early in January 1941 the first Beaufort conversion course was mounted mainly for the pilots

Beaufort I of No 2 Flight, No 3 (C) OTU. (Imperial War Museum)

of No 42 squadron converting from their antiquated biplanes –
Vildebeest IIIs and IVs. The OTU would operate from the airfield until
July, when it was replaced the following month by one of the two new
Coastal Command OTUs – No 5.

On 1st December 1940, No 252 squadron arrived from Bircham
Newton with its Blenheim IFs and IVFs, under the command of
Squadron Leader R.G. Yaxley, MC, specifically to convert to Beaufighter
F1Cs, followed, in April, by another Blenheim squadron – No 272. The
conversion was a prolonged affair, mainly because Fighter Command
had preference for this scarce new fighter. Nevertheless, on 6th April
No 252 made the first operational sortie by a Coastal Command
Beaufighter, from Aldergrove and ten days later would claim its first
victory of the war – Fw 200. The squadron would be the first to operate
Beaufighters outside the United Kingdom. No 272 was also posted
overseas, to Malta. The departure of these two squadrons abroad
brought about an unfortunate delay in Coastal Command's plans for a
strong Beaufighter fighter and anti-shipping strike force, which
ultimately proved to be so successful.

For just over three years KLM, the Dutch national airline, operating
under the auspices of British Overseas Airways Corporation, would use
Chivenor as a staging post on its regular wartime passenger service
from BOAC's land-base at Whitchurch, Bristol to Lisbon, Portugal. The

Beaufighter IC of No 252 squadron, early 1941. (via H. Morris)

first flight landed on 24th December 1940 and until Hurn in Dorset became the country's major international airport in February 1944, Chivenor would be used by a number of 'civil' aircraft, mainly Douglas DC-2s and 3s. It is interesting to note that when KLM received its first DC-3 in October 1936, it was advertised as a 'luxury airliner'! These flights across the Bay of Biscay were fraught with danger and when fighters were available, escort support was provided. Surprisingly few incidents occurred, although a KLM DC-3, G-AGBB, was shot down in June 1943 by a Junkers 88; amongst the missing passengers was the film star Leslie Howard.

In early 1941 the airfield's main runway was extended and concrete taxiways and hardstandings were laid, which seemed to be the signal for the Luftwaffe to strike. In March the airfield was bombed with little damage sustained, but, on 16th April, the Luftwaffe returned and the raid caused substantial damage to parked aircraft, the control tower and the runways, putting the airfield out of commission for several days. Another Luftwaffe surprise was in store for Chivenor on 20th November when a Junkers 88A-6 landed. It had left from Morlaix in France for an anti-shipping patrol over the Irish Sea, and due to a grave navigational error the crew thought Chivenor was an airfield in Brittany! The aircraft duly joined the RAF's No 1426 (Enemy Aircraft) Flight at Duxford; the purpose of this unusual unit was to study and compare the relative performances of the captured aircraft. From

February 1942 onwards, the Flight made tours of RAF (and later USAAF) stations with its motley collection of aircraft, to assist aircrews in aircraft recognition and to enlighten them on their various performances. The 'Chivenor' Ju 88 would return briefly to the airfield in October 1942.

In November 1941 Armstrong Whitworth Whitley Vs of No 502 (Ulster), an Auxiliary Air Force squadron that had been assigned to Coastal Command in November 1938, were detached from Limavady to Chivenor for anti-submarine patrols. The Whitley, a rather cumbersome and inelegant aircraft, commonly known as the 'Flying Barn Door', dated from 1936, and had first entered Coastal Command in the autumn of 1940 mainly because of its operational range – over 1,600 miles; although No 58's Whitley IIIs had been seconded from Bomber Command in late September 1939 to mid-February to fly convoy escorts and anti-submarine patrols. The Whitleys carried ASV Mk.II radar, which the squadron had introduced operationally in October 1940. On the last day of November Flying Officer R. W. G. Holsworth's crew made a radar contact with a U-boat, *U-206*, in the Bay of Biscay and it was claimed to have been destroyed by depth charges. In 1992 this claim was reassessed and amended to the opinion that the Whitley had in fact attacked *U-71* without causing serious damage and *U-206* was sunk in a minefield off St Nazaire. It should be noted that immediately after the war the Admiralty and the US Navy set up committees to assess the accuracy of all claims of U-boats destroyed in the light of German Naval documents. The Foreign Documents Section/Naval Historical Branch has reassessed a number of U-boat 'kills' in recent years, and its current findings or decisions have been reflected in this account.

Despite their inherent faults and obvious antiquity, Whitley Vs and later VIIs would give admirable service to Coastal Command over the next few years, bridging the Command's long-range operational gap until they were replaced by Wellingtons and Liberators. No 502 squadron would move down the coast to St Eval at the end of the year, but a number of Whitley squadrons would be detached to Chivenor later in 1942.

Undoubtedly Chivenor's main claim to wartime fame was in the introduction and operational use of the 'Leigh Light', which became a valuable and effective device in the Command's U-boat offensive. The problem of sighting U-boats at night, when they normally surfaced to cross the Bay of Biscay and re-charge their batteries, had been taxing the scientists and dedicated airmen of the Command's Development Unit since its formation in November 1940; in January 1941 even experiments were being made with parachute flares. However, it would be an ex-World War I pilot serving at the Command's Headquarters, who came up with the ultimate solution. Squadron Leader Humphrey de Vere 'Sammy' Leigh had proposed to the Air Ministry that the answer was to fit a searchlight into a Wellington to illuminate the target once it had been located by radar.

Squadron Leader Leigh had received the encouragement and support of Air Chief Marshal Sir Frederick Bowhill, and had refined his idea by recommending the use of a Royal Navy 22/24 inch carbon arc light; the Air Ministry was somewhat less than enthusiastic about his proposal. Nevertheless, experimental work was eventually authorised and his Light was fitted into a Wellington 1C, P9223, and trials were conducted during April/May 1941. Although they proved successful the new C-in-C of the Command, Air Chief Marshal Sir Philip Joubert de la Ferte wanted to consider a different lighting device – the Helmore 'Turbinlite' – then being trialled by Fighter Command. After considerable delay Joubert decided to back the Leigh Light, and in December the Air Ministry approved the installation of a 'Leigh Light' and ASV Mk II radar into six Wellingtons, which were designated Mark VIIIs, with the promise of another thirty should the experiment prove to be operationally effective. The retractable Light was installed in the ventral turret position with the nose armament removed to accommodate the searchlight operator.

The Wellington was one of the most remarkable aircraft of the Second World War. It had been designed by Barnes Wallis (of 'bouncing bomb' fame), and its unique geodetic design – metal lattices covered with fabric – proved to be immensely strong and durable, able to sustain considerable damage and still survive. The Wellington became a most reliable and versatile aircraft and popular with crews, being dubbed the 'Wimpy' after the famous cartoon character, J. Wellington Wimpy! Its fame with the British public was ensured by the early and successful propaganda film, *Target for Tonight* in which it had the 'starring' part. Wellingtons performed in a diversity of roles unequalled by any other bomber. Over 11,460 were produced, and they were still being used for aircrew training up to 1953, fifteen years after they had first entered the Service.

In order to pursue the operational feasibility of the Leigh Light, No 1417 Flight was formed at Chivenor on 8th January 1942 under the

Wellington VIII of No 172 squadron, October 1942. (RAF Museum)

command of Squadron Leader J.H. Greswell, a pre-war regular officer who had served in the Command's Development Unit. During the next four months the crews eagerly awaited the arrival of their (LL) Wellington VIIIs, but the supply was painfully slow, prolonging the training programme. The crews used the Helwick Light vessel in the Bristol Channel as an 'enemy' target, and it was found that the most effective height for the Light was 250 feet, but at this altitude it would be easy to fly into the sea with the light on; later radio altimeters would be supplied to give greater accuracy and safety. On 4th April the Flight was expanded into No 172 squadron under the command of Wing Commander John B. Russell, with a planned complement of twenty (LL) Wellingtons; it was destined to serve at Chivenor for well over two years with spells of detachment at Wick, Malta, Gibraltar and the Azores. On 14th April one of the original Wellingtons whilst on a local flight to St Eval crashed into a cliff near Hartland Point, killing the crew. Another Wellington would be lost during training when it was mistakenly attacked by a US tanker in the Bristol Channel.

On the night of 3rd/4th June four of the squadron's crews were briefed to make the first Leigh Light operation. The Wellingtons left Chivenor at around 10.30 pm to make a careful sweep of the Bay of Biscay as far as the north coast of Spain at an altitude of about 2,000 feet. Some seven hours later three Wellingtons returned having sighted and successfully illuminated a couple of fishing boats and a small merchant vessel. However, the Wellington captained by Squadron Leader

Greswell located and lighted an Italian submarine, *Luigi Torelli*, some sixty miles north of the Spanish coast. Four 250 pound Mk. 8 Torpex depth charges were dropped, damaging the submarine but not sinking it. The aircraft's navigator, Pilot Officer S.J. Pooley must have experienced some satisfaction as he had developed 'Torpex' whilst serving in the Development Unit; it became the most effective underwater explosive used in the war. The *Luigi Torelli* was forced to remain on the surface whilst making for port for urgent repairs; two days later it was attacked by Sunderlands of No 10 (RAAF) squadron, but again survived.

During the month several more sightings were made using the Leigh Light, but not until 5/6th July was the first U-boat 'kill', *U-502*, made by a (LL) Wellington crew; it was captained by Pilot Officer W.B. Howell, an American volunteer, later awarded the DFC before he transferred to the US Navy. The Leigh Light would play a significant part in the U-boat offensive, not necessarily for the number of 'kills' achieved, but rather because the U-boat commanders became markedly reluctant to surface at night, thus offering greater opportunities for daylight operations. Although best known for its use in Wellingtons, an under-wing version was fitted to both Catalinas and Liberators.

From June 1941 Chivenor became a fully operational station, when it was transferred into No 19 Group, then commanded by Air Commodore A. R. Bromet, CBE, DSO. In the previous month No 5 (C) OTU had moved away to Turnberry in Scotland, having suffered a number of fatal accidents during its time at Chivenor, mainly due to engine failures in its Beauforts; back in February there had been three fatal crashes in two nights. Whitley Vs of Nos 51 and 77 squadrons had arrived on loan from Bomber Command, along with No 612 (County of Aberdeen), another Coastal Command Whitley squadron. Although the bomber crews took some time to acclimatise themselves to this vastly different type of operation, in June over 190 anti-submarine patrols were mounted from the airfield and five Whitleys and one Wellington were lost. Most were victims of the increasing number of Junkers 88s, which were based along the French Atlantic coast. Several Beaufighter squadrons would be detached to Chivenor to give fighter protection; the first was No 235, commanded by Wing Commander H.J. Garlick, DFC, which arrived in July, followed in January 1943 by No 404 (RCAF), which had been equipped with Beaufighters only a few months earlier. Besides escort duties the crews flew convoy and fishery patrols as well as operations over the Bay of Biscay seeking out the

Whitley VII of No 502 squadron. (via D. Howard)

dreaded Junkers 88s and the occasional Fw 200.

Before the Whitleys returned to Bomber Command in October 1942, a crew of No 77 squadron damaged *U-256* on 2nd September, which forced its return to Brest for repairs. The following day Flight Sergeant A.A. MacInnes' crew were credited with the destruction of *U-705*, but this was reassessed in 1987 amending the claim to *U-660* attacked with little damage inflicted. During October and November Chivenor was used as a convenient refuelling point for the numerous RAF and USAAF aircraft flying to Gibraltar and North Africa engaged in Operation Torch. In December another Wellington VIII squadron, No 547, arrived from Holmsley South; it had been formed the previous October under Squadron Leader H.N. Garbutt and would remain until the following June except for a period of detachment at Tain in Scotland for torpedo training. In the New Year one of the three Command's squadrons to be equipped with Boeing Flying Fortress IIAs, operated from the airfield. However, No 59 squadron's stay was relatively brief, mainly on account of inadequacies of the runways; the Fortresses returned to Thorney Island.

From now onwards Chivenor became the Command's premier (LL)

Wellington station, fully engaged in night (and day) operations over the Bay of Biscay and the North Atlantic. No 172 squadron had since March been under the command of Wing Commander Rowland G. Musson, a pre-war officer; it was the first squadron to be supplied with the vastly improved centimetric ASV Mk. III radar encased in a prominent nose radome. In February U-268 was destroyed by Flying Officer G.D. Lundon's crew on the 19th – the squadron's second U-boat 'kill'. Two other U-boats, U-459 and U-614, claimed to have been destroyed in the following two months have since been reassessed. July was a particularly successful month for the squadron, three U-boats were destroyed, U-126, U-459 and U-614. Flight Sergeant A. Coumbis' crew sunk U-126 on the 3rd, and when U-459 was destroyed by Flying Officer W.H.T. Jennings and his crew on 24th July, heavy flak from the U-boat caused the Wellington to blow up; only the rear gunner survived. Wing Commander Musson's crew accounted for U-614 to the north-west of Spain five days later. Sadly a month later the Wing Commander and his crew would be killed when their Wellington crashed a few miles inland from Clovelly shortly after taking off from Chivenor. He was replaced by Wing Commander E. G. Palmer. Another two Wellingtons were lost in August, one to engine trouble and the second due to accidental causes.

Over the next eighteen months No 172 was joined by a number of (LL) Wellington squadrons, and, in September, by a detachment of Seafires of No 748 (FAA) squadron (No 10 (Naval) OTU) from St Merryn, to provide fighter affiliation exercises – simulating enemy fighter attacks – for the Wellington crews. However, during the month the airfield suffered serious flooding, and later in the year the runways began to break up, requiring urgent remedial work. Most of No 172's Wellingtons were temporarily detached to Gibraltar, and the other two (LL) Wellington squadrons, Nos 407 (RCAF) and 612, under the command of Wing Commander J. B. Russell (previously with No 172) moved out to St Eval.

In early 1944 No 172 squadron was back at Chivenor, although some crews were still on detachment at Lagens in the Azores and whilst there two U-boats had been destroyed. The squadron would not be back to full strength until April. By the following month there would be four (LL) Wellington squadrons operating at Chivenor; Nos 407(RCAF) and 612, along with No 304 'Land of Silesia' Polish squadron. No 304 squadron had suffered heavy casualties whilst originally serving in Bomber Command, but its crews were now well experienced in anti-

Wellington XIV: Chivenor was a premier (LL) Wellington station.

submarine operations having been transferred to Coastal Command in May 1942; it had previously operated from Davidstow Moor. The airfield was crammed with some seventy (LL) Wellingtons, all XIVs, which had entered production in May 1943. They carried a retractable Leigh Light amidships and featured a prominent nose radome for its ASV Mk.III radar. The aircraft was armed with seven .303 machine guns, could carry four rocket projectiles under each wing and had an endurance of some ten hours, or about 1,360 miles; the crews would patrol the Bay of Biscay and the coastal waters between Gibraltar and Cape Finisterre. No 407 squadron, under Wing Commander R.A.Ashman, recorded their second U-boat 'kill' on 4th May when Flying Officer L.J. Bateman's crew sunk *U-846* to the north of Spain.

All four squadrons would be engaged in the Command's massive and vital task to ensure that enemy U-boats or surface vessels did not enter the western approaches of the English Channel as the vast armada of Allied vessels were gathering for the invasion of Europe. The operation, code-named Cork, planned that an area of about 20,000 square miles of sea would be patrolled continuously every 30 minutes round the clock, thus the twelve designated interlocking patrol areas required the maximum resources of No 19 Group. On D-Day it comprised no fewer than thirty-one squadrons (RAF, FAA and US Navy) of various aircraft directly involved in the Operation, with the Chivenor Wellington squadrons bearing most of the brunt of the night operations.

Although over 350 individual patrols were mounted from the airfield during June, only one U-boat was sunk. A Polish crew captained by Flight Lieutenant J. Antoniewicz of No 304 squadron was credited with the sinking of *U-441* on 18th June, its six depth charges said to have virtually blown the U-boat into pieces. This U-boat was the first experimental boat to be equipped with two heavily armed 'bandstands' of 20mm guns back in May 1943, and had survived at least two attacks by Coastal Command units (see Predannack). However, a recent reassessment (1997) of this sinking has amended the credit to a Liberator of No 224 from St Eval; 304's Wellington attack 'was very probably directed against a nonsubmarine target, possibly a whale'! During June five Wellingtons were lost with a number being damaged in action or in flying accidents. The first, piloted by Squadron Leader D.W. Farrell of No 407 (RCAF) squadron went missing on the night of the 6/7th. No 172 squadron lost two aircraft and a third would go missing at the end of July.

In September No 304 squadron left for Benbecula, followed by No 172 to Limavady, after over two and a half years of service at Chivenor; the squadron ended the war with seven credited U-boat sinkings. No 179 squadron moved in briefly from Predannack; it had been the second unit to be equipped with (LL) Wellingtons back in September 1942. However, its crews would move down to St Eval, where they would exchange their Wellingtons for Warwick Vs. In October two other Wellington squadrons arrived from the Middle East and Italy respectively, Nos 14 and 36. No 14 would have a detachment at Portreath and the latter squadron, now commanded by Wing Commander G. Williams, had originally been engaged on anti-submarine duties in the Far East. Its crews would mainly patrol off the Channel Islands seeking out the remaining U-boats operating in the area, although from September until the end of the year only five U-boats were sunk by No 19 Group's squadrons. It was the Canadian crews of No 407 (RCAF) squadron that claimed the final U-boat 'kill' for aircraft operating from Chivenor; *U-772* was destroyed by Squadron Leader C.J.W. Taylor's crew in the English Channel to the south of Weymouth on 30th December. This was the squadron's third U-boat victory.

In March 1945 No 36 squadron moved out to Benbecula, where it would be disbanded in early June. Also in March (14th) No 459 squadron reassembled at Chivenor after service in the Middle East, where it had operated Martin Baltimores. However, before it was allocated any new aircraft, the squadron was disbanded on 10th April. No 14 squadron was also disbanded on 1st June, and it was left to the Canadian crews to mount the last wartime operational patrol from

'. . . the neat rows of white headstones . . . tell their own poignant and silent story. . .'

Chivenor on 2nd June 1945. Two days later the squadron was disbanded, having operated in Coastal Command since May 1941, and during this period lost forty-two aircraft (Hudsons and Wellingtons). Appropriately there is a memorial plaque in Heanton Punchardon church dedicated 'in proud and honoured memory of the Canadian air crew who laid down their lives for King and Country . . . and are buried in this churchyard'.

The progress of RAF Chivenor over the next fifty years is not germane to this account; the RAF Ensign was lowered for the last time on 1st October 1995, when the airfield was formally transferred to the Royal Marines. The neat rows of white headstones in the churchyard tell their own poignant and silent story of the airfield's past.

4

CLEAVE

Few wartime airfields are quite as simple to locate as Cleave; the
original site in Cornwall is now occupied by the Composite Signals
Organisation, and the station's large and futuristic dish aerials are
plainly visible from miles away, emanating an uneasy and almost eerie
feeling. The sole surviving remnant of wartime RAF Cleave is a row of
married quarters, aptly named Cleave Crescent, and but for them the
name would have all but disappeared, as the Signals Station has taken
the name of Morwenstow, a village a mile or so due north.

In early 1939 Cleave was planned as a temporary landing ground for
the summer anti-aircraft co-operation and artillery training camps in
the area. The necessary land, perched on cliffs some four hundred feet
above sea level, was requisitioned from the estate of Cleave Manor, and
was situated four miles to the north of Bude close to the village of
Kilkhampton. In May it was first occupied by airmen and aircraft of 'G'
and 'V' Flights of No 1 Anti-Aircraft Co-operation Unit. The airmen
were accommodated under canvas, as indeed were their aircraft! Two
(later increased to three) Bessoneaux hangars had been erected; relics of
the First World War that had been brought out of storage as considered
quite adequate for use at a seasonal landing ground. This Type 'H'
hangar was a large light-weight timber frame construction and covered
with heavy canvas. It dated from 1916 and was French in origin.
Perhaps its main disadvantage was that the canvas doors were apt to
freeze during the winter months!

The aircraft supplied to the two Flights were also of a certain

Westland Wallaces flew from Cleave in its early days.

antiquity. 'G' Flight used Westland Wallaces as target-towers. This two-seater biplane was a direct derivative of the company's successful Wapiti aircraft, and had entered the Service in early 1933. Its main claim to fame was that it had flown at a height of 31,000 feet over Mount Everest during the Houston expedition of 1933. Only five squadrons were ever equipped with Wallaces, but nevertheless at the outbreak of war the RAF had over eighty of them on complement. Such is their renown that there is a full-scale model of the aircraft on display at the Science Museum in London.

The other Flight operated a most unusual aircraft – de Havilland DH.82B or Queen Bee. This was a pilotless radio-controlled aircraft that had been developed by de Havilland as a result of an Air Ministry specification, 18/33, for 'a radio controlled target'. It had first flown in 1935 and was then trialled and developed by No 1 Pilotless Aircraft Unit, initially at Farnborough and subsequently at Henlow in Bedfordshire. Indeed, Squadron Leader Pearce, the Station Commander at Cleave, had served in No 1 PAU at Henlow. Externally resembling a Tiger Moth, the aircraft combined a Gipsy Moth wooden fuselage with Tiger Moth wings and was powered by a 130 hp Gipsy Major engine, giving a cruising speed just in excess of 90 mph; not

DH.82B 'Queen Bee' catapulted from a vessel. (via J. Adams)

particularly taxing for target practice! The Queen Bee was produced both as a land and seaplane with over four hundred being manufactured, and at the beginning of the war the RAF had over one hundred and eighty; perhaps quite amazingly these odd aircraft were still being used in late 1943.

In the early summer of 1939 a crane and Naval steam catapult were erected at Cleave with a concrete plinth projecting over the cliffs to set the Queen Bees airborne. They would be recovered by Naval lighters from either Padstow or Appledore. The first pilotless flights were made in June, although soon successful take offs and landings were made from the grass runway, and the catapult system was abandoned. This was the first time that such radio-controlled flights had been made from landing grounds.

With the advent of war the Air Ministry decided to develop the grassed landing ground into a permanent airfield. In October construction work was put in hand to erect proper living quarters, messes, administration and flight offices for the three Flights that were now using Cleave. Two more substantial Bellman hangars were also provided. By the summer of 1940 the building work had been completed, although like so many wartime airfields further improvements and extensions would be made. The newly furbished airfield had not passed the notice of the Luftwaffe, and on 26th August Junkers 88s dropped twelve bombs, damaging two Wallaces and injuring a civilian worker. Another raid early in October caused superficial damage to one of the Bellman hangars but fortunately the bomb did not explode.

The airfield was under the control of No 22 (Army Co-operation) Group of Fighter Command, and it must be admitted that Army Co-operation did not sit easily in a Command dedicated to the air defence of the country. However, on 1st December 1940 a separate Army Co-operation Command was formed, comprising two Groups, Nos 71 and 72. Its first and only AOC-in-C was a most experienced officer, Air Marshal Sir Arthur S. Barratt, KCB, CMG, MC, who had commanded the RAF squadrons in France. Thus RAF Cleave became one of the relatively few airfields under his Command, and now the number of Flights had increased to six, with the Wallaces being slowly replaced by Hawker Henleys, although some other more ancient biplanes had put in an appearance, Blackburn Sharks of No 2 AACU. They had originally operated from Mount Batten and Roborough, but had come directly from St Eval.

The Hawker Henley was originally designed as a light bomber, but shortly after its maiden flight in March 1937, the Air Ministry decreed that its role would be changed to that of 'a high-speed target tug'. When

Hawker Henleys equipped three Flights of No 1 AACU.

the aircraft began to enter the Service, the *Aeroplane* commented, 'although [it] is officially to be used to tow targets, it is a very good bomber indeed . . . one of the nicest looking aeroplanes, which have so far been produced and it combines good looks with a remarkable performance'. In retrospect it does seem a waste of a well designed aircraft that bore a certain resemblance to its close stablemate – the Hurricane.

The two-seater Henley was powered by a 1030hp Rolls-Royce Merlin III engine, which gave it a top speed of over 270 mph but when towing a target drogue it was restricted to 200 mph, and therein lay the problem. At this unrealistically low speed there were many engine failures, which caused a number of fatal accidents when the drogue could not be released quickly enough. It was largely because of the high number of engine failures that the Henley was ultimately phased out and replaced by the specially designed Miles Martinet target-tug. Only about two hundred Henleys were produced and they were built by Gloster Aircraft Co Ltd at Hucclecote under contract, as Hawker Aircraft Ltd was fully engaged with the production of Hurricanes. The Henleys would, like all similar aircraft, bear broad black diagonal bars to identify them as target towers, and they operated over Penhale and

Aerial view of RAF Cleave. (RAF Museum)

85

Cleave ranges, as well as Cameron Camp at St Agnes.

In 1942 the Flights were officially renumbered to Nos 1602, 1603, 1604 and 1618 for the Queen Bees, which were still gamely soldiering on. When the Army Co-operation Command was disbanded in June 1943 with the formation of the 2nd Tactical Air Force, the airfield returned to the fold of Fighter Command (soon to be known as the 'Air Defence of Great Britain'). However, nothing really changed as the Flights continued their army and anti-aircraft co-operation duties. But in December of that year the Flights were formally made up into a new squadron – No 639 – which remained at Cleave for almost the duration of the war. The Queen Bees had now departed and the squadron began to use Hurricane IVs, the final production version of this splendid aircraft, which had become somewhat outmoded with the advent of the Typhoons. No 639 squadron was disbanded on 30th April 1945, sixteen days later Cleave was placed on a Care and Maintenance basis, drawing to a close the RAF operations at this small and unspectacular wartime airfield.

5

DAVIDSTOW MOOR

Davidstow Moor was one of the few Class A Standard bomber airfields built in the South-West during the Second World War; its three concrete runways were laid down in the classic 'A'-shaped configuration. With the provision of three 'T2' hangars and fifty hardstandings it was a very basic and functional airfield, which with hindsight should never have been built in such an unsuitable and inhospitable location. The site, some two miles north-east of Camelford on Bodmin Moor, is 970 feet above sea level, well in excess of the Air Ministry's upper benchmark of 600 feet, quite apart from the presence of a nearby natural hazard, Brown Willy, the highest hill in Cornwall and rising 405 feet above the airfield. These factors alone ensured that operating conditions at the airfield would be fraught with difficulties, additionally it was often covered in heavy low cloud. In 1943 it was estimated that the weather conditions at Davidstow were unsuitable for flying for almost 80% of the time!

The airfield formally opened on 1st October 1942 in less than a complete state and was allocated to No 19 Group of Coastal Command, although several months would pass before a RAF squadron used its facilities. Within a week or so airmen of the USAAF's Eighth Air Force moved in to occupy the basic accommodation and services, and about three weeks later the first aircraft landed on the new runways. They were Consolidated B-24Ds of the 44th and 93rd Bomb Groups, then the only two Groups in the Eighth to be equipped with these rugged bombers.

The 44th Group, known as 'The Flying Eightballs', had only arrived in England in October and had flown its first operation on 7th November from Shipdham in Norfolk, whereas the 93rd, then stationed at Alconbury in Cambridgeshire, had already completed three operations. The 'Mighty Eighth', as it would later become known, had mounted its first operation in August, and was as yet a relatively small force still feeling its way in the European air war. On 9th November, fourteen B-24s left Davidstow Moor to bomb the U-boat pens at St Nazaire, later to be dubbed 'Flak City' by the American crews, because it had become the heaviest defended target outside Germany. On this occasion all the B-24s arrived back safely – a rare occurrence in the Eighth's early operations. In the coming weeks the USAAF would use the airfield as a staging post when attacking the French Atlantic ports, which figured top of the Eighth's list of priority targets. In December some rather rare American fighters used the airfield whilst en route to North Africa; they were Bell P-400 Airacobras of 360th Fighter Group that had been transferred to serve with the Twelfth Air Force.

Even when the first RAF squadron, No 53, made an appearance early in January 1943, it was operating with American-built aircraft – Lockheed Hudson Vs. These admirable aircraft had been in service with Coastal Command since May 1939. The first Mark Vs, powered by a Pratt & Whitney Twin Wasp engine, had been received by the squadron in July 1941. Since November 1940, when a BOAC Captain, D.G.T. Bennett (later Air Vice-Marshal of Pathfinder Force fame) became the first airman to fly a Hudson across the Atlantic, all new Hudsons had been flown across from Montreal via Gander in Newfoundland.

The squadron had been operating from Quonset Point in America since the previous summer and latterly from Waller Field, Trinidad seeking out the U-boats that were attacking American coastal convoys. Before No 53 moved away to Docking in Norfolk, they were joined by a few Hudson IIIs of No 279 (A/S/R) squadron that had been detached from Bircham Newton, which by coincidence was Docking's control station. These A/S/R Hudsons were equipped with Mk. I airborne lifeboats, which had been specifically designed to be dropped from Hudsons, and the crews would make the first operational lifeboat drop in May.

Other than a couple of Hawker Henleys from Cleave that used the airfield briefly in December, it was not until the spring that British-built aircraft arrived for a more permanent stay. Inevitably they were a

Hudson III of No 279 squadron, with airborne lifeboat.

mixture of Whitley VIIs and Wellington VIIIs and XIIIs belonging to No 612 squadron, which had transferred from Wick in the far north; although in May most of the squadron moved to Chivenor. It will be very noticeable how Coastal Command squadrons would move between the various Command airfields in Scotland, Northern Ireland, Devon and Cornwall. In June they were joined by more Wellington Xs and XIs operating with the Polish No 304 (Land of Silesia) and No 547 squadrons. It now could be said that at long last Davidstow Moor was taking up the operational role for which it had originally been designed – anti-submarine patrols.

During the summer Davidstow Moor was very active mounting anti-submarine operations with relatively little success, despite all the efforts of the crews and the large numbers of flying hours undertaken. On 1st May *U-415* was damaged by a Whitley of 612 squadron captained by Flight Sergeant N. Earnshaw; this U-boat had already been attacked by a Halifax and Sunderland earlier the same day, and it was not finally destroyed until July 1944 running into a British minefield. Another U-boat, *U-230*, was damaged on 8th July by Sergeant S. Kieltyke's Polish crew of 304 squadron; eight days later he and his crew would run out of fuel but all parachuted to safety. A Wellington XI of No 547 squadron piloted by Flying Officer J. Whyte shared the destruction of *U-459* with a (LL) Wellington of No 172 squadron from Chivenor. Whyte and his crew would fail to return from patrol on 15th August. Another of 547's Wellingtons attacked *U-218* on 2nd August and forced it to return to base because of injured crew members.

These anti-submarine operations were not conducted without

Wellington XIV of No 304 (Land of Silesia) squadron. (via M. Novak)

casualties. In July No 304 lost three Wellingtons. One aircraft crashed, on the 29th, shortly after take off and the pilot and navigator were killed, the other four crewmen survived. The Polish squadron would lose another two aircraft in the following month, as did No 547 squadron; several of these aircraft had fallen victims of Junkers 88s, now patrolling the Bay of Biscay in considerable force.

During May, B-24s of the 44th and 93rd Bomb Groups returned once again, for a bombing operation to Bordeaux. Since their previous visits both Groups had been deeply involved in the Eighth's bombing offensive, and in the process had suffered quite heavy losses. On 17th May a total of twenty-seven B-24s left Davidstow Moor with the formations flying well out over the Bay of Biscay at a low altitude before turning and climbing to a height of 22,000 feet to bomb. The operation was a total success, the bombing was reported to be highly accurate causing extensive damage to the port and the lock gates; only one B-24 failed to return, when due to engine trouble the crew were compelled to land at Gijon in Spain. In August the two Groups would be detached to North Africa to take part in the epic low-level bombing raid of the Ploesti oil refineries in Roumania.

Towards the end of the month a couple of A/S/R Hudsons of No 279 squadron were detached to the airfield to be engaged in the large rescue operation mounted by No 19 Group to search for a crew of a Whitley of No 10 OTU from St Eval that had ditched in the Bay of Biscay on the 26th of the month. The crew's dinghy had been spotted by a Sunderland of No 461 (RAAF) squadron, which crashed into the sea when attempting to land alongside. Three days later another Sunderland from the same squadron made contact, and although it managed to land safely to pick up the crews, it failed to take off because of engine trouble. The crew of a Hudson of No 279, piloted by Flying Officer Sherwood finally located the Sunderland and guided a Free French sloop *La Canattante* to the scene. By the end of 1943 the air-sea rescue services had saved 1,684 aircrews out of a total of some 5,460 known to have ditched – a success rate of 30%.

In October a detachment of four Wellington Xs and a single Halifax III of No 192 squadron, then operating from Feltwell in Norfolk, flew into Davidstow Moor to initiate regular patrols that were shrouded in some secrecy. The squadron (previously No 1474 Flight) had been engaged for over twelve months in the investigation, monitoring and gathering of information on the enemy's radio and radar defences; its operations were known as 'Elint', derived from ELectronic INTelligence. The crews would patrol along the Bay of Biscay as far as the north coast of Spain gathering information on the location, volume and direction of the German radio signals and radar patterns, that were tracking the Command's anti-submarine patrols in the Bay. The small detachment would remain at the airfield until the middle of May flying some 50 sorties each month, losing three aircraft in the process. The detached crews returned to Foulsham, also in Norfolk, where the squadron was then based, operating under the control of No 100 (Bomber Support) Group of Bomber Command.

The Wellingtons of No 547 squadron left for Thorney Island in October, although the squadron would soon return to Cornwall (St Eval) in early 1944. The Polish pilots had been taken off operations, whilst they converted to Wellington XIVs, and were given training on Leigh Light operations. In early December they left for yet another Cornish airfield – Predannack. For virtually the next four months the airfield would be solely devoted to air-sea rescue operations, which, at this stage of the war, effectively meant it would become a premier Vickers Warwick station.

This aircraft had originally been designed as a bomber replacement for both Hampdens and Wellingtons, but because of various changes to the original specification, B1/35, the first prototype powered with Rolls-Royce Vulture engines did not fly until August 1939. Then because of the unreliability of this new engine, the second prototype had Bristol Centaurus powerplants when it appeared in April 1940. Delays in the deliveries of these engines resulted in the first production Warwick, in May 1942, being powered by the American Pratt & Whitney Twin Wasps. The aircraft was now much too late to operate successfully as a bomber, it had been superseded by the four-engined Stirlings, Halifaxes and Lancasters. In January 1943 the Air Ministry allocated Warwicks to A/S/R operations (eight years after the aircraft's inception), and planned to have four Warwick squadrons, each with a complement of twenty aircraft, in service by the end of 1943.

The first Warwick A/S/R Mk1s arrived at Davidstow Moor from Portreath on 14th December. They were a detachment of No 280, the first squadron to be supplied with Warwicks replacing its Ansons. They were either provided with Lindholme Gear, which was a set of five buoyant containers comprising a large dinghy and four survival packs, or a Mk 1A lifeboat. On 7th January the squadron made the first operational drop of a Mk 1A lifeboat to a Mosquito crew about 170 miles south of Lands End. It was successful; the two airmen were able to climb aboard the small airborne lifeboat quite easily from their dinghies.

Early in January No 269 squadron was reformed at the airfield, equipped with Hudson IIIs, Walruses and Spitfire Vs. The intention of the squadron was to operate as a general purpose unit from Lagens in the Azores, under the control of No 274 Group of Coastal Command. It would be employed on meteorological reconnaissance flights, anti-submarine duties and search and rescue. Early in March the Hudsons flew to the Azores via Gibraltar, whereas the Walruses and Spitfires were transported by aircraft carrier. During the following month another detachment of Warwick A/S/R Mk1s arrived from Thornaby, No 281, which had only reformed in November from what had hitherto been a fighter squadron.

However, it was No 282 (A/S/R) squadron, which reformed at the airfield on 1st February with Warwick A/S/R Mk1s, that would serve (or suffer?) at Davidstow Moor for the longest period of time – some eight months. This was the fourth Warwick A/S/R squadron to be formed, so the Air Ministry had finally reached its planned target; it would be several months before the squadron received its full complement of aircraft and trained crews, and was fully operational. Indeed, it was not until 27th April that the squadron made its first successful lifeboat drop to a Halifax crew; the crew was finally rescued when the lifeboat was later taken in tow by a rescue launch. Besides operational flying the squadron was also engaged in training Warwick crews, in fact it almost took on the mantle of a Warwick conversion unit. By D-Day there would be twenty-two Warwicks at Davidstow Moor, one of which, HF959, was lost at sea on 8th June.

In March some Fortress IIAs of No 206 squadron used the airfield briefly prior to moving to St Eval, where the crews would convert to Liberators. Then on 7th April No 524 squadron reformed at the airfield with ASV radar equipped Wellington GR MkXIIIs. It had been specifically formed to seek out the enemy's fast torpedo boats, the *Schnellboots* (E-boats), and the *Räumboots* (R-boats) that might be operating in western approaches to the English Channel; another similarly equipped squadron, No 415 (RCAF), was based at Bircham Newton. The crews mounted their first operational sorties on 30th April and forty patrols were flown in the following month. During June the crews would operate closely with the Beaufighter Wing at the airfield, but on 1st July the squadron moved across to East Anglia.

It was on 11th May that Davidstow Moor really came to life with the sound and fury of Beaufighter TF MkXs of No 154 (GR) Wing. These potent, brutal and pugnacious aircraft, once described by the legendary Guy Gibson as 'sturdy, powerful and fearsome', had spearheaded the Command's anti-shipping force since the formation of the first Strike Wing in November 1942. The 'Beaus' really altered the course of the anti-shipping war, at least in the coastal waters of enemy occupied Europe. The crews of the nine squadrons that ultimately made up Coastal Command's four Strike Wings fought ferociously and bravely right up to the end of the war, suffering a high ratio of fatalities, whilst inflicting increasingly heavy losses and substantial damage on the enemy's shipping.

The TF MkXs had first flown in November 1942 and were powered by a modified Hercules VI engine designed to give peak performance at low level, about 300 mph at 200 feet, and it was claimed to be the fastest aircraft of its class at sea level. Armed with four Hispano-Suiza 20mm cannons and a rear facing Browning or Vickers gun in the dorsal cupola, the TFXs were able to carry bombs or a torpedo and eight rocket projectiles, and they certainly 'packed a punch'! Fitted with ASV Mk VIII radar in the so-called 'thimble' nose, and with an operational range of some 1,500 miles, the Beaufighters posed a constant and formidable threat to any enemy shipping operating in coastal waters. The Beaufighters were painted in what was known as the 'Temperate Sea Scheme' – wavy patterns of slate grey and dark sea grey with blue-white undersurfaces – but by D-Day each aircraft would carry black and white 'invasion' stripes on the wings and fuselages.

The two squadrons that made up No 156 (GR) Wing were Nos 144 and 404 (RCAF), both of which had been operating from Wick in

Scotland. No 404 was also known as the 'Buffaloes', and had formed in May 1941, originally with Blenheims; it had briefly served at Chivenor in early 1943. No 144 had commenced the war as a Hampden bomber squadron, and had been transferred to Coastal Command in April 1942. Each squadron was commanded by a very experienced officer. No 144 was led by Wing Commander David O. F. Lumsden, DSO, DFC, a regular pre-war officer, who had served in Bomber Command, the FAA and had commanded the squadron since the previous August. The commander of the Canadian squadron was one of the Command's most famous pilots – Wing Commander A. K. 'Ken' Gatward DSO, DFC Bar – a RAFVR airman who had served in the first Strike Wing.

One of Gatward's claims to wartime fame was an audacious flight to Paris in 1942. On 12th June Gatward, with his navigator, Sergeant George Fern had flown a single Beaufighter daylight sortie from Thorney Island to the centre of Paris – some 160 miles at tree-top height. A tricolour was dropped over the Arc de Triomphe, another was dropped over the German Kriegsmarine headquarters, and for good measure Gatward raked the building with cannons. The Beaufighter landed safely at Northolt where Gatward reported directly to the AOC-in-C of Coastal Command. Two days later leaflets were dropped over Paris recording the success of this courageous mission, said to be, 'In homage to France and the glorious memory of her sons fallen on the field of battle'. Not only had this remarkable flight given a great morale boost to the French people, but it had demonstrated the proven skill and daring of the Command's Beaufighter crews. For this operation Gatward was awarded his first DFC and Sergeant Fern the DFM. After a spell as ADC to the Governor of Gibraltar, Gatward returned to operations as Flight Commander with No 404 squadron, and was given command of the Canadian squadron in March 1944 when its Canadian CO, Wing Commander C. A. 'Chuck' Willis was lost in action.

The Wing's first major strike from Davidstow Moor came on 19th May when twenty-two Beaufighters, escorted by twenty-eight Spitfires attacked two destroyers and four escort vessels near the Brest Peninsula. Wing Commander Gatward led the Wing, with No 404 squadron attacking with 60-pound rockets, and No 144 acting as anti-flak escorts. However, the results were rather disappointing although the enemy flotilla was forced back into Brest because of the damage its vessels had sustained. Squadron Leader P. W. Dunn leading No 144 squadron was shot down, and many Beaufighters were damaged, but all managed to return safely.

Beaufighter X of No 404 (RCAF) squadron, August 1944. (Canadian Aviation Museum)

On D-Day there were fifty Beaufighters on complement at Davidstow Moor, and the Wing carried out what is considered 'the most spectacular strike made by Coastal Command aircraft on that eventful day'. Early in the evening (18.30 hours) 31 Beaufighters left the airfield led by Wing Commander Lumsden, and picked up their escort of eight Mosquito VIs of No 248 squadron from Portreath. Once again No 404 was armed with rocket projectiles, this time with 25-pound armour piercing warheads considered more effective for shipping strikes. Two German and one Dutch destroyers were located in the Gironde Estuary near Belle Ile, and the Beaufighters attacked with devastating accuracy and fury. The three destroyers, *Z.32, Z.24* and *ZHI*, were sunk. Several Beaufighters were heavily damaged, one force-landed at Predannack, but another from No 404 squadron ditched soon after the attack. A Warwick later dropped a lifeboat to the crew, but it was another two days before rather appropriately a Royal Canadian Naval destroyer rescued them. On the last day of the month No 404 shared in the destruction of a submarine chaser, *UJ1408*, in the Bay of Biscay with the two Mosquito squadrons, Nos 235 and 248, from Portreath.

On 1st July the Wing moved away to Strubby in Lincolnshire, although No 404 squadron left a large detachment of their aircraft at Davidstow Moor. On 6th August they were joined by Beaufighter TFXs of No 236 squadron from North Coates, an original member of the first Strike Wing, and by coincidence Gatward's old squadron. It was now commanded by Wing Commander Peter D. F. Mitchell, DFC, and there was another Wing Commander, A. 'Tony' Gadd, DFC, also flying with

A/S/R Warwick carrying an airborne lifeboat.

the squadron. He, along with one of the Flight Commanders, Squadron Leader E. W. 'Bill' Tacon, DFC Bar, AFC, would later command Beaufighter squadrons – Nos 144 and 236 respectively. In addition Wing Commander Gatward had briefly returned to Davidstow to lead the Canadian crews. It seems amazing that so many experienced Beaufighter pilots and leaders were flying from this airfield. The crews' prime objective was to clear the last remains of the German Kriegsmarine that were still operating from the French Atlantic ports, despite the fact that this stretch of coast had become rather isolated because of the rapid advance of the Allied land forces further eastwards.

On the day of their arrival No 236's crews made a successful strike, destroying a *Geleitboot*, a fast escort vessel named *Jupiter*; only one aircraft was lost. Two days later four minesweepers were sunk, but an aircraft from No 404 squadron was shot down by heavy flak. On the 12th a mine destructor ship, the *Sauerland*, was sunk, along with the flak vessel, *Germania*, but the Canadians lost another Beaufighter in action. The following day the Beaufighter force was led by Wing Commander Gadd and two German vessels, totalling 11,460 tons were destroyed; sadly once again a Canadian crew was lost in the action. The trail of destruction continued on the next day when a French harbour defence vessel, *Le Leroux*, was sunk in Arachon Bay, south of the Gironde. Gatward's Beaufighter was hit by flak and heavily damaged, but he managed to limp back to the airfield, carefully shepherded by one of his Canadian pilots, Flying Officer Sydney Shulemson, DSO, DFC. This proved to be Gatward's last operational sortie of the war; he would retire from the post-war Service at the rank of Group Captain. He died in December 1998 aged 84 years.

The final successful Beaufighter strike from Davidstow Moor came on 24th August. The twenty Beaufighters were led by Squadron Leader Tacon, and a destroyer and torpedo boat were sunk in the port of Le Verdon. Three Beaufighters were lost on this operation; they had been heavily damaged by flak, and had landed on Vannes airfield near to St Nazaire on the orders of Squadron Leader Tacon. Fortunately the airfield was unoccupied but one of the Beaufighters crashed on landing. The Squadron Leader, along with a Beaufighter piloted by Flying Officer J. P. Allan, also landed at Vannes, and picked up the crews after they had set fire to the damaged aircraft. The detachment of Beaufighters left during the next few days for their Lincolnshire bases, and the airfield's operational days were virtually over. No 282's Warwicks departed for St Eval on 17th September and a week later the airfield was placed on a Care and Maintenance basis.

Nevertheless, the airfield was used occasionally by diversionary flights, and it was occupied as a training camp by the RAF Regiment who remained there until 5th October 1945. Davidstow Moor was finally closed at the end of the year. Today the airfield site is a peaceful stretch of moorland safely grazed by flocks of sheep. Stretches of the old runways are still intact, as is the control tower, a rather gaunt and eerie reminder of wartime days. Although the hangars have long since disappeared, there are a number of other airfield buildings still standing. The name Davidstow is perhaps now better known as a brand of cheddar cheese, which is made at the large and modern Dairy Crest creamery, built on part of the old airfield.

6

DUNKESWELL

During 1941 George Wimpey & Co Ltd moved into a site about four miles due north of Honiton and bordering the small Devon village of Dunkeswell, to construct a Class A Standard airfield. Originally planned as a fighter station, during its construction the airfield was allocated to No 19 Group of Coastal Command. It was not ready for occupation until the summer of 1943, and further construction work would continue into the summer of 1944; indeed, the airfield was dubbed 'Mudville Heights' by the American airmen. RAF Dunkeswell opened on 26th June 1943 with Group Captain E. C. Kidd as Station Commander, but subsequently the airfield was almost exclusively used by various units of the USAAF and US Navy.

By the end of 1942 the US Antisubmarine (sic) Command had nineteen squadrons operating a total of some two hundred aircraft mainly over the western Atlantic waters and the Gulf of Mexico. Of these just twenty were B-24Ds, although the aircraft had already been 'recognized as the best weapon available for the purpose.' The first direct USAAF involvement in the Battle of the Atlantic from this country, began in November 1942 when B-24Ds of the 480th Antisubmarine Group operated from St Eval, until the Group was transferred to the Moroccan Sea Frontier (MSF) to operate from Port Lyautey in North Africa.

The Consolidated B-24 was one of the two heavy bombers used by the USAAF in Europe. It had been first designed in January 1939 with the prototype taking to the air the following December. The aircraft did not enter the Service until late 1941, and was ultimately produced in greater numbers than any other American wartime aircraft – over 18,470. Unlike its close rival, the Boeing B-17, the B-24 was not a particularly attractive aircraft with its twin tails and rather cumbersome and slab-like appearance, but it proved very reliable, durable and versatile. The B-24 was known as the Liberator in the RAF and one, AL 504, became Winston Churchill's personal aircraft named *Commando*. Eventually several marks of Liberators equipped ten Coastal Command squadrons, their long operational range allied to their bomb capacity making them ideally suited to anti-submarine duties. Without doubt Coastal Command would have readily taken a greater number of Liberators if they had been available. In total, Liberators (both RAF and American) sank seventy-one U-boats and damaged another twenty-seven – a fine record for any maritime aircraft.

On 6th August 1943 the first B-24Ds arrived at Dunkeswell, having made the 'short hop' from St Eval. They belonged to the 4th and 19th squadrons of the 479th Antisubmarine Group commanded by Colonel Howard Moore, which had been operating from the Cornish airfield since July with some success; three U-boats had been destroyed albeit they had been shared with RAF and RCAF squadrons. The Group came under the Eighth Air Force's Bomber Command for administrative purposes, but was operationally controlled by No 19 Group of Coastal Command. Although the 479th was only nominally in the Eighth Air Force, Lieutenant General Ira C. Eaker, its Commander-in-Chief, visited Dunkeswell on 5th October to bolster the crews' morale and also to present gallantry medals to a number of the Group's airmen – thirty DFCs and thirteen Purple Hearts.

The airfield was still not yet fully completed. It would subsequently have a large number of hardstandings, five 'T2' and two US Navy canvas hangars and a rather unusual control tower, as can be seen from the illustration. At first the Americans had to rely on RAF support crews, and the Commander of the 4th squadron, Major Stephen D. McElroy later recalled, 'the splendid cooperation given us by the RAF and the hospitality with which we were received'.

The Group's first operation from Dunkeswell was mounted on 7th August, and on average each patrol would last for about ten hours, although one crew was airborne for fourteen hours on 18th October, due to bad weather, which had resulted in a long search for an airfield open for landings. However, taking account of the various checks of equipment and the pre-flight briefing, plus a similar procedure at the

Strafing attack on enemy boat by a B-24 piloted by Lieutenant Leal, summer 1943. (National Archives & Records)

end of a mission, it really meant that each operational sortie took about fifteen hours. Each crew was expected to fly one operational mission every three days, in addition to a number of training flights. At this time airmen in the Eighth's Bomber Command were required to complete thirty missions for an operational tour, with an Air Medal awarded after two hundred operational hours flown. The 479th Group did not serve long enough in Europe for crews to complete an operational tour whilst serving under the control of Coastal Command.

By the time the Group operated from Dunkeswell, the airborne battle against U-boats had distinctly changed. The heavy losses of U-boats suffered in the previous three months had forced Admiral K. Döenitz to order his commanders to avoid direct confrontation with their hunters, and concentrate on evasion tactics. Largely as a result the number of U-boat sightings fell dramatically in August to a mere thirteen, and only seven attacks were made. The crews of the 479th Group did not record a single sighting during the month. They were joined by the 6th and

22nd squadrons direct from America. It was not until 7th September that a Group's crew made its only U-boat attack from Dunkeswell; B-24 'P/19' piloted by 1st Lieutenant J.O. Bolin made an inconclusive attack. The Group mounted over 350 patrols, or some 3,330 operational hours, without any tangible results – an awesome amount of time spent 'water watching'!

However, what had also changed in the conflict over the Bay of Biscay, was the number of aerial combats with the Luftwaffe's Junkers 88s and Me 410s, from just one in July to a total of fourteen during the crews' time at the airfield. These air battles resulted in the loss of three B-24s in action; on 8th August Captain R.L. Thomas and his nine-man crew of 4th squadron failed to return. Another aircraft was lost on the 11th when it crashed shortly after take off, killing six airmen. A week later a B-24 of 19th squadron went missing, due to enemy fighter action; six airmen were ultimately rescued by a Naval vessel, after spending five days in their dinghies. The last combat took place on 17th October when 'C/22' from 22nd squadron, piloted by Captain J.A. Estes, was attacked by twelve Ju 88s, and although one of the aircraft's engines was disabled in the action, Captain Estes managed to escape and return safely on three engines.

In October the Group was finally stood down from anti-submarine duties, which had now been transferred over to the US Navy; the 4th squadron ceasing operations on the last day of the month. In its brief period under Coastal Command, the Group had mounted 452 patrols, eight U-boat attacks were made with three successes, but in the process five aircraft and thirty-seven airmen had been lost. The Group moved to Podington in Bedfordshire, where it was disbanded on 11th November. Many of the crews formed the nucleus of two bomb squadrons, which would later become the 801st (Provisional) Group, dropping agents and supplies to Resistance forces in occupied Europe, and rejoicing under the name of the 'Carpetbaggers'; it operated from several airfields in East Anglia, and famously and most successfully from Harrington (see *Northamptonshire Airfields in the Second World War*).

Airborne units of the US Navy had entered the ETO (European Theater of Operations) in November 1942 when Catalinas of VP-63 squadron operated from Ballykelly in Northern Ireland under the control of Coastal Command. The US Navy had received their first B-24s during the previous August, designated 'PB4Y-1s', although essentially B-24Ds equipped with American ASV radar. Supplies of B-

24s to the Navy were painfully slow, preference was accorded to the USAAF and to a lesser extent the RAF. But in August 1943 the US Navy detached one of their squadrons, VB-103, to St Eval for its crews to begin training with RAF personnel. They would be followed into St Eval by the crews of VB-105 and VB-110 squadrons, although the latter squadron had been originally scheduled to operate from St David's in West Wales.

On 26th September VB-103 moved into Dunkeswell and by the end of October the other two squadrons had also been transferred; their crews had already flown operationally from St Eval. The three squadrons were part of the Fleet Air Wing Seven of the American Twelfth Fleet, which had set up its headquarters in Plymouth. The Wing had also appointed a Senior Liaison Officer to serve at Coastal Command's headquarters at Northwood to ensure a close working relationship with the Command. Nevertheless, it would not be until 23rd March 1944 that the US Navy formally took over the airfield from the RAF, when it officially became known as the 'US Naval Air Facility Dunkeswell'. Commander Thomas Durfee assumed control of the airfield, with Dunkeswell becoming the US Navy's first and only major operational air base in the United Kingdom.

The first operational loss in action from Dunkeswell came on 8th November when PB4Y-1 of VB-110 piloted by Lieutenant Grumbles' crew failed to return from a patrol over the Bay of Biscay; probably a victim of enemy fighters. Two days later three crews, one from each squadron, captained by Lieutenants K.L. Wright, Hermon, and J.A. Parish, attacked U-966, originally located by a (LL) Wellington of No 612 squadron. They were later joined by Liberators of No 311 (Czech) squadron, armed with rocket projectiles. The U-boat was severely damaged, and later beached at Punta Estaca on the north Spanish coast where it was blown up by its crew. The American crews were awarded a 50% share of the 'kill'! On the 12th, Lieutenant R.B. Brownell's crew of VB-103 squadron attacked U-508 in the Bay of Biscay. Sadly the aircraft did not return to Dunkeswell but the U-boat 'kill' was credited to the crew; the first unassisted victory by the American Naval airmen. In the first month of operations the Naval crews had flown a total of 2,521 patrol hours, they were well and truly 'blooded'.

Although U-boats were still the major priority for Coastal Command, its anti-submarine squadrons did get involved in shipping strikes, and during December the American crews were engaged in several such operations. On the 23rd they attacked a large blockade runner sighted in the Bay, when other Coastal Command squadrons were also in action. The vessel was identified as the 6,000 ton frieghter, *Pietro Orsono*, later located beached at the mouth of the Gironde, obviously severely damaged. The following day a flotilla of enemy merchant vessels was attacked by depth charges, although it was not certain whether any damage had been inflicted. Then on the 28th of the month the crews sighted a force of ten enemy destroyers, and fifteen PB4Y-1s were sent out on a strike. Six crews bombed from about 1,000 feet despite being opposed by heavy and concentrated flak. None of the vessels were heavily damaged, although three were later sunk by British Naval vessels. During November two aircraft were lost in crashes in this country, one near Manchester and the other on high ground close to Okehampton, besides another four either in action or as a result of the weather. Nevertheless, the Wing managed to mount over 220 sorties.

Late in January 1944 (28th) Lieutenant C.A. Enloe's crew of VB-103 squadron accounted for *U-271* off the west coast of Ireland. However, it would be a further fourteen months before the squadrons added to their score. In February a total of 253 sorties were completed despite poor weather conditions. On successive days (26th and 27th) two aircraft went missing off the south-west coast of Ireland; on the latter day an aircraft from VB-110 squadron crashed into Skellig Michael rock, killing Lieutenant John Williams and his ten crewmen. This tragic accident is the subject of a pamphlet entitled *The Fatal Echo*.

In the following month FAW 7 mounted 327 operational sorties, which were said to be 'a considerable improvement on the two previous months . . . due to an improvement in the weather from the severe conditions encountered during the preceding months.' Four PB4-Ys were lost during the month. On the 12th one from VB-110 piloted by Lieutenant Ryan, returning in bad weather was given an incorrect course by flying control and the aircraft passed over Cherbourg. Nothing more was heard of the aircraft. On the last day of the month two aircraft, again from VB-110 squadron, fell victim to enemy fighters (probably Junkers 88s) over the Bay of Biscay.

A certain Lieutenant Joseph Kennedy was serving at Dunkeswell at this time. This Naval pilot was the eldest son of the ex-US Ambassador to Britain and the brother of John F. Kennedy, a future US President. Lieutenant Kennedy had volunteered to serve with a secret US Navy project code-named Anvil, involving the use of 'robot' aircraft, which would become activated as part of the USAAF's own highly secret 'robot' programme code-named Aphrodite. It was planned to use

Control tower at Dunkeswell and the omnipresent jeep – a PB4Y-1 of VB-103

taking off. (National Archives & Records)

A PB4Y-1 of VB-110 returning from 'ops hop over Bay of Biscay' (official caption!). (National Archives & Records)

'battle worn' B-17s or B-24s fitted with radio receiving sets and packed with ten tons of explosives, which would then be directed at known V1 rocket sites. The method of operation was for the 'robot' aircraft to be flown by a two-man crew until radio contact was ensured with the 'guide' aircraft; the two airmen would then bale out to allow the robot aircraft to be guided on to the target.

The USAAF operations would be conducted from a small and secluded airfield in Norfolk – Fersfield. The first Aphrodite mission was launched on 4th August. It went quite well but the second operation malfunctioned and the 'robot' aircraft landed in Suffolk leaving a crater over 100 feet in diameter! Lieutenant Kennedy was selected to pilot the US Navy's first Anvil launch on 12th August, targeted for a large V1 site at Mimoyecques near Calais. The 'robot' B-24 headed out towards the Suffolk coast at Southwold, and at an altitude of 2,000 feet it exploded, killing Kennedy and his radio-engineer. The wreckage was strewn over a wide area, and the bodies of the two airmen were never recovered, but their names, along with hundreds more, appear on the 'Memorial Wall of the Missing' (472 feet long) at the American Military Cemetery at Madingley near Cambridge. Although more 'robot' flights were made by both the USAAF and US Navy, the projects were finally abandoned in November.

During April and May 1944 over 400 operational sorties were flown as well as numerous training flights in preparation for the Wing's involvement in Operation Cork. Although several U-boat contacts were made, no subsequent attacks were recorded and no aircraft lost in action during the two months. It was surmised that the U-boats were remaining in port in anticipation of the imminent invasion. From D-Day onwards each squadron had six, later increased to seven, crews on patrol every day, an operational schedule claimed by the US Navy to be 'the highest sustained effort of any of the Allied Anti-Submarine Air Forces engaged in supporting the invasion'.

Shortly after D-Day Admiral Ernest J. King, the US Chief of Naval Operations, visited Dunkeswell for a formal inspection. Whether by coincidence or as a result of a direct appeal by Commander Durfee, on 19th June six aircraft equipped with searchlights of VB-114 squadron, under the command of Commander I. H. McAlpine, moved in from their base in Morocco. It was maintained that they 'would give the Wing a better balanced effort and to prepare for the coming months when there would be more hours of darkness'. It should be pointed out that since the previous November the Wing's crews had been engaged on night patrols but without the provision of searchlights, flares being used to illuminate any targets contacted. The detached crews of VB-114 began to operate two sorties per day from 26th June.

On 18th June a crew of VB-110 led by Lieutenant-Commander J. Munson accomplished a notable first, when they located and attacked a *Schnorkel* ('Snort') U-boat. This was a fairly recent German development, comprising two vents, that enabled a U-boat at periscope height to expel exhaust gases from its diesel motors as well as suck fresh air from above the surface. The *Schnorkel* allowed U-boats to operate their main engines and charge their batteries without surfacing. The *Schnorkel* U-boats were difficult to locate by radar and visual sightings

PB4Y-1 leaving the coast of England on patrol. (National Archives & Records)

were rare because the *Schnorkel* was only about 20 inches in diameter and extended only six feet above the surface of the water. At this time it was thought that only about a fifth of the enemy's U-boats were fitted with the new device. Munson's crew were only able to inflict minor damage on the U-boat, which had somehow managed to enter the English Channel despite the massive 'Cork' blockade. The first destruction of a *Schnorkel* boat was made by a Liberator of No 224 squadron, with the aid of Naval vessels, towards the end of June.

During June the Dunkeswell squadrons mounted over 470 sorties, more than double that of the two previous months. Twenty-four sightings and seventeen attacks were made but with no confirmed sinkings, although not a single aircraft was lost despite the number of operational hours flown (over 4,680). At the end of the month Commander Durfee was replaced by Lieutenant Colonel Henry W. King. Early in November when the main runway at Dunkeswell was being repaired, the squadrons used nearby Upottery for operations. The fourth U-boat victory was claimed on 11th March 1945 when *U-681* was sunk by Lieutenant R.N. Field's crew from VB-103 squadron. In the following month (25th) *U-326* was destroyed by a homing torpedo fired by Lieutenant D.D. Nott and his crew of VB-103 squadron. It was probably a source of great satisfaction that on 9th May, *U-249* hoisted the black flag of surrender to an American crew on patrol in the English Channel close to the Scilly Isles.

Some 5,000 American officers and men had served at Dunkeswell since September 1943, over 6,460 missions had been flown, totalling some 62,000 operational hours and the names of 183 Naval airmen killed in action are recorded on the Memorial plaque in St Nicholas' church, Dunkeswell. When the American airmen left soon after VE Day, the airfield reverted to RAF ownership; on 6th August it was placed under the control of No 46 Group of Transport Command. Three days later No 16 Ferry Unit moved in; the Unit prepared a variety of aircraft for overseas service. In the following May the Unit left Dunkeswell but the airfield was not finally closed until February 1949.

Today the airfield is still very much alive and well, with flying operations by Air Westward from there still continuing. The control tower has survived plus several other buildings, one of which is the command centre, and at the time of writing there is a current application to make them listed buildings for restoration with the aim to turn them into a permanent interactive museum, depicting wartime activities of the Battle of the Atlantic. The major feature of Dunkeswell

The fine memorial at Dunkeswell.

is a particularly fine private Memorial Museum, which does full honour to the US Navy airmen; it is open every day except Monday, from 1st March to 31st October, and at weekends throughout the year including Bank Holidays. Nearby is a stone memorial erected to the memory of those American crews, which records, 'Many returned home, some stayed forever, none will be forgotten'.

7
EXETER

At the outbreak of war the municipal airfield at Exeter had been in existence for just over two years. It had opened on 31st May 1937 under the management of the Straight Corporation; on the same day Jersey Airlines Ltd began a regular air service to the Channel Islands. The Elementary & Reserve Flying Training School, No 37, that had only been operating since July 1939 by the Straight Corporation under contract to the Air Ministry closed down. Now the airfield came under the jurisdiction of the National Air Communications, which had been established to administer the existing pre-war civil airlines to ensure their efforts were directed towards a common plan. Exeter was designated the sole English terminal for services to the Channel Islands, and during May/June 1940 Jersey Airlines worked to full capacity to evacuate civilians from the threatened Islands. It was strange to see de Havilland Dragon Rapides on the same airfield as Hurricanes. However, with the fall of France, and the reorganisation of internal air routes completed, the need for the NAC ceased. It was accordingly disbanded and the control of the remaining inland flights placed under the Associated Airways Joint Committee.

The first RAF personnel moved into Exeter on 14th September 1939, an unusual unit, known as '02 Detachment', from the Royal Aircraft Establishment at Farnborough bringing a mixture of aircraft, including Battles, a Vickers Wellesley and Virginia and a Handley Page Harrow. It was engaged on experimental work testing the viability of balloon cable-cutters! The Unit used a large hangar, which had recently been erected near the terminal building, and it would remain at Exeter until early 1942. In June 1940 another research unit was formed at the airfield from personnel of the Armament Testing Squadron then at Boscombe Down. The Gunnery Research Unit, as it became known, tested and trialled machine guns, turrets and gunsights for a variety of aircraft, both bomber and fighter. During 1941 a famous post-war airman, Reginald H.E. Emson, served with the Unit, helping to develop the gyro gunsight, for which work he was awarded the AFC. As an Air Marshal, Sir Reginald retired from the RAF in 1969 as its last Inspector-General.

On 18th June 1940 the first Hurricanes arrived at Exeter. This classic fighter had been designed by Sidney Camm, the chief designer of Hawker Aircraft Ltd, as a development of his successful Fury biplane. The prototype first flew at Brooklands on 6th November 1935, and some months later the Air Ministry placed an order for the 'Fury Interceptor monoplane' as the aircraft was known until Camm suggested the name 'Hurricane' in June 1936. The early Hurricanes were powered by Rolls-Royce Merlin II engines, armed with eight .303 machine guns, and were capable of a top speed of 330 mph. When they entered the Service in December 1937 (with No 111 squadron) they ushered in a new era for Fighter Command as the first monoplane fighters. The Hurricane proved to be a very sturdy, reliable and highly manoeuvrable aircraft, able to withstand considerable damage. The 'Hurry' inspired great loyalty in its pilots, it was an outstanding combat aircraft operating in a variety of roles – day and night-fighter, FAA fleet fighter, fighter/bomber and 'tank-buster'. The last Hurricane was delivered to the RAF in September 1944 bearing the legend on its fuselage, *The Last Of the Many*; over 14,000 were produced.

Hurricane II of No 87 squadron.

The Hurricane Is belonged to No 213 squadron, and had been flown in from Biggin Hill after service in France. The squadron, commanded by a New Zealander, Squadron Leader H. D. McGregor, was also known as the 'Hornets' – a name that dated back to its origins in France in 1918. On 5th July it would be joined by another Hurricane squadron – No 87 'United Provinces' – which since September 1939 had operated in France. During May 1940 its pilots had experienced a furious and torrid time; Flying Officer William D. David, DFC, who had been credited with eleven victories in France, later remarked, 'The ten days of fighting in France was hell – a real killer. The Battle of Britain, by comparison, was a picnic'! David would add another 5½ victories whilst serving at Exeter, and he managed to survive the war, retiring as a Group Captain in 1967.

With two fighter squadrons in residence, RAF Exeter formally came into being on 6th July, under the control of No 10 Group, Fighter Command. The first Station Commander, Wing Commander John S. Dewar, DSO, DFC, was an ex-Cranwell College cadet of 'exceptional qualities', who had recently commanded No 87 in France. He quickly proved that he was no mere 'desk bound' commander, on 11th July he claimed two Me 110s, adding another 1½ to his score in August. Both squadrons were fairly representative of those that fought in the Battle of Britain – they were a mixture of regular, short-service and RAFVR officers, with about one third being sergeant pilots. Each squadron had a sprinkling of airmen from Australia, New Zealand, Poland and Belgium, but No 213 had three of the twenty-two seconded FAA pilots. No 87 was also commanded by a New Zealander, Squadron Leader T. G. Lovell-Gregg.

The two squadrons were tasked with the defence of Exeter, Plymouth and its Naval dockyard, but they were invariably drawn into the action elsewhere – most frequently over Portland. The first Hurricane was lost in action on 15th July; Sub-Lieutenant H. G. K. Bramah was shot down near Dartmouth. He baled out injured and did not return to his squadron, No 213. The first day of really heavy and concentrated fighting came on 11th August when the Exeter squadrons claimed eighteen enemy aircraft for the loss of five Hurricanes. One of the three pilots killed was Flying Officer R. V. Jeff, DFC Bar, Croix de Guerre, of 87 squadron, an experienced pilot, who had shot down the first enemy aircraft (Heinkel 111) on French soil in November 1939. The following day eleven victories were claimed by No 213's pilots without a single casualty. On 'Eagle Day' (13th) No 87 lost another battle-hardened pilot,

Flying Officer R. L. Glyde, DFC, an Australian who had served in the squadron since October 1938; Sergeant P. P. Norris of No 213, also failed to return. Two days later, although the squadrons claimed over 20 enemy aircraft destroyed, four aircraft and three pilots were lost, including Squadron Leader Lovell-Gregg, who was replaced by Squadron Leader Randolph S. Mills, DFC, a pre-war regular officer.

By the end of August the two squadrons had claimed a total of over eighty aircraft but for the loss of nineteen Hurricanes and fifteen pilots killed. Each squadron had its share of notable 'aces', those with five or more victories. Perhaps the foremost in No 213 were Sergeant Reginald T. Llewellyn, a pre-war 'Halton brat', who would end up with seventeen victories to his name and be awarded the DFM; and Pilot Officer H. D. Atkinson, DFC, who in a period of seven days had shot down six aircraft but was killed on 25th August. Flying Officers Wilfred Sizer and J. E. J. Sing would both be awarded the DFC in November; they survived the war. Amongst No 87's leading pilots were Flight Lieutenant I. R. Gleed, Flying Officers John R. Cock, Roland P. Beamont, and W. D. David, along with Pilot Officer D. T. Jay.

By the beginning of September 'A' and 'B' Flights of No 87 squadron rotated night-flying duties from Bibury in Gloucestershire, and by the end of the year the pilots would be almost exclusively engaged on night-operations. On the 7th of the month No 213 squadron moved away to Tangmere. Of the 63 squadrons engaged in the Battle of Britain, No 213 suffered some of the heaviest casualties with fifteen pilots lost in action. Its replacement was another Hurricane squadron, No 601 'County of London'.

This Auxiliary squadron, formed in 1925, had been in the thick of the Battles of France and Britain from Tangmere; Air Vice-Marshal Keith Park later said that 'without the Auxiliaries we would not have defeated the Luftwaffe in 1940.' No 601 was also known as the 'Millionaires squadron' from the number of wealthy pilots in its ranks! Its Commander was Squadron Leader Sir Archibald P. Hope, an old Etonian, who had learned to fly whilst at Oxford University, and he would return to command RAF Exeter in February 1944. One of the squadron's pilots, at least from October, was Flying Officer Whitney W. Straight, a pre-war racing driver and wealthy founder of the Straight Corporation, who was certainly no stranger to either the area or the airfield! He was probably the only aviator to have an aircraft named after him – F. G. Miles, in 1936, named his new light aircraft for club flying after Whitney Straight. Fifty were produced and twenty of them impressed into the RAF. This ebullient pilot claimed a Heinkel 111 on December 11th, a rare victory for the squadron whilst at Exeter. As a Squadron Leader commanding No 242, Straight was shot down over France in July 1941; he managed to evade capture and finally escaped via Gibraltar a year later. By the end of the war Straight was a highly decorated Air Commodore.

The squadron's spell at Exeter was not a particularly happy time; morale was at a low ebb, partly because of the frequent changes in personnel, a sad lack of action and also on account of a number of flying accidents that occurred.The most serious and tragic came on 25th October when two Hurricanes collided off Exmouth during a training flight, and both pilots were killed. Sadly only the previous day a similar collision had occurred with two of No 87's Hurricanes, and Pilot Officer D. T. Jay had been killed.

By now Exeter had a new Station Commander, Wing Commander H. S. 'George' Darley, DSO, a regular pre-war officer, who had commanded No 609 squadron during the Battle of Britain and had been dubbed 'the little dynamo' by his pilots! Darley retired from the RAF in 1956 as a Group Captain and died in November 1999 aged 86 years. The previous Station Commander, Wing Commander Dewar, had gone missing on a routine Hurricane flight from Exeter to Tangmere on 12th September. The exact circumstances surrounding his death are still unknown because on that day there was little enemy action as rain and heavy cloud had hampered their operations. Dewar's body was washed ashore on the Sussex coast on 30th September and he is buried in the churchyard at North Baddesley, Hampshire.

As No 87 squadron left Exeter on 28th November, it was replaced by No 263 squadron from Drem bringing their rare fighters – Westland Whirlwinds – which were then still on the secret list. The first prototype flew on 11th October 1938, and in the following January Westland was given a production contract for two hundred aircraft. The Whirlwind was an interesting aircraft – the RAF's first twin-engined fighter. Its performance at low altitude was superior to any other contemporary fighter, and the four 20 mm cannons mounted in the nose, gave it the most formidable firepower of any fighter. These qualities, allied to a long operational range, should have theoretically made it a most useful addition to Fighter Command's armoury. However, its Rolls-Royce Peregrine engines were unreliable and difficult to maintain, further-more its high landing speed resulted in a number of accidents; the aircraft's relatively poor performance at higher altitudes proved a grave

Westland Whirlwind of the much travelled No 263 squadron.

disadvantage on escort missions. Ultimately only 112 were produced, equipping just two squadrons, but they were usefully employed in the fighter/bomber role, able to carry 1,000 pounds of bombs. The squadron was mainly engaged in seeking out E-boats operating in the English Channel, gaining its first success on 8th February 1941- an Arado 196 floatplane – but an aircraft and pilot (P/O K. Graham) were lost in the process. The squadron moved to St Eval towards the end of February; the muddy conditions of the airfield during the winter having made operations most difficult. No 263 would serve at many airfields in the South-West over the next three years, almost assuming the mantle of a 'local' squadron.

They were replaced by Spitfires of No 66 squadron, the first of many Spitfire squadrons to operate from the airfield during the next two years. The airfield now housed both Spitfires and Hurricanes, the latter belonging to No 504 'County of Nottingham', which had been at Exeter since the middle of December. The squadron was commanded by Squadron Leader John Sample, DFC, who would leave in March to form the only other Whirlwind squadron, No 137. Although the airfield had been greatly extended both to the east and to the north-west and considerable improvements made during the previous year, it was still a grassed area. Ground crews were accommodated in tents around the airfield's perimeter whereas the pilots were billeted out at hotels in Exeter. However, John Laing & Son Ltd moved in to lay hard runways, ultimately three – 2,000, 1,450 and 1,000 yards long – hardstandings and a perimeter track 50 feet wide.

Towards the end of April (26th) the third 'Battle of Britain' fighter made an appearance – Boulton Paul Defiants – which because of severe

Beaufighter of No 307 squadron with General Sikorski (C-in-C, Polish Forces), September 1942. (via J. Walentowicz)

losses in the Battle had now been adapted into a night-fighter. Their arrival heralded the first of the countless number of Polish airmen to serve at Exeter, making the airfield quite a 'home from home' over the next few years. No 307 'City of Lwów' had been the first Polish night-fighter squadron to be formed in September 1940, and had been engaged in the night-defence of Liverpool from Squires Gate near Blackpool. The squadron would convert from Defiants to Beaufighter IIFs in September, and claim their first Beaufighter victories on 1st November when two Dornier 17s were destroyed and another three damaged; three weeks later a Junkers 88 was shot down over Plymouth.

The airfield suffered particularly harshly from the Luftwaffe. It was first bombed on 21st August 1940. Then in the following April no fewer than eight raids were recorded, the heaviest on 5th April when a hangar was damaged along with sixteen aircraft. In May the Luftwaffe returned on three occasions and on the night of the 12/13th substantial damage was sustained with bomb craters across the landing ground but mercifully with no loss of life. Three more raids would occur during the year, along with further attacks in both February and November 1942. Without doubt Exeter could lay claim to be the most heavily bombed airfield in the South-West.

Exeter's satellite airfield at Bolt Head was now in full operational use, and during 1942 the airfields at Church Stanton in Somerset and Harrowbeer would come under its control. In July 1941 another Polish squadron, No 317 'City of Wilno', moved in to replace No 504; it had been formed in February originally with Hurricanes but shortly after its arrival at Exeter the pilots would convert to Spitfire VBs. On 2nd August No 2 Polish Wing was formed at Exeter; the other two squadrons, Nos 302 and 316, were operating from nearby Church Stanton. In January the Wing would be commanded by a famous Czech fighter pilot, Wing Commander A. Vasatko, DFC, who had served with the French Air Force in 1940, before escaping to this country to fly with and later command No 312 (Czech) squadron. When No 317 moved away at the beginning of April 1942, it was replaced briefly by another Polish squadron – No 308 'City of Kraków'. The Polish Wing would remain at Exeter until the autumn of 1942 when it moved to Heston. Their night-fighter colleagues had a successful night on 3rd May, when the crews accounted for four enemy aircraft over Exeter. The airfield had a remarkably strong Polish presence, and in 1942 it was officially visited by General W. Sikorski, the Commander-in-Chief of the Polish forces; he had appropriately arrived in one of No 307's Beaufighters. The General was killed in a Liberator which crashed at Gibraltar in July 1943.

In early May when No 308 squadron left, it was replaced by No 310 (Czech) squadron operating Spitfire VBs. The operational days of the Hurricane as a purely day-fighter now were numbered. The last Hurricane squadron to operate from Exeter was No 247; its Hurricane IIAs and Bs arrived from Predannack in mid-May and they would remain until 21st September. Pete O'Brian, the squadron's long-serving commander had left to be replaced by Squadron Leader James C. Melvill, a Battle of Britain pilot who had been treated for burns at Queen Victoria Hospital, East Grinstead and was one of the pioneering plastic surgeon Sir Archibald MacIndoe's 'Guinea Pigs'. The squadron had operated from Roborough, St Eval, and Portreath. Its pilots would be occupied on Intruders as well as flying Roadsteads at night (attacks on enemy coastal shipping). The Czech pilots of No 310 squadron, under Squadron Leader F. Dolezal, would operate from either Exeter or Bolt Head until the summer of 1943, although they did have a brief period of detachment to Redhill in Surrey, whilst engaged on Operation Jubilee – the ill-fated Dieppe raid of 19th August 1942. The squadron would fly four missions, claiming three Dornier 217s probably

Spitfire of No 310 squadron.

destroyed and another six damaged, without any losses.

Early in January 1943 No 266 squadron, under Squadron Leader C. L. Green, DFC, arrived with its Typhoons; this was one of the first squadrons to be equipped with this aircraft. It had already been operating in the South-West mainly engaged on countering low-level raids by Fw 190s, and during its nine months stay at Exeter part of the squadron was detached to Warmwell in Dorset.

During 1943 the airfield was buzzing with aircraft and action. The Polish night-fighter crews were in the process of converting to de Havilland Mosquito NFIIs, and they made their first operational sortie with them on 15th February. However, the squadron's long association with Exeter was fast coming to an end; on 15th April the Polish airmen moved to Fairwood Common. It is appropriate at this juncture to record the immense contribution made by the Polish squadrons; they served in all three operational Commands, flying over 100,000 sorties, destroying 770 enemy aircraft and dropping thousands of tons of bombs, losing 1,973 airmen in action and another 1,388 wounded.

Perhaps the most unusual visitors to the airfield during 1943 were the

Exeter airfield in 1942. (RAF Museum)

black painted Swordfish of several FAA squadrons. These rather antiquated biplanes seemed a little out of place when compared with the Spitfires, Typhoons and Beaufighters also using the airfield. They were specifically detached to Exeter to seek out E-boats operating in the Channel at night. It was a thankless task for the crews, as even with ASV radar the E-boats were difficult targets to locate. No 825 (FAA) squadron, famed for its valiant strike on the German battleships in the Channel in 1942, was the first FAA unit to arrive at the end of 1942, staying for about a month, and then replaced by No 834 (FAA) until the middle of April. Sadly on 5th March one of its Swordfish crashed at the airfield, killing its pilot Sub-Lieutenant R. L. Knight. During May/June No 816(FAA), under the command of Lt Cdr P. F. Pryor, RM, made several contacts and attacks, notably on the nights of 30th/31st May and 6/7th June, but it was virtually impossible to ascertain whether they were successful or not. From July onwards until November No 841 (FAA) squadron, equipped with Fairey Albacore torpedo bombers, operated from the airfield on anti-shipping patrols. The squadron had spent most of its time, since its formation in July 1942, attached to Fighter Command; it was disbanded after leaving Exeter in late November.

The gap that had been left by the Polish Mosquito night-fighters was filled by Beaufighter VIFs of No 125 (Newfoundland) squadron, which was now commanded by Wing Commander Rupert F.H. Clerke, DFC, one of the Service's leading night-fighter pilots. He had been a Flight Commander with the first Mosquito night-fighter squadron – No 157. The Mark VIs had entered Fighter Command in March 1942 and were powered by two Hercules radial engines giving them a maximum speed of 330 mph. They were armed with four 20mm cannons in the nose and six .303 machine guns in the wings. Over 1,840 Mark VIs were produced for both Fighter and Coastal Commands, ultimately equipping fourteen night-fighter squadrons.

The Beaufighter crews had a successful night on 13th June during a raid on Plymouth when four enemy aircraft were destroyed and another three were damaged; a Junkers 88 was claimed by Clerke. Because the Luftwaffe's night-operations were becoming very few and far between, the squadron had only one more night-combat during the year, although the crews were often sent out on A/S/R patrols. When No 125 moved away to Valley in November (14th) it was commanded by another famous pilot, Wing Commander J. G. Topham, DSO, DFC Bar. The squadron was replaced by another Beaufighter VIF unit, No 406 (RCAF), which was a straight exchange as it had been operating from Valley since March, and had previously served at Predannack during 1942/3.

During the early months of 1944 the airfield was used by the Canadian Beaufighters and the Spitfires of Nos 616 and 610 squadron. The former was an Auxiliary Air Force squadron known as 'South Yorkshire' and was commanded by Squadron Leader L.W. Watts, DFC. Since the spring of 1942 the squadron had mainly been engaged on high-altitude patrols originally with Mark VIs and now with Mark VIIs with extended wings and the more powerful two-stage Merlin 60 engines. The other Auxiliary squadron, No 610 'County of Chester', operated Mark XIVs and was the first squadron to be equipped with these Griffon 65-powered Spitfires. However, although D-Day was looming, by the middle of April the three fighter squadrons had departed, No 406 (RCAF) to nearby Winkleigh, No 610 to Culmhead and No 616 to West Malling, where its pilots would later take on the V1 rockets.

The airfield was about to take on a completely different role, that of 'Station 463' of the USAAF. Exeter had been one of a number of West Country airfields planned to house a Ninth Air Force fighter group during the winter of 1943/4, though this had not materialised. The Stars and Stripes was raised with due ceremony at Exeter on 15th April when the Ninth's 440th Troop Carrier Group moved in from Bottesford in the east Midlands, where its four squadrons, 95th to 98th, had been training with paratroops of the US 82nd Airborne Division since the middle of March. The Group was commanded by Lieutenant Colonel Frank X. Krebs. Exeter also became the headquarters of the 50th TC Wing, under Brigadier General Julian M. Chappell, who also controlled three other Carrier Groups based at Upottery, Merryfield and Weston Zoyland.

On 26th April over seventy of the Group's C-47s flew in from Bottesford. The Douglas C-47 'Skytrain', or 'Dakota', was the military version of the most successful DC-3 civil airliner. Despite their subsequent ubiquity C-47s did not enter the USAAF in any great numbers until 1942. It proved to be an excellent and reliable transport aircraft, which could double as a troop-carrier, capable of carrying twenty-eight fully-equipped airborne troops, who could exit safely and quickly from its wide side door. More details will be noted on this aircraft under 'Upottery'.

By the afternoon of 5th June all the C-47s at Exeter had been painted with their 'Invasion Stripes' of alternating black and white bands completely around the fuselages and wings, to indicate to the Allied vessels that they were friendly aircraft. The crews had been briefed on the coming massive operation, and the airfield was then completely sealed. They were to drop US airborne troops near Carentan at the south of the Contentin peninsula. In the early hours of the 6th the C-47s took off at eleven second intervals. Two crews in each Group had been trained in pathfinder techniques to lead their respective Groups to within visual sight of the dropping zones. Of the 805 troop carriers engaged, twenty-one were lost, of which three came from 440th. The following day an even larger armada – 1,662 – was assembled to drop 'parapacks' of supplies and arms; 42 were shot down, again three C-47s failed to return to Exeter. In the following weeks the crews were transporting supplies and returning with wounded servicemen. The first Advanced Landing Ground in Normandy was established on 19th June, and A-10 ALG at Carentan completed on the 26th, which the Group used. The 440th was awarded a Distinguished Unit Citation for its operations during this period.

During the middle of July three of the Group's squadrons, 95th, 96th and 97th, were transferred to Ombrone in Italy to deliver supplies to Rome. They also took part in the airborne invasion of southern France on 15th August. The Group's remaining squadron, 98th, was now operating from Ramsbury near Marlborough, but by the end of the month the four squadrons were back in Exeter, although their stay would be short-lived. By 11th September the Group had established a new headquarters at Rheims in France, and on that day the C-47s moved out to Fulbeck in Lincolnshire preparatory to taking part in Operation Market Garden (Arnhem). In two days, the 18th and 19th, the Group mounted 170 sorties; Lt Col Krebs' C-47 was shot down on the 18th, but he managed to evade capture, and was hidden by the Dutch resistance for a month. Although all of the Group's personnel had left for France by 13th September, Exeter remained under USAAF control until November.

On its return to RAF control, 'A' Flight of No 275 (A/S/R) squadron equipped with six Walruses used the airfield until the New Year, when it was transferred to No 23 Group of Flying Training Command, and No 3 Glider Training School arrived from nearby Culmhead. The ill-fated Arnhem operation had resulted in over 460 glider pilots being killed or captured, and as a result the Army had reluctantly agreed that RAF pilots should be trained in glider flying to fill the vacancies in the Glider Pilot Regiment. It was proposed that the RAF would contribute over 500 glider pilots by April 1945.

The School was still using General Aircraft Hotspur gliders, which was the standard wartime training glider, but Miles Master IIs had now replaced the Hawker Audax and Hector biplanes as glider-tugs. The

Hotspurs were the standard training gliders. (Museum of Army Flying)

course normally lasted twelve weeks, after which the pilots would pass into an Operational Conversion Unit with Airspeed Horsas, the main operational glider. However, in July the airfield was passed back to Fighter Command, and No 3 GTS moved away to Wellesbourne Mountford, but continued its training until the end of 1947. The RAF airfield finally closed down in October 1946, and on 1st January 1947 Exeter airfield was handed over to the Ministry of Civil Aviation.

Nowadays Exeter and Devon Airport is an important and thriving airport with summer charter services to numerous European holiday locations, as well as regular scheduled services to the Channel Islands, the Scillies, Birmingham and Dublin. A new arrivals building was opened in June 1999 to cope with the two million or so passengers that fly from there each year.

8

HARROWBEER

On 15th August 1981, forty years to the very day that Harrowbeer opened as an airfield, a granite memorial stone was unveiled at Leg O'Mutton Corner, Yelverton, to commemorate all the airmen that served at the airfield during its wartime existence, and especially those who gave their lives. Precious little other evidence now remains of the airfield. The site has assuredly returned to nature, largely comprising of scrub and heathland that is now grazed by sheep. However, unlike the majority of wartime airfield sites, Harrowbeer is on common land and as such freely accessible to the public. How many realise that once, not so long ago, this land echoed to the raucous sounds of Hurricanes, Spitfires, Typhoons and Swordfish?

This Devon airfield was situated along the A386 road from Plymouth to Tavistock, some six miles out of the city, and on the edge of the village of Yelverton. It was built during late 1940 and early 1941, and specifically planned as a fighter airfield, to act as a satellite for Exeter in No 10 Group of Fighter Command. Even in 1940 the concept of satellite airfields was a fairly recent innovation. The first trial 'satellite landing ground' was established at Alconbury in May 1938, with the minimum of facilities as it was expected that the pilots would be transported daily from the parent station, and their aircraft would also return for fuelling, servicing and repair. However, the exigencies of war and the pressure on airfield space quickly changed that original concept. Fighter Command was the first to use satellite airfields during the summer of 1940 when their main stations came under continual heavy attacks from the Luftwaffe. Most fighter satellites were relatively small grassed landing grounds blessed with the minimum of refinements – Harrowbeer would be different.

During late 1940 the Air Ministry had decided that 'firm' runways would be laid down at all new fighter airfields. The harsh winter of 1939/40, which had severely restricted operational flying at purely grassed airfields, had been one factor in the change of policy, but also the success of the 'firm' runways provided at six major fighter airfields had decided the matter. Thus it was that Harrowbeer was provided with three asphalt or tarmacadam runways; concrete was then only considered necessary for airfields operating heavier types of aircraft. Two Bellman and eight Blister hangars were erected, the latter being familiar landmarks on fighter airfields, along with a number of double fighter blast pens or shelters, one of few wartime features to have survived at Harrowbeer.

The airfield was considered ready for occupation in August 1941, although the building contractors were still on site, and the control tower was not ready for use until the following April. The first Station Commander was Group Captain the Hon. E. F. Ward, who would have little idea that forty years later he would be called upon to unveil a memorial stone on the site! Towards the end of August the first aircraft put in an appearance – Bristol Blenheim IVs, which could not really be described as fighters.

This famous Second World War aircraft was the military version of the Bristol Type 142, which owed its development to Lord Rothermere. He benevolently presented the first aircraft called *Britain First* to the Nation, after the Air Ministry had shown an interest in its potential as a light bomber. The aircraft's performance during trials was most impressive, it was able to out-pace all the current biplane fighters, and the Air Ministry considered that it had a winner on its hands. The Blenheim I duly came into service in March 1937, and in the following year a new version was developed, the so-called 'long-nosed' or Mark IV, which was capable of speeds in excess of 260 mph, carried 1,000 pounds of bombs and was armed with five .303 machine guns. The brave and valiant exploits of Blenheim IV crews in the early war years, when they suffered horrendous losses, have rightly become legendary and the aircraft continued to operate as a light bomber until August 1942.

The Blenheim IVs were a detachment of No 500 'County of Kent' squadron under Wing Commander G.I. Pawson, which was operating

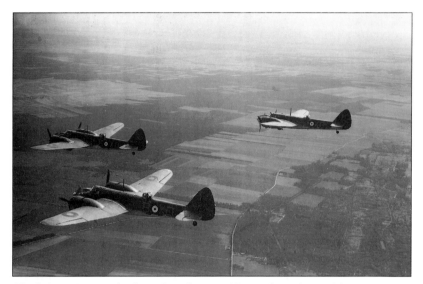

Blenheim IVs were the first aircraft to use Harrowbeer. (Imperial War Museum)

in Coastal Command from Carew Cheriton in West Wales, although the squadron was permanently based at Bircham Newton in Norfolk. This Auxiliary Air Force squadron, then operating Ansons, had made the first airborne attack on a U-boat on 5th September 1939, but its claim of a possible 'kill' was not upheld. The crews were now engaged in a mixture of operations, mainly anti-shipping strikes along the north-west French coast, but also bombing enemy airfields in Brittany. Towards the end of the year No 500 would exchange its Blenheims for Hudson IIIs and serve at both St Eval and Portreath before being posted out to the Middle East.

It was over two months before the first 'genuine' fighters arrived at Harrowbeer, and at this stage of the war it was perhaps not surprising to discover that they were Spitfires, Mark IIAs. This was the first design development of this quite remarkable fighter and it was powered by a 1,175 hp Merlin XII engine. They first entered the Service in 1940 and were operational by the end of that year. Over 900 were produced, the majority (750) being designated 'A' armed with eight .303 machine guns. The Spitfire IIAs of No 130 squadron moved in from Portreath on 25th October. It was quite a fledgling unit, having been formed earlier in June and its pilots had flown their first operational sorties at the end of September. They had been mainly engaged on shipping patrols along the coasts, and occasionally acting as bomber escorts. Their new commander, Squadron Leader E.P.P. Gibbs, DFC, was still in the process of 'breaking his pilots in', especially as they began to receive the newest mark of Spitfires – Vs.

Four days earlier the airfield had seen the formation of a new squadron – No 276 (A/S/R). It directly owed its existence to a change in the organisation of the RAF's A/S/R units. In August the executive control of A/S/R had passed from Fighter to Coastal Command, and the Directorate of Sea Rescue, which had been set up in the Air Ministry in January 1941 to co-ordinate such operations, was absorbed into a new organisation – the Directorate of Aircraft Safety. In September, to emphasise the prime importance of A/S/R operations, a very senior retired officer was appointed as its Director General – Marshal of the RAF Sir John Salmond, DSO – who had been Chief of the Air Staff from 1930 to 1933. Almost immediately Sir John authorised the upgrade of the existing A/S/R units into squadron strength, and they were re-designated Nos 275 to 278. The new squadrons were also given an increased operational remit – 40 miles from the coast – which was twice the previous range. One of the main features of A/S/R operations was the way these squadrons maintained detachments of aircraft at various airfields in the area to extend their scope; for instance the Headquarters and 'A' Flight of No 276 would move down to Portreath, whereas 'B' Flight equipped with Walruses and Lysanders would cover the Exeter sector, though it would later move to Warmwell in Dorset. In 1942 the squadron would be supplied with Defiants, followed by Ansons and later with some Spitfire VBs.

A second Spitfire V squadron arrived on 1st November – No 302 'City of Poznań'. These Polish airmen were no mere beginners in the trade, it had been the first Polish fighter squadron to be formed in this country in July 1940, and its airmen had been involved in the Battle of Britain notably from Duxford and Northolt, where they had flown with great verve. However, now they were getting accustomed to their new aircraft, as previously they had flown Hurricanes. When No 130 squadron left for Warmwell at the end of the month, the airfield became the sole preserve of the Polish airmen. During the winter of 1941/2 they were gainfully employed on convoy patrols, Circuses and escort missions for No 2 Group's bombers operating mainly from Exeter over Northern France. They also temporarily moved to airfields in No 11 Group (such as Redhill) for fighter sweeps. By the end of the year the pilots had claimed at least three Me 109s destroyed and before they departed for Warmwell towards the end of April, a Me 109 was shot down over Cherbourg docks whilst escorting bombers.

No 302 was replaced by another Spitfire V squadron, No 312, manned by Czechoslovakian pilots, which had recently been operating from Fairwood Common in South Wales. From Harrowbeer they would fly fighter sweeps, bomber escorts, Rhubarbs and Ramrods, the latter being the codename for an operation where a specific target was the objective. It was during one of these operations, on 3rd June, that the pilots had quite a combat with Fw 190s. The squadron claimed one destroyed and two probables but lost two pilots in action. In mid-August they moved up to Redhill in Surrey and were engaged in the air battle over Dieppe. Led by Squadron Leader J. Cermak the squadron completed three missions, claiming two Dornier 217s and two Fw 190s as probably destroyed, as well as Flight Sergeant J. Pipa probably sinking a E-boat and damaging another in a brave strafing attack; just one of their Spitfires was damaged in this massive air battle. The squadron remained at Harrowbeer until 10th October.

The departure of the Spitfires resulted in the arrival of a different aircraft – Hurricane IIBs. This famous fighter had been developed during 1941 for a new role, that of a fighter/bomber when they were known as 'Hurribombers'. Strongly armed with twelve .303 machine guns and able to carry two 250 or 500 pound bombs, the Hurribombers proved to be more than effective strike aircraft, especially later when they were armed with rocket projectiles. The Hurricanes of No 175, commanded by Squadron Leader J. R. Pennington-Legh, DFC, Bar, had also been engaged over Dieppe. During the two months that No 175 served at Harrowbeer, its pilots would be mainly engaged on anti-shipping strikes in the English Channel.

Just a week before Christmas 1942 a new squadron was formed at Harrowbeer, No 193, under the command of Squadron Leader W. H. A. Wright. It was the intention that the new squadron would be equipped with Typhoons, but there were none available. The teething problems (earlier described) had only just been resolved, and full production of the Typhoon recently resumed. Meanwhile the pilots were attached to two Typhoon squadrons, Nos 257 and 266, then at Exeter/Bolt Head and Warmwell. However, in the New Year the first 'Tiffies' began to arrive at Harrowbeer, and for the next four months the pilots under Squadron Leader G. W. Petre would be working up to operational readiness. There was a current Service joke that you could tell Tiffy

Typhoon Ibs of No 193 squadron at Harrowbeer in October 1943.
(RAF Museum)

pilots, because they were 'always blue in the face on account of the speed of their aircraft'!

Like all RAF squadrons, the Typhoons quickly acquired the squadron's unique two-letter identification code – 'DP'; they were painted in bold block letters on the fuselages, normally to the left of the RAF rondels, but most Typhoon squadrons had them emblazoned to the right. Thus 'DP' would identify the squadron's aircraft until it was disbanded in August 1945. The squadron became operational in April, mounting anti-shipping patrols and acting as escorts for fast motor torpedo boats. During February and March they shared the airfield with the Whirlwinds of No 263 squadron, continuing its tour of airfields in the South-West! Briefly in April six Swordfish of No 834 (FAA) squadron, which had been seconded to Coastal Command, used Harrowbeer for night patrols of the English Channel. In late May and early June North American Mustangs (better known as P-51s) of No 414 (RCAF) under Squadron Leader J.M. Godfrey, were detached to the airfield. This was a tactical reconnaissance unit, which had formed in August 1941 for army co-operation duties; it was one of a number of squadrons that had been temporarily allocated to Fighter Command on the disbandment of the Army Co-operation Command, and prior to the formation of the 2nd Tactical Air Force. The Canadian pilots flew a number of shipping reconnaissance patrols, as well as some Roadsteads, which were effectively low-level operations to attack vessels at sea or in harbour, by fighters or bombers escorted by fighters.

On 5th June Harrowbeer really became acknowledged as a 'Tiffy' airfield with the arrival of No 183 squadron, commanded by Squadron Leader Arthur V. Gowers, DFC, an ex-Battle of Britain pilot who would be killed in action in October. Like No 193, the squadron had only received its Typhoons earlier in the year. For the next two months or so the two squadrons made coastal patrols and sweeps seeking out Fw 190s attacking coastal targets and towns, which were quaintly known as 'anti-Rhubarbs', as well as escorting bombers engaged on anti-shipping strikes. Both squadrons left Harrowbeer in August, although No 193 returned in September (18th), after spending a month at Gravesend. It would be joined three days later by yet another Typhoon squadron – No 266 (Rhodesia). From now until well into the New Year the two squadrons would be fully operational from the airfield, and towards the end of 1943 they began to carry bombs, working up to the role each would play in the Typhoon wings of the 2nd TAF.

In October, No 193 squadron was adopted by Brazil, with that country's Ambassador making a formal visit to the airfield to inspect the squadron. It now acquired the strange name 'Fellowship of the Bellows' from a patriotic organisation of Anglo/South American businessmen, who had raised considerable funds to purchase RAF aircraft. No 193 was not the only RAF squadron to carry this name, the peripatetic No 263, along with a Mosquito squadron of Bomber Command, No 692, were also known as such. When No 193 squadron left for Fairlop in Essex, it had become the longest serving squadron at Harrowbeer.

In March 1944 No 266 was replaced by another Typhoon squadron – none other than No 263! The squadron had finally relinquished its Whirlwinds at the end of 1943, and it was now commanded by a well-known Belgian pilot, Squadron Leader Henri A. C. Gonay, C de G (Croix de Guerre). Like all airfields situated close to the fierce action in the skies over Normandy, Harrowbeer would experience a couple of months of intense operational activity, without doubt the busiest and most hectic time of its wartime existence.

Towards the end of March (24th) the dulcet tones of Rolls-Royce Merlin engines were heard over the airfield once again, heralding the return of Spitfires; they were Mark VIIs of No 131 squadron. The squadron was led by the ebullient Squadron Leader J. J. O'Meara, DFC, Bar, a famous Battle of Britain pilot with No 64 squadron with twelve victories to his name. For the next two months the pilots would fly high-altitude patrols, fighter sweeps and bomber escorts. When the squadron left for Culmhead on 24th May, it was immediately replaced

Spitfire XIV of No 610 squadron.

by No 610 'County of Chester' squadron, from Bolt Head, flying their special Spitfire XIVs. For over twelve months the squadron had been operating from a number of airfields in the South-West. It was now commanded by Squadron Leader R.A. Newbury, DFC, Bar.

Just four days earlier a number of Fairey Swordfish IIs 'lumbered' into the airfield, or so it would appear in comparison to the Typhoons and Spitfires also there. This valiant biplane's maximum speed was about 138 mph, little more than the Typhoon's landing speed! The Swordfish squadron, No 838 (FAA), commanded by Lieutenant Commander J.M. Brown, RNVR, DSC, was part of Coastal Command's No 156 (GR) Wing, the other members operating from Perranporth. Back in March the Admiralty had agreed to make six FAA squadrons available to Coastal Command for D-Day operations, with the proviso they were returned by 1st August. The Swordfish IIs had entered the FAA in 1943. The lower wing had been strengthened and metal skinned to carry rocket projectiles, and they were powered by more powerful Pegasus XXX engines. The aircraft, still with open cockpits, were equipped with the latest ASV Mk.X radar with a radome to carry the scanner positioned between the landing gear. On their first operation from Harrowbeer on the night of 30th April/1st May one Swordfish was shot down by coastal batteries when the squadron was attacking a beached enemy vessel; another two also failed to return. Later in the month one Swordfish crashed into a hillside after practice over Treligga Range, but the three airmen survived.

As D-Day approached the airfield housed over fifty aircraft – Typhoons, Spitfires and Swordfish. The 'Tiffy' pilots, their aircraft

Swordfish of No 838 (FAA) squadron served at Harrowbeer during 1944.

armed with rocket projectiles, would operate over the western approaches to the English Channel to engage any enemy vessels attempting to enter the area. They were especially briefed to look out for fast patrol boats. On the two days following D-Day No 263 squadron lost two aircraft, MN515 and MN449, and then just five days before the squadron moved on to Bolt Head on the 19th of the month, Squadron Leader Gonay was lost in action. He was replaced by Squadron Leader Robert D. Rutter.

The Spitfire pilots were given specific areas to patrol, usually south of Plymouth, although they were also engaged over the Solent. Their Spitfires, often operating in pairs, left Harrowbeer regularly during daylight hours, and not a single aircraft was lost on any of the days up to 19th June, when the squadron moved to West Malling in Kent. The nightly patrols of the Swordfish crews proved to be relatively uneventful, but before the squadron departed on 8th August three aircraft had been lost, with two crews safely rescued from the sea.

The odd Hurricane II appeared at the airfield during late May and June. They were operating what was known as the Air Despatch Letter Service (or No 1697 Flight), which as the name suggests had been formed as a mail courier service. The ADLS ultimately flew with messages and documents into the first Advanced Landing Grounds in Normandy. The Flight had established a detachment at Thorney Island, with Harrowbeer as one of the airfields on its scheduled internal mail flights. The Flight was commanded by Squadron Leader James E. Storrar, DFC, Bar

With the departure of the Typhoons, Harrowbeer became the home of Spitfires of various marks until the end of August. In total five Spitfire squadrons, Nos 1, 165, 611, 64 and 126, used the airfield, some staying briefly – the odd day or so. By August the airfield had become rather detached from the action in Normandy with the land battles moving further eastward, and its operational days were nearing their end. On 30th August the final two Spitfire squadrons left, and the airfield was placed on a Care and Maintenance basis. However, some form of flying still continued, mainly communications aircraft of the US Navy for visitors to its Fleet Air Wing's headquarters in Plymouth.

On Monday 28th August there was a buzz of excitement when a couple of USAAF C-47s landed from Twinwood Farm in Bedfordshire. The aircraft had brought Major Glenn Miller and the American Band of the AEF to play three concerts in Plymouth – at the US Navy Field Hospital at Manadon, the Odeon cinema, and HMS *Drake* at Shapter's Field. Since July, Glenn Miller and the AEF Band had been making an exhausting countrywide tour of American military bases and airfields. The Band was due to leave the following day but heavy fog delayed their departure until the 30th. On 15th December Major Glenn Miller would fly from Twinwood Farm bound for Paris; the aircraft was never seen again.

The airfield was resuscitated in January 1945 when Exeter was

The granite memorial unveiled in August 1981.

transferred to Flying Training Command and Harrowbeer took over control of Bolt Head. Walruses of No 275 (A/S/R) squadron moved in, only to be disbanded in mid-February. The various target-towing aircraft of No 691 squadron, then based at Roborough 'just down the road' also arrived for a relatively short stay. There was some excitement in May when Spitfire IXs of No 329 (Free French) squadron arrived from Skaebrae in Scotland and was to take part in a special Air Pageant over Paris in celebration of victory in Europe. However, the squadron moved to Fairwood Common in July and was disbanded in November whilst at Exeter. No 691 squadron would leave for Exeter in August, and from then on there was little flying activity; the airfield was closed down in May 1946.

The Ministry of Civil Aviation now took possession, and there was a proposal to use it as Plymouth's airport, in preference to the smaller airfield at Roborough, but due to strong local opposition this did not materialise. Aircraft of No 19 Group's Communications Flight used the airfield for about nine months, but when they departed in August 1948, Harrowbeer's flying days were over.

9

MOUNT BATTEN

At the outbreak of the war RAF Mount Batten had been operational for some ten years, although its origins dated back to the First World War when the sheltered waters of the Cattewater at the estuary of the river Plym and to the north-east of Mount Batten Head, had been first used by RNAS flying boats and floatplanes. Mount Batten, along with Pembroke Dock, operated as a major flying boat station within No 15 (GR) Group of Coastal Command, then under the command of Air Commodore R. G. Parry, DSO. There could not have been a greater or more striking difference in the size of the aircraft that shared the station's facilities; the small and compact Shark floatplanes were dwarfed by the massive and majestic Sunderland flying boats – more than a touch of David and Goliath!

Blackburn Sharks had first appeared in the FAA during 1935 and when production ceased three years later over 230 had been delivered. This biplane operated for less than three years as a torpedo/ reconnaissance bomber before being superseded in this role by the remarkable Fairey Swordfish. Although Sharks were involved in the evacuation of Dunkirk and the Channel Islands in 1940, they were now mainly used for target towing, hence their presence at Mount Batten; they operated in No 2 Anti-Aircraft Co-operation Unit towing drogues to provide firing practice for the Naval Gunnery School at Devonport. Some idea of the great disparity in size between the two aircraft can be gained by the fact that the Shark's maximum laden weight for take off was 3½ tons set against the Sunderland's 29 tons. Furthermore the

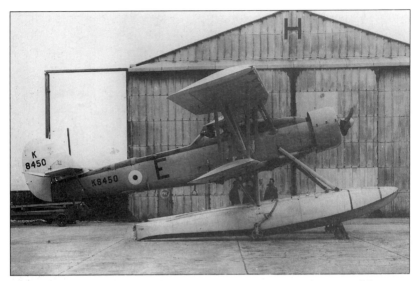

Blackburn Sharks of No 2 Anti-Aircraft Co-Operation Unit operated from Mount Batten. (RAF Museum)

aircraft's overall length was a mere 35 feet with a 46 feet wing span compared with the 85 foot long Sunderland and its large foot wing span – over 112 feet. The Sunderland was, by some distance, the largest aircraft in service with the RAF.

Without doubt the Short S.25 Sunderland will forever epitomise Coastal Command's operations during the Second World War. The aircraft was designed to meet the requirements of the Air Ministry's specification R22/36 for a long-range reconnaissance flying boat, which did not state that it should be a monoplane, but was essentially a military version of the Company's 'C' Class 'Empire' flying boat produced for Imperial Airways in July 1936, which proved to be so successful. The Sunderland made its maiden flight in October 1937, and the first production aircraft entered the Service in the following June with No 230 squadron in Singapore. It was the Service's first monoplane flying boat, and also the first to feature power-operated turrets. Its strong armament (eight .303 machine guns ultimately in three turrets – nose, tail and dorsal) gained for it the German nickname – *Fliegende Stachelschwein* or 'Flying Porcupine' – by bitter experience the Luftwaffe seldom attacked a Sunderland in less than pairs.

The first three marks were powered by four Bristol Pegasus XXII or

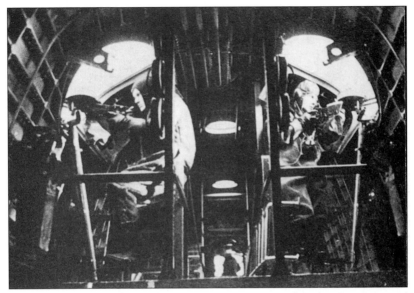

Part of the fire power of the Fliegende Stachelschwein or 'Flying Porcupine'. (via S. Cox)

XVII radial engines, and they cruised at about 115 mph with an operational endurance of 12½ hours. ASV Mark II radar was fitted to the early Sunderlands, identified by the four vertical masts on the top of the hull and the loops along the fuselage. The Mark V, the last of the famous breed of which 150 were produced, was generally introduced in early 1945; they had been provided with the more powerful Pratt & Whitney Twin Wasp radial engines, which gave them an increased range of close to 3,000 miles. In August 1945 there were twenty RAF Sunderland squadrons, and when production ceased in June 1946 over 700 had been built. It was one of the most successful and longest serving of all RAF aircraft, even famously operating in the Berlin Airlift of 1948. Sunderlands were not finally retired from service until May 1959 when operating in the Far East.

The Sunderland was much more than just an aircraft to its twelve man crew; many lived aboard it between operations, preferring it to their quarters. The aircraft was fully appointed with a galley, wardroom, flush lavatory, bunks and wash basins, becoming 'a home from home'. One crewman maintained that throughout his two operational tours the only time he was really contented was when he was on board! Despite its enormous size and bulk the Sunderland was, according to Lettice Curtis (one of the few women Air Transport Auxiliary pilots qualified to fly it), 'a delightful aeroplane to fly, being light on the controls . . . and very manoeuvrable on the water.' Flight Lieutenant Vic Hodkinson, DFC, a pilot with No 10 (RAAF) squadron, summed it up with the words: 'the Sunderland was a dream to fly'.

On 3rd September 1939 there were just six Sunderland Is at Mount Batten equipping No 204 squadron, which had received them in June, making it the third Sunderland squadron in Coastal Command. Soon they would have Mount Batten to themselves as the Sharks, which could be adapted into land planes, left for nearby Roborough, the small municipal airfield that had been smartly requisitioned by the Admiralty.

No 204 squadron could trace its origins right back to December 1916, first as a bomber unit and later a fighter squadron, but it had reformed at Mount Batten on 1st February 1929 as a general reconnaissance flying boat squadron, with its motto saying it all – *Praedam mare quaro* or 'I seek my prey in the sea.' It was commanded by Wing Commander K.B. Lloyd, AFC, and his crews had already completed their conversion from the biplane Saro Londons, and were ready to take their handful of Sunderlands into action. The first convoy escorts were mounted at dawn on 4th September and over the next five days at least five attacks were made on U-boats but with no conclusive results. A further attack was made by Flight Lieutenant Harrison's crew on the 18th, they returned to Mount Batten to claim a probable destruction but the evidence was not considered to be conclusive and the 'kill' was not confirmed.

On the same day distress signals were received from a merchant vessel, *Kensington Court*, that was sinking after being torpedoed about seventy miles to the west of the Scillies. Flight Lieutenant J. Barrett's crew responded to the SOS as did two Sunderland crews from Pembroke Dock and the three aircraft arrived over the stricken vessel at about the same time. Flight Lieutenant Barrett, along with a Sunderland of No 228 squadron, decided to land on the open sea despite the heavy swell, whilst the other Sunderland circled overhead. Ultimately thirty-four survivors were picked up by the two aircraft – the first 'open sea' rescue of the war; later such rescues were strictly forbidden because of the high risk of crashing. Flight Lieutenant Barrett was awarded the DFC in November and by the end of the war he was a Wing Commander with No 201 Catalina squadron.

For the rest of the winter the Sunderland crews were operating on A/S/R patrols and convoy escort duties despite the severe weather conditions; however, there were precious few U-boat sightings let alone attacks. In October two aircraft were lost, one with fatal results. Much to the crews' dismay the squadron was posted to a most inhospitable station – Sullom Voe in the Shetland Islands. This would be followed by a spell even further north in Iceland; although later the squadron would move to far warmer climes – Bathurst in West Africa. No 204 was immediately replaced at Mount Batten by another Sunderland squadron – No 10 of the Royal Australian Air Force – which, except for a seven month spell of detachment at Pembroke Dock during 1941, would serve at Mount Batten for the duration of the war.

The Australian airmen had originally arrived in this country to transport Sunderlands back to Australia, but the outbreak of war and the acute shortage of aircraft changed the original plan. In October the Australian Government decided that No 10 squadron should remain in this country and serve with Coastal Command. The Australian crews had received their first Sunderland on 11th September 1939, and the crews, including those transferred in from Australia, commenced conversion training at Pembroke Dock with Sunderland crews of No 210 squadron. By 1st February the squadron was declared fully operational bringing the Command's Sunderland squadrons to four; the first operational patrol was made on 6th February by Sunderland, P9605. This aircraft would survive all the rigours of operational flying until March 1942.

The squadron's first U-boat success came on 1st July 1940 when Flight Lieutenant W.N. 'Hoot' Gibson's crew searched for the attacker of a torpedoed merchant vessel, *Zarian*, about 250 miles to the west of the Scillies. It was finally sighted to the south-west of Ireland and four 250 pound AS (Anti-Submarine) bombs were dropped just as the submarine submerged. The U-boat surfaced minutes later and Gibson dropped his remaining four bombs. The crew were seen to abandon the U-boat before it was scuttled by its Captain; forty-eight of the survivors were subsequently rescued by a Naval vessel. The U-boat, *U-26*, had already been damaged by depth charges from HMS *Gladiolus*, so the squadron's first U-boat 'kill' was shared with the Royal Navy. It was not the first U-boat to be sunk by a Sunderland crew, that had been accomplished by No 228 squadron on 31st January, also with the assistance of Naval vessels.

Sunderland 'RB-C' of No 10 (RAF) squadron. (via S. Cox)

On 1st July, No 1 Air Despatch and Receipt Unit was formed at Mount Batten to transport VIPs to Gibraltar, North Africa and the Middle East, although already the Australian crews had made several flights. On the 29th, Flight Lieutenant Birch's Sunderland was attacked by a Dornier 18 flying boat en route to Gibraltar, it suffered damage and the aircraft was forced to return to Mount Batten. One of the squadron's Sunderlands, N9049, was destroyed at Malta on 10th May 1941 during an air attack.

The following month three Short S.26 'G' Class flying boats, named *Golden Hind*, *Golden Fleece* and *Golden Horn*, arrived at Mount Batten. These aircraft had originally been built for Imperial Airways for long-range mail and passenger services; the first was handed over to the Airways in late September 1939. However, the three aircraft were requisitioned by the Air Ministry for these special VIP flights. They formed a Special Flight of No 119 squadron based at Bowmore, Islay under the command of Wing Commander A.G.F. Stewart. The aircraft (known as S.26M) had been strongly armed with twelve .303 machine guns and a considerable amount of armour plating was added for the protection of the fuel tanks, crew and passengers. When No 119 squadron effectively became non-operational in June 1941, the three aircraft were attached to No 10 squadron pro tem, and they operated from Mount Batten, although the rest of the squadron was based at Pembroke Dock. Sadly, on 20th June 1941, the *Golden Fleece* was lost due to a double engine failure off Cape Finistère when it was forced to land in a heavy swell; the survivors were rescued by a U-boat. The remaining two aircraft, after a number of close escapes, were transferred to British Overseas Airways Corporation at the end of 1941; BOAC operated from Poole Harbour throughout the war. The *Golden Horn* would crash in the river Tagus in January 1943 as a result of an engine fire, but the *Golden Hind* continued in service with BOAC until September 1947.

The Australian crews continued their long and arduous anti-submarine patrols, convoy escorts and A/S/R patrols for the rest of 1940, and although the crews managed to make a number of attacks on U-boats, no further 'kills' were recorded; in fact the destruction of *U-26* would be Coastal Command's second and last victory of 1940. From 2nd July the squadron's Sunderlands were armed with depth charges, rather than AS bombs, for the first time. During the summer many of the crews were engaged on photo-reconnaissance patrols over French ports seeking evidence of invasion craft.

In August four crews were detached to Oban in Scotland and one Sunderland was lost there in a night-landing accident on 2nd September. The crews found themselves increasingly involved in air combats with Junkers 88s, Me 110s, Heinkel 111s and Dornier 17s. In September (25th) Squadron Leader W.H. Garing and his crew spotted a lifeboat, and from the message held up by one of the survivors, it was identified as belonging to the liner *City of Benares*, which had been torpedoed eight days earlier whilst carrying child evacuees to Canada. Squadron Leader Garing attempted to land near the lifeboat but the sea was too rough. He managed to contact another Sunderland (of No 210 squadron) and informed the crew of the lifeboat's precise position. This aircraft guided HMS *Anthony* to pick up 46 survivors, six of them children, all suffering from severe exposure The *City of Benares* had been carrying 421 passengers and crew, of which only 150 were rescued and just 13 of the 100 children. The tragic sinking of this liner, with the loss of so many children, made front-page news during the dark days of 1940. Almost a month later (16th October) another of the squadron's Sunderlands was also involved in a famous rescue. The crew operating from Oban sighted a lifeboat from the vessel *Stangrant*, and they landed on the open sea, to pick up twenty-one survivors, who had been afloat for 3½ days.

During November the squadron lost two aircraft in a heavy bombing raid over Plymouth. On the evening of the 27th, Sunderland, N9048, was destroyed when a hangar received a direct hit from an oil bomb

A hangar at Mount Batten received a direct hit on 27th November 1940. (via M. Jones)

and was destroyed. Another aircraft, P9601, was heavily damaged at its moorings and sank with its load of depth charges and anti-submarine bombs. Other bombs set oil tanks on fire at Turnchapel about a quarter of a mile way, which burned for over ninety hours.

The horrendous night-blitzes on Plymouth during March to early May 1941 resulted in the decision to move the squadron to Pembroke Dock on 28th May. On one of its first operational patrols from there a Sunderland came down in the Bay of Biscay; the aircraft (T9075) was piloted by Pilot Officer (then) Vic M. Hodkinson, and he and his crew were fortunate to be picked up by a merchant vessel after some six hours on the water. By mid-1942 Hodkinson had completed two operational tours with the squadron and he returned to Australia with over 1,800 hours of flying time logged. Later, as a Wing Commander, he commanded two flying boat squadrons in Australia. After the war he returned to England to become a BOAC Captain flying their 'Empire' flying boats. For interest it should be noted that it was laid down in May 1943 by the Air Ministry that 800 operational hours comprised a tour in flying boats, and the Air Ministry produced figures showing that the percentage chance of completing one tour was 66% and two tours 43%; this compared with 44% and 19½% respectively in Bomber Command.

During the squadron's absence from Mount Batten, the facilities were used by a detachment of Sunderlands from No 210 squadron, then based at Oban, which would by coincidence destroy six U-boats during the war, the same number as No 10 squadron. The 'G' Class Sunderlands mentioned above, as well as some of BOAC's 'Empire' flying boats from Poole used Mount Batten as a staging post. Mount Batten's 'old' resident squadron, No 204, appeared briefly in July before leaving for service in Gibraltar.

Early in January 1942 No 10's Sunderlands returned and on the morning of 16th January the largest flying boat in the world, the Boeing 314, landed after a 3,300 mile flight across the Atlantic from Baltimore via Bermuda. On board were Winston Churchill, Lord Beaverbrook and Captain Harold Balfour, as well as Lord Portal and Admiral Pound (the Chiefs of Staff for Air and the Navy) and their advisers; they had all been attending a summit meeting with President Roosevelt in Washington. It was the first time that a British Prime Minister had flown the Atlantic. The Boeing flying boat, named *Berwick*, was under the command of Captain Kelly-Rogers of BOAC, and was one of three such aircraft purchased by Captain Balfour, the Under-Secretary of State for Air; they were forever afterwards called the 'Balfour Boeings' because of the political furore that their purchase caused (each aircraft cost $1,050,000)! However, the three massive Boeings would fly over four million miles with BOAC during the war without a single accident or incident, and were finally returned to the United States in 1948.

The Boeing 314 was the largest flying boat in the world. (National Air & Space Museum)

Towards the end of April (25th) a new RAAF Sunderland squadron, No 461, was formed at Mount Batten, its nucleus being made up from crews from No 10 squadron. The squadron was placed under the command of Wing Commander N.A.R. Halliday and by June its crews were flying A/S/R missions. In the following month they were cleared for anti-submarine patrols. For the three months that the crews operated from Mount Batten there was no shortage of incidents. On 6th July Wing Commander Halliday successfully rescued the crew of a Whitley from No 10 OTU based at St Eval, followed a month later by another successful 'open sea' rescue. However, on 10th August the squadron lost its first aircraft in action, and two days later the Wing Commander's Sunderland crashed whilst attempting to land near a dinghy to rescue the crew of a Wellington of No 172 squadron from Chivenor. As a result of this incident official orders were issued to prohibit such rescues unless specific permission was obtained from Group headquarters, though in truth the Australian crews appeared to pay scant heed to such instructions!

When the squadron moved to RAF Hamworthy in Poole Harbour at the end of August, Squadron Leader (later Wing Commander) R.C.O. Lovelock, previously a squadron Flight Commander, had been given command of the squadron. However, when the crews were engaged on night-operations, they moved back to Mount Batten which was considered far safer for night-landings. On 1st September one of its

Sunderland of No 461 (RAAF) squadron.

Sunderlands, T9113, was shot down over the Bay of Biscay, the twelve crewmen were all posted as missing.

Perhaps the closest No 10's crews had come to success since their return to Mount Batten was on 5th June, when Flight Lieutenant S.R.C. Wood's crew damaged *U-71*; it managed to limp back to La Pallice for urgent repairs. This U-boat had been commissioned in December 1940 and quite amazingly survived until 5th May 1945. Later in the month (18th) the squadron's crews were involved in a large A/S/R operation that was mounted to locate the survivors of a Naval escort destroyer, HMS *Wild Swan*, which sank off the southern coast of Eire. Flight Lieutenant Maurice L. Judell and his crew left Mount Batten at 03.00 hours on the 18th and about seven hours later they located two dinghies and a number of life-rafts from the vessel. A Naval destroyer HMS *Vansittart* was guided to the area to make the rescue. Sadly, four days later Judell's crew would be lost whilst on another A/S/R patrol. Their Sunderland, W3999, was shot down by an Arado Ar196 seaplane, there were no survivors.

In January 1943 the level of U-boat sightings in the Bay of Biscay fell dramatically with only two U-boats being destroyed, and yet intelligence reports coming into the Admiralty indicated that at least 45 U-boats would be crossing the Bay during the first two weeks of February. Coastal Command mounted Operation Gondola, an intensive concentration of day/night patrols over a relatively small area. The Sunderland squadrons, then eight in number, were allocated the inner section of the Bay, and Gondola lasted for twelve days as far as No 19 Group's crews were concerned. Gondola was followed in March by Enclose I and II, a similar type of operation but of rather shorter duration. Over the next months a serious of special operations variously coded Derange, Musketry and Seaslug, were introduced by Coastal Command. They were basically regular sweeps across closely delineated areas of sea, which were further to the west and south of the Bay of Biscay, with at least seven A/S aircraft continually flying parallel patrols in the areas.

A rather ominous feature of the offensive was the tactic of the U-boats to remain on the surface and fight back with their greatly strengthened armoury of 20 or 30 mm guns placed on the conning towers. Frequently two or more U-boats operated in conjunction producing an even greater concentration of flak, thus making U-boat attacks an even more hazardous task. As a result four fixed forward-firing machine guns were installed in the Sunderlands' nose turrets to add more firepower to their frontal attacks. Nevertheless, during May to August forty anti-submarine aircraft were lost in operations over the Bay, many of these falling to flak from U-boats.

On 1st April 1943 Group Captain J. Alexander, OBE of the RAAF took over command of RAF Mount Batten from Group Captain L. Martin, AFC, thus making the station almost exclusively Australian. From May to August it may be said that the U-boat offensive reached its climax with the Command's squadrons achieving considerable success. The Australian crews now led by Wing Commander G.C. Hartnell managed to destroy three of the fifty-seven U-boats sunk by Coastal Command during these months – quite 'a killing ground'. On 7th May Flight Lieutenant Geoffrey C. Rossiter's crew was credited with the destruction of U-663; it is thought to have sunk as a result of a diving accident due to the heavy damage inflicted by Rossiter's Sunderland. Originally the destruction of U-663 was credited to a Halifax of No 58 squadron, but this was amended in 1989. At the end of the month U-563 was destroyed off the north-west coast of Spain by Flight Lieutenant Maxwell Mainprise's crew. It was shared with a Halifax of No 58 squadron and another Sunderland of No 228 squadron. The U-boat had left Brest only two days earlier and it was on its eighth wartime patrol.

At the end of June, Flight Lieutenant H.W. Skinner's crew made a most determined attack on U-518 in the face of severe and heavy fire with one of the crew being mortally injured in the action; this U-boat was sunk in April 1945. Flight Lieutenant Skinner and his crew would be lost on 18th August when their Sunderland was shot down by Junkers 88s. On the first day of August Flight Lieutenant Kenneth G. Fry's crew was on a Musketry patrol when they sighted a U-boat and they made a brave attack on U-454 despite heavy and concentrated fire. After the U-boat sank the heavily damaged Sunderland crashed into the sea about six miles from a Naval escort vessel. Only six of the crew, who were clinging to the remains of their Sunderland, were saved by HMS *Wren*, but Flight Lieutenant Fry was not amongst them. During the intensive campaign another four Sunderlands were lost to Junkers 88s, with a fifth being destroyed in a fatal training accident. Despite the official orders to the contrary Flight Lieutenant Rossiter landed on the open sea, on 19th May, to rescue two members of a Liberator of No 224 squadron ex-St Eval, which had been shot down by Junkers 88s six days earlier. Unfortunately only the pilot, Pilot Officer G. B. Willerton, survived the long ordeal; he later received the DFC.

Early in January 1944 No 10 squadron had a successful strike when a

Sunderland captained by Flying Officer J.P. Roberts sank *U-426* on the 8th of the month. Towards the end of the month six Sunderlands crewed by tour-expired Australian airmen left for their homeland, to be followed in February by another four Sunderlands. Nevertheless, by D-Day No 10 squadron still had eleven Sunderland IIIs on complement. One of these, ML839, had been converted to Pratt & Whitney engines. These more powerful engines had been introduced to overcome the problem of engine wear, which had resulted from the need to run the Pegasus engines almost continuously at full power. The new engines produced an improved cruising speed and enabled the Sunderland to fly on just two engines if necessary. Back in November 1942 No 10 squadron had put forward the idea of maybe using the American engines in the Sunderlands, and thus a converted Mark III arrived at Mount Batten in early May. It was first trialled by Group Captain Alexander on the 4th; this aircraft, the forerunner of the Mark Vs, was used on operations for the first time by Flight Lieutenant Chilcott's crew on 12th September and they completed a 13½ hour patrol.

Although there were seven Sunderland squadrons in the United Kingdom by D-Day, totalling ninety-four aircraft (fifty of them serviceable), only eight operational Sunderland sorties were made on 6th June – one by JM721 of No 10 squadron. During the month over 90 sorties were mounted by the squadron, quite an achievement considering the number of invasion vessels that were crowded in and around the port. On 8th July *U-243* was sunk about 130 miles south-west of Brest by Flying Officer W.B. Tilley and his crew. Machine gun fire from the Sunderland's rear turret killed the U-boat commander and coxswain. After the attack the U-boat was seen to sink and the crew launched dinghies. Tilley's crew dropped a spare dinghy to survivors swimming in the water, as well as food packs before radioing their exact position to a nearby convoy and 38 seamen were rescued. This was the sixth and final U-boat to be destroyed by No 10's Australian crews. By September 1944 virtually all the U-boats had departed from the Bay of Biscay, and Coastal Command's anti-submarine operations were concentrated into other areas. In the last four months of the year only twenty-nine attacks were made and just four U-boats destroyed. It is interesting to note that Sunderland crews accounted for thirty-three U-boats during the war.

With the squadron's long war completed, No 10's crews finally left for Australia on 31st October 1945 having completed over 3,100 operations in which twenty-five aircraft were lost, nineteen from enemy action. There is a plaque at the Barbican, which commemorates all the Australian airmen that flew from Mount Batten during the Second World War. The demise of the flying boat effectively brought about the end of Mount Batten as a flying operational station, although in 1961 it became the principal station of RAF Marine Branch until 1986. The base was handed over for civilian use in 1992 but now most of the Service buildings have been demolished. Two of the large hangars survived and are used for marine industries and in association with the nearby marina.

10

PERRANPORTH

The RAF's urgent and compelling need for operational airfields in South-West England for both Coastal and Fighter Commands during the early war years, forced the Air Ministry's Aerodromes Board to compromise somewhat in its existing strict criteria for suitable and viable airfield sites. Largely on account of the unfavourable terrain found in both Devon and Cornwall, the Board had little alternative than to accept some unlikely and rather unsuitable locations, and of these perhaps none was more uncongenial than Perranporth in Cornwall. The airfield was built high on the clifftops above the town, 320 feet above sea level, and close to the village of Trevellas, by which name it was originally known by the local community. The bleak and exposed location made flying conditions somewhat arduous and at times more than a little hazardous, and it is quite surprising to discover that there were not more flying accidents at the airfield. No doubt the building contractors experienced some difficult and trying times during the airfield's construction in the hard and harsh winter of 1940/1.

In December 1940 the partially completed airfield received its first unexpected visitor when a Blenheim IV of No 236 squadron, based at St

Eval, attempted a forced landing in bad weather. The aircraft struck some cables placed across the runway and crashed; it was then normal practice to place obstructions on airfields in the throes of construction as the threat of an enemy airborne invasion was considered very real. The airfield was finally ready in late April 1941, and it opened as a satellite for nearby Portreath, which itself had only become operational some six weeks earlier.

Three tarmacadam runways linked by a perimeter track had been laid, along with a number of double fighter blast shelters. One large 'T2' hangar and a number of smaller Blister hangars had been erected, as had the control tower and flight huts; hardly the most generous or comfortable facilities. Initially personnel were accommodated away from the airfield. Although the airfield was originally planned to house one fighter squadron, invariably there would be two operating from the airfield and by the end of 1942 at least three; during 1943 the airfield was extended and developed to account for the increased complement of aircraft and personnel. A much improved control tower was brought into operation during the summer of 1943.

No 66 squadron was the first to occupy Perranporth, its Spitfire IIAs arriving from Exeter on 27th April. The squadron could trace its origins back to June 1916 and had been the second unit to receive Spitfires in October 1938. It had been fully engaged in the Battle of Britain from Coltishall and later Gravesend and continuously since, flying fighter sweeps from Biggin Hill. Only days before being posted 'to the West for a rest', four aircraft and one pilot were lost to Me 109s. The squadron had also lost a number of aircraft on the ground during a Luftwaffe attack on Exeter. It had been commanded by Squadron Leader Athol S. Forbes, DFC, since October, who during his time at Perranporth would bring his tally of victories to 10½ and be awarded a Bar to his DFC. He and his pilots were mainly engaged in defensive patrols along the coasts, as well as covering the vital Western Approaches to the English Channel. In October Forbes would be replaced by Squadron Leader Hubert R. Allen, DFC, previously a Flight Commander with the Squadron.

In May (18th) a rather large aircraft, an Avro Manchester, attempted a forced landing at the small airfield. This twin-engined aircraft of No 207 squadron from Waddington in Lincolnshire was on an air test when it developed an engine fire over the Bristol Channel. Its pilot, Squadron Leader J. C. Macintosh, had completed an excellent single engine landing when the aircraft hit a truck and broke in two; fortunately all

Spitfire IIA; No 66 squadron arrived with IIAs in April 1941.

crew members survived. The Manchester was one of the less successful of wartime bombers; constant problems were experienced with its new Rolls-Royce Vulture engines, and at the time of the accident all Manchesters had been temporarily taken off operations. Only 220 Manchesters were produced, but perhaps the aircraft's saving and lasting grace was that its design led directly to the immortal Lancaster.

For periods during the summer and autumn Spitfire IIAs of No 118 squadron, on detachment from Ibsley in Hampshire, used the airfield, and its pilots would continue to be regular visitors well into 1942. By then the squadron had moved into Predannack, the second satellite airfield provided for Portreath. In a similar way No 66 squadron would leave for periods of detachment to Coltishall in Norfolk, where its aircraft acted as escorts for No 2 Group's light bombers on daylight operations to various targets in Holland. On one such spell of detachment, in August, two sergeant pilots were lost in action, and when the squadron returned to Cornwall, Sergeant F.H.M. Green was shot down off the Lizard on 25th September.

In mid-December the squadron moved to the parent station at Portreath, leaving Perranporth in the hands of another Spitfire squadron, No 130. The pilots had brought their new Mark VAs from Harrowbeer via Portreath earlier in the month. No 130 had the dubious honour to make Perranporth almost its permanent home; other than some short spells of detachment it would operate from the airfield until the end of March 1943, the longest spell of tenure of any squadron.

Spitfire IIA of No 118 squadron. (via J. Adams)

During this period there were several changes in squadron commanders. Squadron Leader Peter J. Simpson, DFC, a Battle of Britain 'veteran', who had been a Flight Commander with No 66, was promoted to command No 130 in July 1942. Simpson would later command the Portreath Wing. Shortly before the squadron finally left Perranporth for Dyce at the end of March 1943, Squadron Leader W.H.A. Wright had taken over the reins. During its brief operational life so far the squadron had experienced relatively few losses of pilots, but on the last day of the year Sergeant J. Cox failed to return from a convoy patrol off the coast near Falmouth.

When the Spitfire VBs of No 310 (Czech) squadron flew in from Dyce on Christmas Eve 1941, Perranporth was beginning to acquire a somewhat unlikely reputation as a Spitfire station, more especially when one considers its location so far west well away from Fighter Command's main action over North-East France. Until April 1944 all but one of the squadrons serving at the airfield operated Spitfires and mostly Mark Vs. By June 1943 Perranporth was one of only two fighter stations in the whole of Fighter Command to house three Spitfire squadrons; this was a time when Typhoons were entering the Command in some numbers.

In retrospect 1942 may be viewed as a relatively quiet period for the airfield, at least in purely operational terms. This despite the fact that by the end of the year over fifty Spitfires had used the airfield at various times for fighter sweeps, convoy patrols and escort missions, although these latter operations were restricted because of the operational range of the Mark Vs. The pilots were also sent on Jim Crows, coastal patrols to intercept any enemy aircraft; the term originated from 1940 when such patrols had been first introduced, when they had the added advantage of spotting any signs of an enemy invasion. It is not clear how these patrols received their unusual code-name! As each Spitfire squadron left Perranporth, it was immediately and duly replaced by another.

However, in early February, the other renowned Battle of Britain fighter – Hurricane – appeared briefly at Perranporth; they were Mark IICs operating in the role of fighter/bombers, known as 'Hurribombers'. Just eight aircraft of No 402 (RCAF), which was the second Canadian fighter squadron formed in Britain, flew down from Warmwell. The detachment was led by Squadron Leader R.E. Morrow, DFC, and its Hurricanes were to join the mixed Fighter and Coastal Command force tasked with preventing the two German battleships, *Scharnhorst* and *Gneisenau*, along with *Prinz Eugen* from leaving Brest, where they had been sheltering since March 1941. Operation Fuller, which had been planned and put in place since April 1941, was a combined Air Ministry and Admiralty operation to prevent the flotilla making its escape from the port. On 8th February the Admiralty's intelligence sources had revealed that the vessels were preparing to leave Brest and it was wrongly assumed by the Admiralty that the German Commander, Vice Admiral Ciliax would leave in daylight; nor indeed did the Navy think that the enemy vessels would use the English Channel. However, the German vessels successfully slipped out of Brest in the late evening of the 11th, taking full advantage of the appalling weather and heavy low cloud, which gave them maximum concealment. The Canadian pilots, along with other squadrons, had been given the five accompanying destroyers as their specific targets. The infamous 'Channel Dash' was completely successful, as has already been noted, despite the fact that 30 fighter squadrons (almost 400 aircraft) were ultimately committed to the Operation, the combined efforts of Bomber and Coastal Commands, and of course the FAA. It is thought that one of the destroyers was destroyed and another damaged in a separate airborne action off the coast of Brittany as the destroyers were returning to Brest.

The Czech pilots left for Exeter in early May, and they were replaced by perhaps the most famous Spitfire squadron in Fighter Command – No 19. Back in August 1938 this squadron became the first to be equipped with the new Spitfires, and as a result received considerable publicity from the aviation and national press. No 19 had operated from Duxford during the Battle of Britain, becoming part of the famous Duxford Wing under Douglas Bader. Its pilots were the first to test cannon-armed Spitfires in August 1940, with scant success due to continual problems with the cannon's drum feeds. They also first operated the Mark IIAs. By November 1942 the squadron had notched up its 100th victory of the war, whilst under the command of Squadron Leader Victor H. Ekins, DFC. In the following month the squadron was acting as an escort for the USAAF's B-17s attacking Lille.

Both Nos 19 and 130 squadrons would be engaged in Operation Jubilee on 19th August 1942. No 19 temporarily moved to Rochford in Essex and No 130 to Thorney Island in Hampshire. Both would lose two aircraft in this huge air battle; No 19's Sergeant E.A. Blore was killed. Wing Commander M.V. Mindy' Blake, DSO, DFC, who was the Portreath Wing Commander, flew as a 'guest' with No 130; he was shot down and taken prisoner. Another of the squadron's pilots, Sergeant A.W. Utting was killed. Both aircraft were thought to have been shot down by 'friendly' Naval vessels. As Squadron Leader Simpson wrote in his log book, 'What a show, W/C M. Blake and Sgt Utting missing – the RN could brush up on their aircraft recognition'! The two squadrons accounted for one Fw 190 destroyed plus four probables.

Briefly during the summer of 1942 the airfield was allocated to the USAAF Eighth Air Force for use as a fighter base. However, Perranporth was situated too far distant from its bomber groups operating in East Anglia, and by September this decision was rescinded; the USAAF never occupied Perranporth. Although on 1st June 1943 a USAAF B-17 carrying a number of special passengers from North Africa made a successful landing at the small airfield after 'missing' Portreath. Perhaps more amazingly its pilot managed to successfully take off from the short runway on the following day.

During 1943 fourteen Spitfire squadrons operated from Perranporth at various times. Besides British squadrons, there was a mixture of Canadian, Australian, Polish and Free French squadrons, which clearly showed the cosmopolitan nature of Fighter Command. Many were commanded by very experienced pilots, who had fought in the Battle of Britain, and it is rather invidious to name only two of all these fine and brave airmen. However, Squadron Leader Michael F. Beytagh, DFC, was outstanding. He was an Irishman and a pre-war officer who had flown in the Battle of Britain, and had also led No 602 'City of Glasgow'

Spitfire VB of No 602 squadron.

with great verve for twelve months from October 1942. This squadron had replaced No 234, which flew during the Battle of Britain from St Eval, on 20th January and remained until mid-April. Also at Perranporth at this time was Beytagh's close friend, Squadron Leader James E. Storrar, DFC, Bar, commanding No 65 squadron. He had flown Hurricanes with No 145 squadron during the Battle of Britain, and since then had served in the Middle East, as had Beytagh. They had each crash-landed in East Africa, and together they walked through jungle terrain to escape capture. The friends would fly with No 1697 (ADLS) Flight, already noted under Harrowbeer.

The first Canadian squadron, No 412 (RCAF), to serve at Perranporth, arrived from Fairwood Common on 13th April. Also known as the 'Falcon' squadron, its badge incorporated the bird; the falcon was indigenous to Canada, and known for its skill and aggressiveness in dealing with enemies. The Canadian pilots were mainly engaged on coastal and convoy patrols, but they did move to a number of ALGs (Advanced Landing Grounds) near the south coast for fighter sweeps and Ramrods. As indeed did No 610 'County of Chester' squadron, which shared the airfield with the Canadians during May and June. The squadrons were also called upon to act as escorts for No 263's Whirlwinds, then operating in a bomber role from Predannack. When the Canadians left Perranporth in mid-June, followed five days later (26th) by No 610, they were replaced by two Polish squadrons, Nos 302 'City of Poznań' and 317 'City of Wilno', both of which have been mentioned earlier.

In August the two Polish squadrons moved east to Fairlop in Essex, and the gap was partially filled by a RAAF squadron, No 453, which had been reformed in this country in June 1942 from Australian pilots serving in RAF squadrons. The Australians were engaged on convoy patrols, fighter sweeps, and making anti-shipping strikes especially near the Channel Islands. On 13th September there was a sad accident at the airfield when one of No 453's Spitfires crashed into a cottage at Trevellas after striking overhead cables; the pilot was killed as was a child in the cottage. In September (17th) No 66 squadron made a welcome return to the airfield. It was now commanded by Squadron Leader K.T. Lofts, DFC, and was equipped with Mark LFIX Spitfires. The pilots flew standing patrols over Brest and in the following month went over to Insteps, which were interceptions of enemy aircraft attacking Coastal Command operations in the Bay of Biscay. On 8th October the two squadrons accounted for a total of seven enemy aircraft for the loss of two Australian pilots, although two Spitfires collided over the airfield on their return.

During September Typhoons of No 183 squadron moved down from Harrowbeer. For about one month the pilots attempted to operate from the airfield. However, try as they may they faced considerable difficulties at Perranporth. Landings and take offs in these heavy fighter aircraft (some seven tons) were not easy even for experienced 'Tiffy' pilots; also the Typhoon was prone to swing on take off and its high landing speed (120 mph) allied to its weight, meant that it needed a fair stretch of runway. Nevertheless a number of operations were mounted from Perranporth, mainly over the Brest Peninsula. On 3rd October Flight Lieutenant Dring claimed a Fw 190, the squadron's only success from the airfield. Eleven days later it was decided that the restrictive nature of the airfield was not really suitable for Typhoon operations and they moved to Predannack.

Previously, in October, the first Free French squadron had landed at Perranporth. It was No 341 or 'Gruppe Chasse Alsace', which had been formed in January 1943 from French pilots serving with other fighter squadrons in the Western Desert. The squadron had only recently lost its charismatic commander – Commandant R. Mouchotte, C de G, DFC – and was now commanded by Commandant B. Dupier, C de G. All of the seven Free French squadrons that served in the RAF were led by French airmen. The 'Alsace' squadron, as it was known, had also 'lost' to No 602 squadron, perhaps the most famous wartime Free French pilot – Pierre Clostermann; he would later command a Fighter Wing and his wartime RAF experiences are vividly recalled in his book *The Big Show*, published in 1951.

In early November (9th) a second Free French squadron arrived, effectively replacing No 66 squadron, which moved east to Hornchurch. This was No 340 or 'Ile de France' and each of its Spitfire VCs carried the Cross of Lorraine badge just below the cockpit. The pilots flew a mixture of bomber escorts, fighter sweeps, coastal patrols and Insteps. In the New Year (22nd January), the two squadrons were joined by a newly formed Free French squadron, No 329 or 'Cigones', although its pilots were not ready for full operations until early March. For the brief period that the squadrons were operational they formed No 145 Free French Wing, and would move to Merston in Sussex to be re-equipped with Mark LFIX Spitfires and prepare for the invasion of their homeland, when the Wing operated under the 2nd Tactical Air Force.

By 18th April 1944 the Free French squadrons had left Perranporth, which proved to be a sad and final farewell to all the Spitfires that had graced the airfield for almost three years. The main reason for their departure was that on 15th April the airfield had been transferred out of Fighter Command and into No 19 Group of Coastal Command. Perranporth would now be used by several of the FAA squadrons loaned to Coastal Command. The first FAA aircraft appeared at Perranporth on the 20th, twelve Swordfish IIs of No 816 squadron, commanded by Lieutenant Commander P. Snow, RN. It will be recalled that this FAA squadron served briefly from Exeter in the early summer of 1943. The squadron's Swordfish were armed with rocket projectiles and would, on occasions use the FAA base at St Merryn. They were shortly followed by Nos 849 and 850 (FAA) squadrons both equipped with twelve Grumman Avenger Is.

The Grumman TBF-I Avenger, although of a pre-war design, had first flown in August 1941, and essentially from its entry into the US Navy in the following January, had become the Navy's standard fleet torpedo-bomber operating in the Pacific. This aircraft would make its first appearance with the FAA in January 1943, and was originally known in the FAA as the Tarpon I, although soon the American name was adopted. The Avenger had a top speed of about 265 mph, it was armed with five machine guns, and carried either 2,000 pounds of bombs, a single torpedo or eight rocket projectiles – quite a formidable aircraft. The Avenger had a clean design with a powerful Wright R-2600 Cyclone engine, and perhaps its most distinctive feature was the long

Grumman Avenger II: Nos 849 and 850 (FAA) squadrons operated these aircraft from Perranporth. (National Air & Space Museum)

'glasshouse' canopy, which provided an excellent field of vision for its three-man crew. The Avenger remained in service with the US Navy until 1954.

Only one Swordfish was lost whilst the squadron operated from Perranporth; it flew into the sea on 23rd May after completing bombing practice in Harlyn Bay near St Merryn, and two airmen were rescued. The D-Day operations at Perranporth started on the previous evening when two Swordfish left at about 2000 hours for a three hour patrol. From then on throughout the night Swordfish left at regular intervals, the last crew landing back at Perranporth about 0700 hours on the 6th. By then the first three Avengers of No 849 squadron had left to patrol the French coasts, which continued throughout the morning. The other Avenger squadron would take over the 'afternoon shift', and in the evening the Swordfish crews left on their nightly patrols; in that way continuous twenty-four hour patrols could be maintained.

It was not until July that the Avengers met any real opposition or action. On the 20th they engaged two Heinkel 177s, the large *Greif* heavy bombers, attacking Allied shipping near Ushant; one was shot down, and the other damaged. Four days later a couple of enemy vessels were sighted not far from St Peter's Port off Guernsey, one was sunk and the other damaged. The Swordfish and Avengers of No 850 squadron left the airfield on 1st August, and No 849 moved out to St Eval eight days later. Thus ended Perranporth's existence as an operational station, and it was placed on a Care and Maintenance basis at the beginning of September 1944.

In late November Perranporth was handed over to No 46 Group of Transport Command, and the airfield was used as a Staging Post for

Swordfish of No 816 (FAA) squadron armed with rocket projectiles. (Imperial War Museum)

military personnel awaiting detachment on the Continent. By May 1945 the airfield had been put into 'mothballs', and was finally closed by the Air Ministry on 6th April 1946. Nowadays, what is left of the old wartime airfield is used by the Cornish Gliding and Flying Club, and its name has reverted to Trevellas.

11

PORTREATH

Portreath was quite an unusual wartime airfield. It started life as a fighter station in No 10 Group of Fighter Command, before taking on the role of a major ferry transport terminal, both for the USAAF and the RAF. However, by late 1943 it had returned to the offensive with Coastal Command's anti-shipping strike aircraft. Also in common with virtually all coastal airfields, A/S/R units operated from Portreath. It was one of the earliest wartime airfields to open in Cornwall and almost sixty years later it is still occupied by the RAF.

The airfield is situated almost 300 feet above and to the east of the village, and as such prey to the full ferocity of the North Atlantic elements. Nevertheless, it proved to be in a most propitious location, well-positioned for flights to and from the war fronts in the Middle East and North Africa and ideally situated for operations over the Bay of Biscay. In the late summer of 1940 Richard Costain Ltd moved into the site on Nancekuke Common, which until then had been farmed. Fields and hedges were flattened, a number of houses demolished and by dint of rapid construction work, the airfield was considered ready for occupation approximately six months later – one of the speediest completions on record.

Portreath was planned as a fighter airfield specifically to replace Coastal Command's base at St Eval, which had been hastily used by Fighter Command since the Battle of Britain; in May 1941 it would take over the Sector's responsibilities from that airfield. Some idea of the urgency to get the airfield operational can be gained from the fact that its operations room was originally sited above a bakery in Portreath Road outside Redruth, though it would soon move to Tehidy Barton some two miles from the airfield. Portreath had another unusual feature for a wartime airfield, it was originally provided with four rather than three runways. They would ultimately measure 5,480, 4,500, 3,400 and 3,000 feet in length. The eight Blister hangars were later augmented by four larger and more substantial 'T2' hangars. The airfield opened on 7th March 1941 with Wing Commander J. Heber-Percy, AFC, as its first Commander.

Eleven days later the first aircraft arrived, Whirlwinds of the itinerant No 263 squadron, which had already served at Exeter and St Eval and was now commanded by Squadron Leader Arthur H. Donaldson, the youngest of three brothers that served in the RAF – one of a number of 'RAF families'. The eldest, Jack, had commanded No 263 from October 1939 to the following June when he was lost in the tragic sinking of HMS *Glorious* in the North Sea. To my knowledge this is the only instance of two brothers commanding the same RAF squadron during the war. The middle brother – Squadron Leader Edward 'Teddy' Donaldson, DSO, AFC, Bar – commanded No 151 squadron during the Battle of Britain, and would retire as an Air Commodore.

During the squadron's time in the South-West it had lost three aircraft; one crash-landed at Portreath on 14th March seriously injuring its pilot. In the few weeks that the Whirlwinds, or 'Crikeys' as they became known, were based at Portreath, Flight Lieutenant D.A.C. Crooks, DFC, was killed when his aircraft was shot down by a Dornier 215 off the Lizard coast, crashing near Helston. The Whirlwinds left for Filton on 10th April, but the squadron would return to Devon and Cornwall on several more occasions.

In their place came Spitfire IIAs of No 152 (Hyderabad) squadron, which had flown down from Warmwell losing one aircraft en route. The squadron had become 'the gift of the Nizam of Hyderabad' and fought most valiantly from the Dorset airfield during the Battle of Britain, losing fourteen pilots – few squadrons suffered heavier losses in the Battle. No 152 was commanded by Squadron Leader P.A. Boitel-Gill, DFC, or 'Bottled Gull' as he was known to his pilots! He had been a pilot with Imperial Airways before joining the pre-war RAF as well as sometime being the personal pilot to the Nizam. In June he was promoted to Wing Commander, and three months later sadly was killed in a flying accident at Carlisle. He had been replaced by Squadron Leader J. Darwen. Several of its Battle of Britain pilots were still serving

Whirlwind of No 263 squadron.

with the squadron, perhaps the most famous being Flying Officer Eric S. 'Boy' Marrs, DFC. Marrs was probably the public's image of a fighter pilot – young (only nineteen), an ex-public schoolboy and a graduate of RAF Cranwell College – yet despite his tender years Marrs was a most experienced and successful fighter pilot.

One of the pilots later recalled the conditions they found at Portreath: 'we'd never heard of this place . . . and when we got there it was only half-built . . . with no completed runways and no buildings we could move into, we were all accommodated in Bell tents on the clifftop. There was only one solid building and this was used as an office and parachute store. Later on we went into digs in the village, which was quite nice . . .' However, by the summer of 1941 much of the construction work had been completed and the station could then house over 1,000 personnel. But like so many wartime airfields further construction and improvement work would continue almost throughout the war years.

The pilots were mainly sent out on convoy patrols, although during late April they were seeking out the high flying Junkers 88 recon-naissance aircraft photographing and collecting weather readings for the Luftwaffe's night-bombing operations over the South-West. On 10th May the black painted Hurricanes of No 247 squadron, which had been engaged on night-operations from St Eval and Roborough, moved into Portreath. The use of Hurricanes as night-fighters will be noted further under Roborough. They remained at the airfield until mid-June before transferring to Portreath's other satellite airfield at Predannack.

Early in April the airfield suffered its first raid, followed by another on Good Friday night (11/12th) and then again on the 27th and 29th, but little damage was sustained. However, in another raid on 11th May some forty high explosives fell and a number of aircraft were damaged with one airman killed. In order to provide some increased night-fighter protection for the South-West the Spitfire pilots were sent out on a number of tentative night-patrols. These led to the loss of two pilots in unfortunate flying accidents, so the squadron quickly reverted to day-patrols. They also often flew as escorts for the Blenheims of No 2 Group of Bomber Command that were temporarily detached to the airfield for bombing raids over Northern France.

On 20th June a new squadron was formed at the airfield – No 130 (Punjab) – with Squadron Leader C. J. Donovan as its first Commander. Equipped with Spitfire IIAs, its pilots would take about ten weeks 'working-up' to operational readiness. As has already been noted, the squadron would spend much of its early existence operating from the other satellite airfield at Perranporth. During June the airfield was first used as a staging and ferry airfield for flights to Gibraltar and Malta. A number of Blenheim IV squadrons were temporarily detached to Luqa airfield, Malta, and the crews flew from their bases in East Anglia to Portreath, before setting out on their long flights to Gibraltar for refuelling before the final stage. Gibraltar was well over seven hours away, crossing the Bay of Biscay and around the Iberian peninsula, and the distance was close to the maximum operational range of the aircraft – a most daunting and hazardous flight. No 82 squadron, then based at Bodney in Norfolk, was the first to make the trip, followed over the next six months by other Blenheim squadrons in rotation. Some suffered heavy losses during their brief spell of duty at Malta; for instance, No 107 squadron from Great Massingham in Norfolk left Portreath on 18th August and on its return in January, only three of its original crews remained.

No 152 squadron became increasingly used on escort missions for bombing raids on the French Atlantic ports. On 24th July Bomber Command mounted a major daylight operation, code-named Sunrise against the German battleships at Brest; although *Scharnhorst* had moved to La Pallice and fifteen unescorted Halifaxes would make a separate attack. Eighteen Hampdens would be escorted by three Spitfire squadrons, Nos 152, 66 and 234, led by Wing Commander

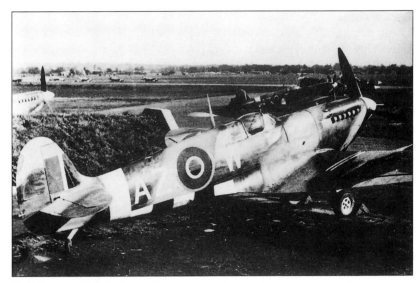

Spitfire VB of No 234 squadron. (RAF Museum)

Heber-Percy, and for this operation the Spitfires were fitted with long-range fuel tanks. The largest bomber force, comprising seventy-nine Wellingtons and just three Flying Fortresses were not given any escorts as none were said to be available! On this occasion the Luftwaffe's fighter opposition was far greater than expected and the flak was heavy and accurate. Ten Wellingtons and two Hampdens were lost (12%), along with two fighters, both from No 152. Sergeant Short was posted as missing but the other pilot, Flying Officer 'Boy' Marrs, DFC, was shot down by anti-aircraft fire and killed. Only six days earlier he had shot down a Heinkel 111 whilst on patrol near the Scillies and had recently celebrated his twentieth birthday. Marrs is buried in Brest cemetery. The squadron left for Snailwell in Cambridgeshire on 26th August, and from late 1942 until the end of the war, it would serve in the Middle East and later India.

The Spitfire IIAs of No 313 (Czech) squadron, formed earlier in the year, arrived on the following day. They took on the task of escorting mainly Blenheims to and from their targets, as well as flying fighter sweeps over Northern France to strafe enemy airfields. When they moved east to Hornchurch in mid-December, they were replaced by another Spitfire II squadron, No 66, which moved down from Perranporth. During its time at Portreath the pilots would convert to

Mark VBs, and some were detached to operate from Warmwell.

During the autumn there was a marked increase in the use of the airfield by a variety of aircraft. The first detachments of Coastal Command's Beaufighters began to operate from Portreath – No 248. This squadron could trace its origins back to 1918 and had been reformed in October 1939, transferring to Coastal Command in the following February. Its crews had recently converted from Blenheims and flew interception patrols off the Scilly Isles, which were known for some unaccountable reason as Operation Milktrain! Some anti-shipping strikes were mounted and the crews managed to claim a couple of enemy aircraft before they moved north to Dyce during March 1942. The squadron would later return to Portreath during early 1944. Beaufighters of No 89 squadron also used the airfield briefly before leaving to serve in Egypt.

In October 1941 No 1 Overseas Aircraft Despatch Unit, which had been formed at Honeybourne in Worcestershire, established a detachment at Portreath for the ferrying of flights and squadrons out to North Africa and the Middle East. The first aircraft to use the Unit's ferry facilities were four Flying Fortresses of No 90 squadron, which left on 28th October bound for Shallufa in Egypt. They would be followed, on 5th November, by Hudson Vs of No 500 squadron and later by Beaufighters of No 600 squadron, that had been operating from Predannack. Also a number of Coastal Command's Wellingtons left for spells of detachment at Gibraltar. Such large influxes of crews, if only on a very temporary basis, placed a great strain on the existing facilities at the airfield. Briefing rooms were needed, as were messes, and the problem of sleeping quarters was solved by bringing the Bell tents out of storage. To add to all this aircraft activity the first A/S/R aircraft arrived during October, a Flight of Walruses and Lysanders of the recently formed A/S/R squadron, No 276, from Harrowbeer.

The German battleships sheltering in Brest were a constant thorn for the Air Ministry and became regular targets for Bomber Command during the winter. Most of these operations were conducted at night and thus were unescorted. However, in December five small daylight bombing raids were mounted, involving escort duties for the Spitfire pilots. On the 30th of the month sixteen Halifaxes were despatched, three of which failed to return; however, the escort fighters claimed six enemy fighters destroyed. Bomber Command's night-operations over Brest continued until 6/7th February 1942, and proved to be costly with few tangible results to show for all the crews' valiant efforts.

No 66 squadron was now commanded by Squadron Leader B.L. Duckenfield, AFC, who had served with No 504 during the Battle of Britain. He was promoted in March and replaced by Squadron Leader D.E. Cremin, DFC before the squadron left for Ibsley on 27th April, although it would return to Cornwall later in the year. There was a straight exchange with No 234 squadron, making a return to Cornwall, where it had previously operated from St Eval. Its erstwhile popular New Zealand Commander – M.V. 'Mindy' Blake, DFC – had been promoted to command the Exeter Wing, but in the summer he would join his old squadron at the airfield, as Portreath's Spitfire Wing Commander and be awarded the DSO in July. No 234, now commanded by Squadron Leader E. W. Birchfield, was equipped with Spitfire VBs and Cs. The squadron would remain in the area, either at Portreath or Perranporth, until January 1943, with its pilots engaged on a variety of convoy patrols ranging from Brest to Cherbourg, bomber escorts and Jim Crows. In the summer of 1944 the squadron would return to Cornwall (Predannack).

Perhaps one of the major events of 1942 was the airfield's involvement in Operation Cackle, the movement of USAAF aircraft, supplies and airmen to Gibraltar and North Africa, to join the Twelfth Air Force, and to be engaged in the Allied invasion of North Africa. Lieutenant-General Luther W. Sweetser, Jr was the master-mind of Cackle, and had set up his headquarters at Hurn in Dorset; on 1st November Lieutenant-Colonel Simenson arrived at Portreath to assume command of the USAAF aircraft and airmen detached to the airfield. It would be from Hurn and Portreath that the majority of the USAAF aircraft, airmen and supplies would leave for North Africa. During the latter three months of the year Portreath was literally swamped with USAAF personnel and American aircraft of all descriptions – C-47s, B-17s, B-24s, DB-7s (Bostons), and P-38s (Lightnings). The logistical problems of handling so many aircraft was not helped when, on 9th November, 19 rather battered B-17s of 306th Bomb Group made emergency landings after suffering a harsh bombing mission over St Nazaire, during which three B-17s had been shot down. One B-17, flown by Major Henry J. Holt, a Squadron Commander, made a heavy crash-landing, and was 'written-off'.

During December a detachment of long-range Mustang Is of No 400 (RCAF) squadron, based at Middle Wallop, provided some meagre escort support for the massive movement of aircraft and supplies. There were also a couple of 'old' B-17Es of the 92nd Bomb Group,

B-24s of the US Eighth Air Force used Portreath in 1942. (USAF)

operating a courier service for VIPs and urgent supplies to and from North Africa, and this service continued well into the New Year. Amongst this welter of USAAF aircraft, RAF squadrons were also despatched to both Gibraltar and Malta. In December, No 23 squadron's Mosquito IIs (ex Bradwell Bay) left for Luqa, and Beaufighter VIfs of No 153 squadron went out to Maison Blanche in North Africa. On 6th December, twenty-four B-24s of the 93rd Bomb Group left for what was stated to be a short detachment in Morocco. They returned to Portreath in February 1943 when the Group acquired the nickname of 'Ted's Travelling Circus', due to its frequent moves and their popular Commanding Officer – Colonel E. 'Ted' Timberlake, Jr.

The departure of No 234's Spitfire Vs to Perranporth in late December really brought about the demise of Portreath as a fighter station, as far as Fighter Command was concerned. During the early months of 1943 the OADU was fully engaged in aircraft movements abroad, from some two hundred and ten in January to over three hundred by the end of March. Then in June there was a great flurry of activity when Halifax Vs of 'A' Flight of No 295 squadron, under Squadron Leader A.M.B. Wilkinson, arrived from Hurn preparatory to towing Airspeed Horsas out to Morocco; by far the longest distance that gliders had been towed. The Halifaxes had been fitted with extra fuel tanks and the dorsal turrets removed to lighten the aircraft. The technique of glider towing was still relatively new and the Horsas would take part in Operation Husky – the invasion of Sicily – the first *major* airborne troop landing of the war. The Halifaxes were followed in by Armstrong Whitworth Albemarles of No 296 squadron, also from Hurn, which would ultimately tow the American Waco GC-4 gliders into Sicily.

Towards the end of the month over one hundred and twenty B-24s from the Eighth Air Force were despatched to North Africa. The 93rd Bomb Group (on the move once again!) left Portreath on the 25th, followed two days later by the 44th Bomb Group, and finally on the 31st the 389th Bomb Group left the airfield. The three Groups would mount a number of bombing missions over Sicily and Italy before taking part in the epic low-level attack of the Ploesti oil refineries in Roumania on 1st August when fifty-three aircraft were lost, and over four hundred airmen killed; it was an operation that ranked alongside the Dam Busters. The three Bomb Groups finally returned to Portreath in October *en route* to their respective bases in East Anglia.

Whilst all these large and heavy bombers were moving in and out during June, detachments of Mustang Is of Nos 414 (RCAF) and 613 'City of Manchester' squadrons were also using the airfield. They were mainly engaged in Insteps, escorting flights of Mosquitos over the Bay of Biscay. One Canadian pilot was unfortunately lost on 17th June, when his aircraft was shot down in error by Spitfires whilst on patrol near the Scilly Isles. No 414 left for Dunsfold in late June, and No 613 moved to Snailwell in the following month. Nevertheless, the airfield was still used as an emergency landing field. For instance, on 4th July a B-17 *Ruthie* of 92nd Bomb Group suffered severe battle damage over Nantes, and Lieutenant R. L. Campbell managed to bring the stricken aircraft into Portreath, but the B-17 was so badly damaged it was 'written-off'.

Portreath would now enter into its third and most successful wartime phase when, in September, Mk. VIC Beaufighters of No 143 squadron moved in from St Eval, under the command of Wing Commander R.N. Lambert, DFC. The squadron had received its first Beaufighters in June 1941, and in November 1942 had become part of the first Beaufighter Strike Wing set up at North Coates. The crews became increasingly engaged on long-range anti-aircraft patrols over the Bay of Biscay – some six hour flights often in atrocious weather conditions – but slowly their victories over the omnipresent Junkers 88s began to mount. In November one of Coastal Command's celebrated pilots moved in to take over command of No 143 squadron – Wing Commander Edric H.

McHardy, DSO, DFC, Bar – until December 1944. McHardy was a New Zealand airman, just one from that small country that made such an immense contribution to the wartime RAF, in all three operational Commands. The Wing Commander was on his third operational tour, having started with No 248 Blenheim squadron in early 1940. He had then commanded No 404 (RCAF) squadron, and had followed this tour of duty by flying Liberators to and from Africa for Ferry Command. McHardy retired from the RAF in 1958 and returned to his homeland.

Although the weather during December 1943 and January 1944 was less than ideal for operational flying, No 143 managed to mount over 100 sorties during each month. On 12th December three Junkers 88s were shot down but for the loss of two Beaufighters – two of the enemy aircraft were claimed by Wing Commander McHardy. By now the airfield's A/S/R services had been augmented by a number of Warwicks from Davidstow Moor. On 1st February No 235 squadron, which was also operating Beaufighters but Mk. XIs, joined No 143. The squadron, led by Wing Commander R. H. McConnell, DFC, could be considered as 'local'; it had been formed at Newlyn in August 1918. Both Beaufighter squadrons were flying anti-aircraft patrols directed by a Naval vessel. They also mounted a number of convoy patrols and were used occasionally as escorts for A/S/R patrols by Warwicks and Walruses. On the 11th of the month No 143 squadron was posted to North Coates in Lincolnshire. Five days later one of 235's Beaufighters crewed by Squadron Leader R.R. Wright and Flying Officer P.F. Ross, whilst on a convoy patrol, shot down a Junkers 290A – a large and long-range maritime aircraft. On the 20th the squadron moved to St Angelo in Northern Ireland, though it would return in April.

The Beaufighters were replaced by de Havilland Mosquito VIs of No 248 squadron which was now commanded by Wing Commander O.J.M. Barron, DFC. The crews had received their first Mosquitos the previous December whilst serving at Predannack but the first operational sorties with Mosquitos took place from Portreath on 20th February, just three days after their move from Predannack.This remarkable and versatile aircraft was, in the opinion of Air Vice-Marshal Sir Basil Embry, 'the finest aeroplane, without exception that has ever been built in this country.' It had entered the Service in July 1941, with over 7,700 being produced in forty-three different marks, at least according to Sir Geoffrey de Havilland. Mosquitos served in all three operational Commands with equal facility and success, and the aircraft's war record in the three operational Commands is unrivalled by any Allied, or indeed enemy, aircraft. Reichsmarshal Hermann Göring is reported as saying, 'I turn green with envy when I see the Mosquito. The British knock together a beautiful wooden aircraft . . . There is nothing the British do not have . . .'

The Mosquito FBVI was a natural development of the IV, which was the first fighter/bomber version. It was provided with two powerful Rolls-Royce Merlin 25 engines, probably giving the aircraft a slight edge in speed of some 20 knots at sea-level over the Beaufighter TBXs. The FBVIs were heavily armed with four .303 machine guns and four 20mm Hispano-Suiza cannons and they could carry four rocket projectiles under each wing along with 1,000 pounds of bombs. Their range could be extended by 50 gallon (later 100 gallon) drop tanks in place of the wing bombs. Compared with the heavy Beaufighter, which had the attributes of a medium bomber, the Mosquito handled more like a fighter, and has been described as 'an Arab steed by comparison with the war horse of the Beaufighter'!

Early in March the squadron received a small detachment of Mark XVIIIs – it never had more than four and only 25 in total were produced for Coastal Command. This Mark had been specifically developed to carry Barnes Wallis' Highball, a type of 'bouncing mine' designed to be used against enemy battleships, and really more specifically for attacking the *Tirpitz*. The Command's Mk. XVIIIs had been modified to accept the 57mm Molins anti-tank gun in place of the four cannons, and greater armour plating was added for the protection of the crews and its engines. In recognition of its far greater 'bite' because of its six pounder shell, the aircraft was called a 'Tsetse'! On 25th March, two of the squadron's XVIIIs, piloted by Flying Officers D.J. Turner and Aubrey Hilliard sank a U-boat, *U-976*, off the Ile d'Yeu to the south of St Nazaire, and two days later, in the same location, another U-boat, *U-960*, was heavily damaged. Fourteen of its crew including the Captain, were wounded, and the U-boat was sunk in the Mediterranean about a month later.

During April No 235 squadron returned to Portreath and further successes came to both squadrons, especially on the 11th when a disabled U-boat was attacked; six of its escorting Junkers 88s were shot down and another five damaged for the loss of two Mosquitos. On D-Day there were eighteen Beaufighters and twenty-four Mosquitos at the airfield, and operations continued from dawn until dusk. The two squadrons were, like most Coastal Command units, fully engaged in ensuring that neither U-boats nor surface vessels entered the English

Beaufighter TFX fitted with rocket projectiles. No 235 squadron operated TFXs on D-Day.

Channel. Although, as has already been noted, when No 248's Mosquitos escorted Davidstow Moor's Beaufighter Wing on its anti-shipping strike at Belle Ile, the crews claimed a solitary Junkers 188, a reconnaissance aircraft that had the misfortune to be in the area at the time. The squadron's crews flew over 270 sorties during June. On the 10th of the month the squadron shared in the destruction of *U-821* to the west of Brest, four crews along with a Liberator of No 120 squadron completing the sinking. A few months earlier this U-boat had successfully fought off a determined attack by another Liberator. By the end of the war the squadron would be credited with five U-boat 'kills'.

During June although No 235's crews were busy converting to Mosquito VIs, they still managed to mount eighty Beaufighter sorties during the month; on the 9th a Beaufighter crew claimed a Junkers 88. The last Beaufighter patrol was sent out on the 22nd, but already the first Mosquito sorties had been made on 16th June, when the two squadrons formally became Coastal Command's first Mosquito Strike Wing – No 153(GR). Towards the end of the month the Wing began to see some success as a result of anti-shipping patrols. On the 29th an oil tanker and six escort vessels were attacked, the tanker was set on fire, and several of the other vessels damaged. On the following day, along with Beaufighters of No 404 (RCAF) squadron, a small convoy was attacked off Concarneau, north of Lorient. One of the escort vessels, *UJ 1408*, was destroyed but a Mosquito from No 248 squadron – HR134 – was shot down.

On 4th July Wing Commander A. D. Phillips DSO, DFC, the Commander of No 248 squadron, along with his navigator, Flying Officer Thompson, DFC, were killed in action when attacking minesweepers near Brest. He was replaced by yet another New

Mosquito FB Mk.XVIII of No 248 squadron. (Imperial War Museum)

Zealander, Wing Commander G.D. 'Bill' Sise, DSO, DFC, who was well versed in Strike Wing tactics, having served at North Coates during and since their inception. On the 15th of the month the Mosquito Wing sank a German flak vessel – *Mars*; six days later Wing Commander J.V. Yonge, now the Commander of No 235 squadron, claimed two Dornier 217Rs. These aircraft carried two Henschel Hs 293 anti-shipping guided missiles or 'glider bombs', which were proving to be quite an irritation to Royal Navy vessels operating in the Bay of Biscay. The Mosquito crews were often flying 'air umbrella' patrols over Naval vessels operating in the Bay.

During August both Mosquito squadrons were active on anti-shipping strikes in the Bay of Biscay, although by now only a few German vessels were still operating in those waters. On the 9th of the month a couple of Dornier 217Rs were shot down, and three days later two minesweepers, *M370* and *M4204*, were sunk near the Gironde estuary, with another, *M292*, destroyed on the 21st. These attacks on enemy Naval and flak vessels could prove costly, the Mosquito was far

Supermarine Walrus on A/S/R practice training. (via T. Woods)

more vulnerable to flak than the resilient Beaufighter; in early September No 248 lost five crews in operations over the Gironde. The last Mosquito sorties from Portreath were flown on 7th September, and the two squadrons left for Banff in Scotland, where they would serve for the rest of the war.

The airfield was now bereft of operational aircraft, just the A/S/R Warwicks and a small detachment of Walruses remained, although they would leave in February 1945. The OADU detachment was still in residence, but their operations were petering out as the overland European route to the Middle East had become available. In May 1945 the airfield was transferred to No 44 Group of Transport Command with some 200 aircraft being delivered overseas, but in early October its air traffic control facilities closed down. By the end of the year the airfield had been placed on Care and Maintenance status, and the following July transferred to Technical Training Command. In May 1950 the airfield was passed over to the Ministry of Supply. However, thirty years later, on 1st October 1980, RAF Portreath reopened to operate a Control Reporting Point, plus a Reporting Point, an essential part of the United Kingdom's air Defence Radar system.

12

PREDANNACK

Predannack was the most southerly wartime airfield in the country and the third Cornish airfield to become operational during 1941. It is situated on the Lizard close to the major First World War base at Mullion. The large exposed moorland site, some 290 feet above sea level, was not particularly suitable for airfield construction – except perhaps in respect of its location. The dense china clay subsoil meant that huge quantities of hardcore were needed to provide a reasonable and secure foundation for the four runways, hangars and various operational and technical buildings. Trethowan of Constantine was appointed as the main contractor, assisted in the task by No 1 Works Area (Field) of the RAF Works Service. Besides the inherent construction problems, the building work was further delayed by a Luftwaffe attack on 10th April when the new runways were damaged.

Nevertheless, like the majority of wartime airfields Predannack opened, in May 1941, before all the construction work had been completed. It was planned to operate as the second satellite airfield for Portreath, and perhaps more specifically to accommodate night-fighters, who would work closely with the GCI station at Treleaver. The first aircraft arrived from the parent airfield on 18th June. They were Hurricane IIAs of No 247 'China-British' squadron, which had already operated from Roborough (originally with Gladiators), St Eval and Portreath. It was still commanded by Squadron Leader 'Pete' O'Brian, who would be awarded a DFC in December and remain in charge whilst the squadron served at Predannack.

Hurricane IIC of No 247 squadron.

A number of Hurricane squadrons had hastily transferred to night-operations during the autumn of 1940, and according to Squadron Leader (later Group Captain) Peter Townsend, '[it] could not remotely qualify as a night-fighter'; Townsend commanded No 87 squadron during the Battle of Britain, and it was the first to experiment with Hurricanes as night-fighters. Being a single-seater the aircraft was incapable of carrying the cumbersome early AI radar, and perhaps the only concessions to its new night-role were a headlight mounted in the wing, which aided landings and take offs, two small adjustable lamps that gave a faint orange glow in the cockpit, a lighted optical gunsight and the aircraft's overall matt-black finish. Townsend described night-operations in a Hurricane as 'an exhausting and frustrating sort of war'!

Shortly after the squadron's arrival at the airfield two new Flight Commanders were appointed – Flight Lieutenants John C. Carver and Kenneth W. Mackenzie, DFC – both Battle of Britain 'veterans'. It was the latter airman that claimed the squadron's first night victory, when on 7th July he shot down a Junkers 88, and in the following month a Dornier 17 was destroyed by Flight Lieutenant Carver. The squadron was now operating Roadsteads, with Mackenzie claiming a Heinkel 111 in September. As the Luftwaffe's night-bombing operations began to tail off, the squadron's pilots were increasingly engaged on fighter sweeps over airfields in Northern France. During an attack on Lannion airfield on 29th September Flight Lieutenant Mackenzie's Hurricane was damaged by flak. It crashed into the sea and Mackenzie managed to make it to the French coast, where he was captured and made a prisoner of war.

In early October the first 'real' night-fighters arrived – Beaufighter IIFs of No 600 'City of London' squadron. It was commanded by Squadron Leader G. Stainforth, AFC, until December when Wing Commander H. M. Pearson took over. This change reflected the Air Ministry's acknowledgement that the responsibilities of commanding an AI night-fighter squadron demanded a higher rank; Bomber Command had already up-graded their squadron commanders. It had been Group Captain Sir Basil Embry, DSO, DFC, AFC, then Station Commander at Wittering, who had finally convinced the Air Ministry of the arduous and demanding nature of night-fighter operations.

The following month saw the arrival of No 1457 'Turbinlite' Flight from Colerne. The concept of these Flights was that Douglas Havoc 1s would be equipped with a large Helmore searchlight (originated by Group Captain Helmore), which was capable of throwing a wide beam of light for a distance of about a mile. The 'Turbinlite' aircraft would be guided onto an enemy contact by GCI and its own AI radar, and would illuminate the target for the following 'parasite' fighter to move in and destroy the aircraft; No 247's pilots operated in conjunction with the Flight. This rather bizarre idea is said to have originated with Winston Churchill, and it was because of his enthusiasm for the project that the ten 'Turbinlite' Flights were so quickly formed.

The Flight made its first operational patrols on 29th January off Land's End, but it was not until June that the crews made their first contacts with enemy aircraft, without any result. Despite a conspicuous lack of success by all the Flights they were made up to squadron

Boston III modified with a Turbinlite and used by No 1457 Flight.

strength and in September the Flight became No 536 squadron. However, by then No 247 squadron had departed for Exeter on 17th May, although some Hurricanes had been left behind to operate with the Flight. Problems were experienced with this method of night-interception; frequently the Hurricanes lost touch with their Havocs in heavy cloud or bad visibility, and there were drawbacks in using the searchlights in bad weather. In October No 536 squadron moved away to Fairwood Common where it was disbanded the following January.

Since December 1941 Spitfire VBs of No 118 squadron had operated from the airfield with a small detachment of pilots at Perranporth. In January John Carver returned to Predannack as Squadron Leader to command the squadron. On 13th March he was shot down over the English Channel and managed to survive in the water for two and a half days before being rescued by a Naval vessel. Carver was awarded the DFC in April, but sadly he was posted as missing on 6th June in action over Cherbourg. The new squadron commander was Squadron Leader E. W. Wooten, DFC, Bar, whose subsequent Service career has already been noted; Wooten led his squadron to Tangmere in July.

During the year the airfield would become a temporary home for several detachments of Coastal Command aircraft, such as Beaufighters of No 236 squadron, and Liberator 1s of No 120 squadron. The latter squadron was then based at Leuchars, and one of its Flight Commanders, Squadron Leader Terence M. Bulloch, DFC, became Coastal Command's leading U-boat 'ace'. Bulloch came from Northern Ireland, and had joined the RAF in 1936. He was known as 'The Bull' and considered an 'exceptional' pilot, who already had 2,300 hours of flying time in his log. Whilst the squadron operated from Predannack during August Bulloch attacked two U-boats, *U-89* and *U-653*; both had to return to port for urgent repairs and would later be destroyed by FAA aircraft. Another two U-boat attacks were made during the month but for the loss of two Liberators. No 120 squadron would destroy fourteen U-boats during the war. These operations presaged an anti-shipping and anti-submarine role that Predannack would increasingly undertake from 1943 onwards, the airfield being ideally placed for patrols over the Bay of Biscay and the Western Approaches.

Nevertheless, it would be Beaufighters that would be the permanent residents for most of 1942. When No 600 squadron left on 2nd September, it was replaced two days later by No 406 (RCAF) squadron, which had formed in May 1941 as the first Canadian night-fighter unit under Wing Commander D.G. Morris, DFC. For some of their time at

Beaufighter VIFs of No 600 squadron.

the airfield the Canadian crews conducted A/S/R patrols. At the end of the year they were followed into the airfield by perhaps Fighter Command's most famous Beaufighter squadron – No 604 'County of Middlesex' – the first to be equipped with Beaufighters in September 1940. Its reputation as a successful night-fighter squadron rapidly grew under Squadron Leader John 'Cat's Eye' Cunningham, DSO Bar, DFC, who would ultimately claim twenty night-victories. The squadron remained at the airfield until 18th February 1943.

Like Portreath the airfield was ideally situated for flights to Gibraltar and North Africa, and during November 1942 it was used by the USAAF as a staging post for aircraft transferred to its Twelfth Air Force in North Africa. On 9th November three B-17s arrived from Gibraltar, having four days earlier transported Generals Eisenhower and Clarke and their military staffs. For the rest of the month numerous USAAF aircraft left Predannack, many of the B-17s belonging to the 97th Bomb Group, then at Polebrook in Northamptonshire. On the 17th of the month, a B-17 of the Group's 341st squadron left for North Africa; it was piloted by Major John Knott, the squadron's commander, and shortly after take off the aircraft crashed into the English Channel with a total loss of life. One of the passengers was Brigadier General Duncan. This was one of the few fatal accidents of this massive movement of aircraft and airmen.

Over the next twelve months or so Predannack would be used for emergency landings by several aircraft. It was the first English airfield to be encountered on the long Southern ferry route used by the Eighth Air Force to bring their B-17s and B-24s across the Atlantic during the winter months. However, many of the USAAF aircraft were suffering from battle damage, and perhaps the most dramatic emergency landing occurred on 1st May 1943. A B-17 of 306th Bomb Group had suffered severe damage over St Nazaire, and its pilot, 1/Lt Lewis P. Johnson, managed to bring the stricken aircraft to a safe landing at Predannack. On board was S/Sergeant Maynard 'Snuffy' Smith, a tail gunner who was on his first operation. For about ninety minutes Smith had fought the fires on board, and tended to injured crewmen as well as manning the guns. For this bravura performance Smith was awarded the Medal of Honor (equivalent to the Victoria Cross). He was the first living Eighth Air Force airman to receive the MOH and one of only seventeen in the Eighth (for further details see *Hertfordshire and Bedfordshire Airfields in the Second World War*). To my knowledge the last emergency landing by a damaged USAAF aircraft was on 31st March 1944 by a B-17G from the 381st Bomb Group from Ridgewell in Essex; another of the Group's aircraft crash-landed at Exeter.

In December a detachment of Whirlwinds of No 263 squadron operated from Predannack, making it the fourth airfield in Devon and Cornwall to house the much travelled squadron. It would return for a longer stay in the following spring, having then also flown from Harrowbeer! Also Spitfire IXs of No 64 squadron briefly occupied the airfield. This squadron had, in June, been the first to be supplied with the new Mark, specifically developed to counter the impressive Fw 190. Early in January (2nd) the Spitfires returned to their previous station – Fairlop in Essex.

The end of the year also saw the arrival of a detachment of Beaufighter VICs of No 248 squadron, then based at Talbenny. This squadron had served in Coastal Command since February 1940, and its crews settled down at Predannack for a long stay. No 248 was the airfield's first permanent Coastal Command squadron, and destined to become its longest serving, although it did maintain a detachment of crews at Gibraltar. For most of the squadron's time at Predannack it was engaged on anti-aircraft patrols in the Bay of Biscay and the Western Approaches, seeking out Junkers 88s and Focke-Wulf Condors. In July Wing Commander F.E. 'Monty' Burton, DFC, took over the command; he was a pre-war officer, who in October 1939 had shared in the destruction of a Dornier 18 flying boat – the first enemy aircraft to be shot down in the war.

With the departure of No 604's Beaufighters in February, another famous night-fighter squadron, No 141, moved in to replace them. It was commanded by one of the most successful fighter pilots of the war – Wing Commander J.R.D. 'Bob' Braham, DSO, DFC Bar; one of the youngest Wing Commanders at twenty-two years. In the words of a colleague, '[His] 100% dedication and commitment to the task, whatever it may be, set him apart from other people and lesser mortals.' With his AI operator, Squadron Leader W.J. 'Sticks' Gregory, DSO, DFC, DFM, they formed a most effective night-fighter crew. When Braham was shot down over Denmark in June 1944 and taken prisoner, his total stood at twenty-nine confirmed victories. The squadron left for Wittering at the end of March to be immediately replaced by another renowned squadron, No 264, under Wing Commander W.J. Allington, DFC, AFC. The squadron had introduced the Defiant into the Service in late 1939, but quite horrendous losses sustained during the Battle of Britain resulted in the Defiants being seconded to night operations. The crews were now flying Mosquito NFIIs and spent most of their time at Predannack on shipping patrols.

These were not the first Mosquitos to grace the airfield; about a month or so earlier NFIIs of Nos 456 (RAAF) and 307 'City of Lwów' squadrons moved in, along with the return of the Whirlwinds; the airfield was crowded with aircraft and airmen. Early in February the Mosquito crews claimed three Junkers 88s on a single mission, but April was a sorry month for No 263 squadron, when five Whirlwinds were lost in action. For the rest of 1943 Predannack would be used by Beaufighter VICs, Hampden Is, Wellington XIVs, Mosquito IIs, VIs and XIIS, as well as Typhoons; all would be engaged in some form of

Mosquito II of No 456 squadron. (RAF Museum)

Coastal Command's anti-shipping and anti-submarine operations, as the battle over the Bay of Biscay reached its peak.

In May a detachment of Beaufighter XICs of No 236 squadron, under Wing Commander H. Neil G. Wheeler, DFC, arrived armed with a highly secret new weapon – rocket projectiles. The squadron's first rocket strike against a U-boat took place on 29th May with no obvious success. However, three days later Flying Officer Mark C. Bateman, along with the Navy's U-boat expert, Lieutenant Commander F.J. Brookes, RN, sighted U-418 to the south-west of Brest. The aircraft's four 25 pound rockets were fired and the U-boat was seen to sink. This was the first time that rocket projectiles had been used successfully in the Atlantic. The action was recorded as 'U-boat probably sunk by depth charges', a deliberate attempt to maintain the secrecy of this new weapon.

On 14th June the Mosquito crews of No 307 also managed to get into some action. A Mosquito flown by Squadron Leader Szablowski strafed two U-boats with cannon fire and caused sufficient damage and injury to their crews, that the two boats, U-68 and U-155, were forced to return to port; although the latter would survive the war. Several days later a patrol of three Mosquitos again led by Squadron Leader Szablowski managed to destroy a Blohm & Voss 138, a three-engined flying boat. Later in the month another Bv 138 would be shot down by Wing Commander Allington of No 264 squadron.

During June detachments of Nos 25, 151 and 410 (RCAF) operated from the airfield, all equipped with various marks of Mosquitos. The crews found plenty of action, mainly engaged in attacking Fw 190s and Junkers 88s. Unfortunately on 13th June three Mosquitos failed to return, two from No 25 squadron and the other from No 410. Eight days later a Mosquito patrol led by Squadron Leader B.D. 'Joe' Bodien, DFC, of No 151 squadron managed to damage U-462; about a month later this U-boat would be destroyed by the combined efforts of a Coastal Command aircraft and Naval vessels.

Perhaps one of the most valiant attacks on a U-boat was made by Beaufighter VICs of No 248 squadron. On 12th July the crews located a U-boat not far out from Brest and the three aircraft led by Flight Lieutenant C.R.B. Schofield went into the attack, little knowing that it was U-441, a special U-boat known as a Unterseeboot-flugzeugfalle or 'Submarine-aircraft-trap' because of its greatly increased armament, which had already accounted for a Sunderland. The crews pressed home their attack despite fierce and heavy flak until the U-boat submerged. *U-441* was sufficiently damaged to force its return to Brest with most of its officers killed or wounded. *U-441* was finally sunk in June 1944 by a Liberator of No 502 squadron from St Eval.

In direct contrast to all the Mosquitos and Beaufighters operating from the airfield was a detachment of Handley Page Hampden Is of No 415 (RCAF) squadron, which had arrived from Thorney Island, a return to Cornwall for some of the crews because a detachment had operated from St Eval in the previous April. The Hampden had first entered the Service in 1936 and it proved to be rather vulnerable to enemy fighters being the only bomber not blessed with power turrets. The accommodation for the three-man crew was so restricted and cramped that it gained the nickname of 'The Flying Suitcase'! Hampdens were taken off bombing operations and were then almost exclusively used as torpedo bombers and mine layers. Ultimately six Coastal Command squadrons were equipped with Hampdens.

No 415 squadron had been formed in August 1941 as a torpedo bomber unit with Beauforts, but in the following January it began to re-equip with Hampdens. By now the Hampden was severely outclassed as a torpedo bomber, and on 14th June Squadron Leader J.G. Stronach and his crew were shot down by Junkers 88s over the Bay of Biscay. Nevertheless, despite its lack of speed and inferior armament Squadron Leader C.G. Ruttan's crew managed to heavily damage *U-706* on 2nd August and the U-boat was finished off by a USAAF B-24 of 4th Antisubmarine squadron operating from St Eval. This was the only instance of a Coastal Command Hampden making a U-boat 'kill', albeit shared. Rattan was promoted to Wing Commander on the same day and given command of the squadron. He was awarded the DSO in the spring of 1944; he would return with his squadron to Winkleigh in the summer of 1944.

In October (14th) the Typhoons of No 183 'Gold Coast' squadron moved across from Perranporth; it was now commanded by Squadron Leader W. Dring, who earlier in the month had claimed a Fw 190. The pilots continued their operations over the Brest Peninsula, as well as giving escort support to anti-shipping strikes, often in conjunction with 248's Beaufighters, although in December that squadron began to convert to Mosquito FBIVs.

It was during October that Coastal Command introduced yet another new weapon into the U-boat offensive – the Molins anti-tank gun – which has already been noted under Portreath. A handful of Mosquito FBXVIIIs of No 618 squadron, based at Benson in Oxfordshire, were

Handley Page Hampden: this one with No 455 (RAAF) squadron. (RAF Museum)

Typhoon IB of No 183 squadron. (via S. Morris)

detached to Predannack to trial the new weapon with No 248's Beaufighters. No 618 had been specifically formed to develop the use of Highball – the so-called bouncing mine. The first operational use of the 57mm Molins gun came on 7th November when a Mosquito FBXVIII, piloted by Flying Officer A.J.L. Bonnett, RCAF, attacked U-boat, *U-123*, near its home port of Lorient. Although several of the six pounder shells were seen to hit the U-boat, it survived and made its escape back to its home port.

Blockade runners into the French Atlantic ports had continually posed problems for both the Royal Navy and Coastal Command. On 26th November a PR Spitfire had spotted and identified a known blockade runner, *Pietro Orseolo*, near the port of Concarneau. This Italian vessel designated a 'Class I' target by the Admiralty, now had a German crew (since Italy's surrender in early September) and it was decided to mount a special strike against the vessel. Three Mosquito FBVIs of No 487 (RNZAF) were detached from their base at Sculthorpe in Norfolk. This squadron would gain lasting wartime fame for its part, in February 1944, in Operation Jericho – the bombing of the walls of Amiens prison. The strike against the blockade runner was activated on 1st December. The Mosquitos would be escorted by twelve Typhoons of Nos 193 and 266 squadrons from Harrowbeer. Only one Mosquito, flown by Squadron Leader A.S. Cussens, managed to attack the vessel, and its four 500 pound bombs caused only superficial damage. The Typhoons managed to account for two Junkers 88s but for the loss of the same number.

Twelve days later a detachment of 'Torbeaus' of No 254, under the command of Wing Commander A.W. Darley Miller, flew in from North Coates to try their luck. The crews had named their squadron '254th Light Foot' because of the number of times they had been detached to other airfields! Bad weather frustrated a number of planned strikes, but on 18th December orders were received that the operation should go ahead irrespective of the weather conditions. Six 'Torbeaus' and six 'anti-flak' Beaufighters from No 248 squadron, escorted by eight resident Typhoons, left Predannack in very poor weather; the Typhoons would be operating almost at the limit of their range. Two torpedoes struck the *Pietro Orseolo*, badly damaging the vessel, and it sank three days later whilst under tow. Despite intense flak all the aircraft returned safely to Predannack. Just six days later the 'Torbeaus' crews returned to Predannack specifically to attack another blockade runner, the *Pietro Orsono*, which had been sighted in the Bay. This time the torpedo strike was unsuccessful as the force failed to find its target; the *Pietro Orsono* managed to make the Gironde estuary, although it did strike a wreck and was beached at Le Verdon.

There were a number of changes at the airfield during the first three months of 1944. The Typhoons moved out to Tangmere on 1st February, and during the month No 248 squadron moved to Portreath after more than twelve months service at Predannack. The Leigh Light Wellingtons of No 304 'Land of Silesia' Polish squadron departed for Chivenor, and they were smartly replaced, on the 23rd, by Liberator Vs of No 311 squadron, under Wing Commander J. Sejbl, DFC, from Beaulieu. This squadron had been formed in Bomber Command in July 1940 from Czech personnel, and before its transfer to Coastal Command in August 1942 it had completed over 150 bombing raids. Its Liberators were armed with rocket projectiles, and the Czech crews had gained no mean reputation on anti-submarine operations, especially whilst serving at Beaulieu.

Towards the end of March (25th) Mosquito NFXIIIs of No 151 squadron moved in from Colerne under the command of Wing Commander G.H. Goodman, DSO, DFC. The crews would be fully extended on night-patrols, Rangers and anti-shipping escorts. On 11th April whilst escorting No 248's Mosquitos to St Nazaire, the squadron claimed seven enemy aircraft, which brought its wartime total to one hundred, although two aircraft were lost. The Wing Commander, along with his AI operator, Flying Officer W.F. Thomas, had a 'field' day on 4th May destroying four Heinkel 111s near Dijon airfield, which brought his personal total to twelve.

April heralded the return of Spitfires – LFIXBs; first with No 165 squadron and about four weeks later with No 1 squadron, which had only recently received this Mark. The two squadrons would operate as the Predannack Spitfire Wing, flying Insteps as well as bombing raids, when their targets would vary between coastal radar installations, shipping, airfields and rail communications. No 1, as its number suggests, was the senior squadron in the RAF, having been formed on the same day as the Royal Flying Corps – 13th May 1912. It was commanded by a South African airman, Squadron Leader H.P. Lardner Burke, DFC Bar. Today the squadron is still going strong, operating Harrier GR.7s from Wittering.

The final squadron to operate from Predannack in those hectic summer months was No 179; its Wellington XIVs were transferred from Gibraltar on 24th April, where the crews had been serving since

November 1942. In June there would be seventeen Liberator Vs and VIs and fourteen Wellington XIVs at Predannack all engaged on Operation Cork; six were in action on the night of 5/6th. During the month over 240 anti-submarine sorties were mounted from the airfield with No 179 losing three Wellingtons in action. On the 24th, No 311 squadron recorded its second U-boat 'kill' when Flying Officer J. Vella's crew destroyed *U-971* just to the south of Land's End. The squadron shared the victory with two Naval vessels, HMCS *Haida* and HMS *Eskimo*. When the squadron moved north in August, it would destroy another U-boat in Norwegian waters. Before No 179 squadron left for Chivenor in September its crews had flown over 100 sorties in the previous month but, despite a number of attacks on U-boats, there were no confirmed successes.

Both Spitfire squadrons were fully engaged on D-Day flying almost continuous patrols and Rodeos. On this day No 165 lost three aircraft in action, and another three would be lost before both squadrons moved away to Harrowbeer on the 20th of the month. The Mosquitos of No 151 squadron were equally active; one, MM450, failed to return from a Ranger misson to Kerlin Bastard, and four days later (10th) another Mosquito was lost in action. Yet another Spitfire squadron, No 264, made a return to Cornwall, on the 19th, with their rather out-moded Mark VBs. They would be briefly joined during the month by No 611 'West Lancashire' squadron, which was in the process of converting back to Mark LFIXs.

Towards the end of October the airfield had assumed an almost deserted air, certainly compared with a few months earlier; the Spitfires, Wellingtons, Mosquitos, and Liberators had all departed. However, on 15th December two Spitfire squadrons, Nos 33 and 222, arrived from the Continent to exchange their LFIXs for Hawker Tempest Vs. This was yet another classic fighter designed by Sidney Camm, which has been described as 'a superb combat aircraft . . . and a pleasure to fly.' Its design owed much to the Typhoon, very rugged, powerful and fast (over 425 mph) and really making its name against the V1 rockets; over one third of them destroyed by the RAF fell to Tempest pilots. A Luftwaffe test pilot, on evaluating a captured Tempest was forced to admit 'this exceptional aircraft is an improvement on the Typhoon, which in performance and aerodynamics was quite stunning, but there is no doubt about this one; the Tempest is an impressive highly powered aircraft by any standards' – praise indeed! For such a superlative aircraft the Service life of the Tempest was relatively short, from April 1944 to 1949, when it was out-classed by the jet-fighters.

Hawker Tempest Vs were in evidence at Predannack in 1945.

The two newly equipped squadrons returned for service with the 2nd Tactical Air Force at Gilze Rijen on 21st February 1945, and No 33's pilots were quickly back in the action, claiming four Me 109s four days later. Meanwhile another two Spitfire squadrons, No 349 (Belgian) and No 485 (RNZAF), arrived from the same Dutch airfield, to also convert to Tempests. However, there were certain reliability problems with the aircraft about this time, so after about a week the pilots were temporarily given Typhoons. When the two squadrons ultimately moved back to the Continent on 19th April they were equipped with their 'old' Spitfire IXs.

In May No 151 squadron returned to the airfield. They were now equipped with the high-altitude Mosquito NFXXXs, as indeed was No 406 (RCAF), which arrived from Manston two months later. The Canadian squadron was disbanded on 1st September 1945 with Wing Commander R.G. Grey, DFC Bar, as its final commander. In over four years of night-operations the squadron had claimed twenty-three enemy aircraft destroyed in the air, with another three on the ground. No 151 soldiered on at Predannack until June 1946 when it moved to Exeter, where it, too, would be disbanded a couple of months later. The airfield was placed on a Care and Maintenance basis but it has survived, and now operates as a satellite for nearby RNAS Culdrose, which was commissioned as HMS *Seahawk* in April 1947.

13

ROBOROUGH

Roborough is one of the earliest municipal airports in the country –
seventy years is quite an achievement in civil aviation. The Devon
airport was officially opened on 15th July 1931 by HRH the Prince of
Wales, who only two years earlier had learned to fly at Northolt. The
Prince was an enthusiastic advocate of aviation and he famously
predicted that 'Britain would possess a great air organisation on the
same lines as our Merchantile marine.' Although the Prince owned a
de Havilland Gypsy Moth, he wrote in *A King's Story,* 'I was content to
leave the piloting from then on to experts'!

In the immediate pre-war years this small airport went from strength
to strength. In March 1936 the Straight Corporation was appointed to
manage it on behalf of the Plymouth City Council, and regular internal
services were established to a number of cities, as well as flights to
Jersey and the Scilly Islands, along with a flourishing Aero Club.
Roborough's close proximity to the Royal Naval Dockyard at
Devonport ensured that the Admiralty was not slow to take advantage
of its facilities. During the summers of 1937 and 1938 Nos 801 and 810
squadrons with Hawker Ospreys and Swordfish used Roborough. At
the outbreak of war the Admiralty requisitioned the airfield although
Swordfish of No 814 (FAA) squadron had been in residence since late
August, along with No 15 Group of Coastal Command's Communications Flight, which had been operating from there since July, brought
about by the move of the Group's headquarters from its temporary
home at Lee-on-Solent to Mount Wise Barracks, Plymouth.

In October No 814 squadron, under the command of Lieutenant Commander N. S. Luard, DSC, RN, left for service on HMS *Hermes*, but it would return briefly in the New Year. The Swordfish were quickly followed by other rather antiquated biplanes, Blackburn Sharks from Mount Batten, for use by No 2 Anti-Aircraft Co-operation Unit to tow target drogues to provide firing practice for the Naval Gunnery School at Devonport. The Unit moved away to St Eval in April, and would later operate from Cleave before returning to Roborough for a more permanent stay of residence. During May and June 1940 other Swordfish arrived for a brief period with two (FAA) squadrons, Nos 819 and 815; they would leave in mid-June to serve on HMS *Illustrious*.

Towards the end of July more biplanes appeared – Gloster Gladiators, the RAF's last biplane fighters. A splendid aircraft and perhaps the ultimate in biplane design, it was the first fighter to be provided with an enclosed cockpit. Their pilots were all agreed that the Gladiator was 'a delight to fly'. However, only months after the prototype was delivered to the Air Ministry for trials in July 1935, the Gladiator had effectively become obsolete with the emergence of the Hurricane and the initial flight of the prototype Spitfire in March 1936. Nevertheless, the production of Gladiators went ahead and they entered the Service with No 72 squadron in January 1937. By the outbreak of war the RAF had over 300 Gladiators and they served valiantly in France and Norway during May 1940. They would also equip seven FAA squadrons where they were known as 'Sea' Gladiators, and a handful fought gallantly in the defence of Malta. For all its sterling qualities the Gladiator certainly lacked speed and adequate firepower, a maximum of about 250 mph and armed with four .303 machine guns. Over 740 were produced, and they operated in liaison and meteorological flights until 1944, but only seven remained on RAF charge at the end of the war.

The Gladiators formed what was known as the Fighter Flight, Shetlands, which had been raised at Sumburgh in January 1940 specifically for convoy protection and to defend the RAF's flying boat base at Sullom Voe. During its stay at Sumburgh the Flight mounted almost five hundred patrols and claimed two enemy aircraft – a Heinkel 111 and a Dornier 17. Its handful of pilots began the long flight south on 21st July. Two Gladiators were damaged *en route*, but in each instance the pilots survived the crashes unharmed.

On 1st August the Flight was reformed at Roborough as No 247 squadron, known as the 'China-British', acknowledging it as a gift from that community; the squadron's motto was appropriate – 'Rise from the

No 247 was the only squadron to fly Gladiators during the Battle of Britain.

East'. The squadron comprising just a single Flight, was temporarily placed under the command of Flight Lieutenant George F. Chater, a pre-war officer from South Africa, who had recently been a flying instructor at the RAF College at Cranwell and would receive the DFC in September. Its pilots had been given the task of the night defence of Devonport dockyard, and for this reason six Gladiators left each evening for St Eval, returning the following morning; St Eval was considered a safer airfield for night-operations. Four aircraft were kept at continual readiness at Roborough for day operations and scrambles.

Facilities at Roborough were, at first, less than congenial. The pilots were 'housed' in Bell tents on the airfield, although some of the crews were more fortunate, they were boarded out at a nearby hotel; ultimately a number of temporary huts were erected to the north-west of the airfield. The two grassed landing runs were extended to 2,340 and 2,160 feet respectively, a Blister hangar was erected in addition to the three small flying club hangars, and later some blast pens to protect the fighters were also constructed. Nevertheless, Roborough always looked what it was, a hastily requisitioned small civil airfield with precious little wartime development or improvement.

During August, the airfield began to get rather crowded. The squadron now had eighteen Gladiators on strength, and they shared the airfield with a detachment of Lysander IIs of No 225 squadron from Tilshead in Wiltshire. This squadron had only reformed in October 1939 for army co-operation duties and the Lysander crews were employed on regular nightly patrols off the coasts seeking any signs of an enemy invasion or suspicious activities. These patrols were conducted nationwide, left at dusk and returned early the flollowing morning. The entire coastline from Land's End to Duncansby Head had been divided into separate 'beats', which were continually patrolled by Lysanders throughout the hours of darkness. No 225's 'beat' covered the coast from Lyme Regis around to St Eval. In September it was replaced by another (AC) Lysander squadron – No 16.

This squadron was one of the oldest, having been originally formed on 19th February 1915 at St Omer in France as a reconnaissance unit for the artillery, and it had pioneered the use of air-to-ground wireless communication with the Army. Although disbanded in late 1919, it was reformed in 1924 as an Army Co-operation squadron, and was the first to be equipped with Lysanders in June 1938. Two years earlier the squadron had had its badge authorised; it was in June of 1936 that the now familiar standard frame for RAF squadron badges – the King's crown and scroll – was approved. Each squadron was required to send its selected design and motto to the Inspector of RAF badges for formal approval. No 16's badge (illustrated) used Roman numerals, as did several other old squadrons but really only No 15 bomber squadron

Westland Lysander: No 16 (AC) squadron operated from Roborough.

was known as 'XV' throughout the war. The squadron's motto *Operata Aperta* or 'Hidden things are revealed', emphasises its reconnaissance role since its inception and the keys are said to be indicative of its Army role in revealing hidden enemy positions.

Besides the squadron's nightly patrols, which continued until the end of the year, the crews were also engaged on A/S/R duties. Like all (AC) squadrons No 16 would lead quite a peripatetic existence in the early wartime years. It had already served in France, as well as at a number of airfields and in November it moved away to Weston Zoyland in Somerset. However, No 16's Lysanders would become fairly regular visitors to Roborough at least until 1942. At the time of writing No 16 (Reserve) is still operating in the Service, as an operational conversion unit for the Jaguar force at Lossiemouth.

The Gladiator pilots of No 247 flew their first operational sorties on 13th August, and despite conducting regular nightly patrols from both St Eval and Roborough made no contacts with enemy aircraft until almost the end of the Battle of Britain. Night-flying was not without its mishaps; on 27th August Sergeant R.T. Thomas was returning to Roborough after a night patrol over Plymouth, when he misjudged his landing approach and crashed into trees at Werrington but he survived the ordeal. Three months later (21st November) he was killed on a night patrol when he lost his bearings and crashed into high ground near Okehampton. It was Flying Officer R. A. Winter, a RAFVR airman who had served with the Flight at Sumburgh, that made the first night-interception – a Heinkel 111 over Plymouth on 28th October – but was unable to bring it down. Eight nights later he made another contact and this time claimed to have damaged the enemy aircraft.

Since 24th September the squadron had been commanded by Squadron Leader Peter St.G. O'Brian, a Canadian airman who had been awarded the 'Sword of Honour' at Cranwell College as the top Flight Cadet passing out in December 1937. O'Brian had flown during most of the Battle of Britain as a Flight Commander with No 152 squadron at Warmwell, and would remain in charge until May 1942. Towards the end of the year the squadron began to exchange their Gladiators for Hurricanes, and the last Gladiator sortie was flown on 3rd February 1941. During that month the squadron left for St Eval but a detachment of Hurricanes remained at Roborough, until the squadron moved completely to Portreath in May. Their departure really brought the brief operational life of the airfield to a close. In truth Roborough suffered from its relatively small landing area, but more especially from the

PLAYER'S CIGARETTES

No. 16 (ARMY CO-OPERATION)
SQUADRON, R.A.F.

Squadron badge of No 16 (AC) squadron.

presence of a new airfield at Harrowbeer, just a few miles away.

The formation of 19 Group of Coastal Command at Mount Batten in
February 1941 resulted in a new Communications Flight, to replace No 15
Group's Unit which moved to its new headquarters in Liverpool. In June
No 2 AACU returned with Hawker Hectors and the odd Gladiator. The
Hector was another biplane dating from the mid-thirties, which had been
superseded on army co-operation duties by the Lysander; although most

Hectors would be employed as glider tugs rather than target towers. On 9th February there was a serious flying accident at the airfield when a Lysander of No 16 squadron, on detachment from Weston Zoyland and piloted by the squadron's commander, Wing Commander Hancock, crashed whilst taking off, killing the crew. Squadron Leader Walker temporarily assumed command, but the following day he and his gunner were killed as their Lysander was shot down by four Me 109s near Exmouth – the twin losses were a body blow for the squadron.

On 16th August the largest aircraft ever to attempt a landing at Roborough came to a tragic end. A Flying Fortress of No 90 squadron overran the landing run, hit a tank trap and was destroyed by fire. The squadron operated from Polebrook and was the only squadron in Bomber Command to fly Flying Fortresses. Two crews had been detailed to bomb Brest, and one of the Fortresses, AN523, was severely damaged in sustained attacks by seven Me 109s at an altitude of 32,000 feet, the highest fighter interception yet recorded. Three of the crew were killed and one injured but the other three crew members, including the pilot, Pilot Officer Sturmey, managed to survive the crash. Despite the subsequent success of the Eighth Air Force's B-17s, the RAF's Fortress experiment proved to be a dismal failure; only 51 sorties were made, half of which had to be abandoned, and less than 50 tons of bombs were dropped all for the loss of three aircraft in action.

For the duration of the war the airfield would play host to a number of different aircraft – FAA Swordfish and Albacores, RAF Ansons, de Havilland Dominies, A/S/R Spitfires and Lysanders; and despite the airfield being handed over to the Air Ministry in May 1942, nothing really changed. 'C' Flight of No 2 AACU continued to be the permanent residents, along with No 19 Group's Communications Flight. In February 1943 'C' Flight was numbered 1623 and was now operating Defiants, Battles and the faithful Gladiators. Then, on 1st December, it was made up to a full squadron, No 691.

One rather unusual and fairly rare aircraft operated in the squadron – Vultee A.31 Vengeance. They were American-built two-seater dive-bombers and some 700 were ordered by the British Purchasing Commission in 1940. The RAF belatedly found that they were totally unsuitable for operations in Europe, and the majority were transferred to four squadrons operating in Burma, where they were successful against difficult jungle targets. The remainder were converted to target towers, known as 'TT.IVs'. The squadron remained at Roborough until February 1945 when it moved to Harrowbeer, although by this time the

Miles Martinet TTI: used by No 3 Armament Practice Group

Vengeances had been replaced by Barracudas. However, the detachment of Miles Martinet TTIs of No 3 Armament Practice Camp Unit which also used Roborough, soldiered on until May. The Martinet was the only specifically designed target tug to operate from the airfield. It had first flown in April 1942, and was so successful that between 1942 and 1945 more than 1,700 were produced; they remained in the service well into the post-war years.

Roborough returned to civil aviation in 1946, and continued to be operated by Straight Corporation on behalf of Plymouth City Council although No 19 Group's Flight still used the airfield until late 1947. The fortunes of the small civil airfield varied considerably until 1975, when the contract was passed to Brymon Airways, who proceeded to build up the number of services. Brymon Airways, now owned by British Airways, are still in residence, as is Plymouth Flying Club. There is a modern passenger terminal at what is now 'Plymouth Airport', to cater for passengers using the wide range of regular internal services.

14

ST EVAL

During the Second World War St Eval in Cornwall was almost a microcosm of the Royal Air Force; predominantly a Coastal Command airfield, but it also operated as a fighter Sector station. Day and night-fighters served there; bombing raids, anti-shipping strikes, anti-submarine operations, photographic and meteorological patrols as well as air-sea rescue missions were all mounted from there – virtually the whole gamut of RAF wartime operations! It is difficult to think of another wartime airfield that housed such a diverse range of operational aircraft in a bewildering array of squadrons, flights and detachments – more than fifty – making it impossible to do justice to them all in such a brief account.

In 1938 construction work commenced on the site, about six miles to the north-east of Newquay and within the parish of St Eval, where a small hamlet near the church was demolished. The fine Norman church became a prominent landmark on the northern edge of the airfield, and was later incorporated into the station's badge. By the outbreak of war the area had been cleared and foundations laid for four hangars and the administrative buildings but very little else accomplished. Nevertheless St Eval eventually had many of the trappings of a 'Expansion' station, including a parade ground, officers' and airmen's married quarters and the inevitable squash court! The three tarmac runways, ultimately 1,960, 1,900 and 1,600 yards long, would not be completed until the following year and not fully extended until late 1943. However, largely due to pressure of time the airfield was not levelled properly with the result that the main runway rose quite sharply for its initial 200 yards, creating St Eval's infamous 'hump'.

The airfield opened on 2nd October 1939, allocated to No 15 Group of Coastal Command, when Ansons of No 217 squadron arrived from Warmwell. The Anson became one of the best loved aircraft of the wartime RAF, known affectionately as the 'Faithful Annie' to all the aircrews that were trained in them. In March 1936 it was the first monoplane to enter the Service and also the first to employ a retractable undercarriage. Over 20,000 Ansons were built and they were not retired until June 1968 – over thirty years of 'faithful' service. The squadron, under Wing Commander A.P. Revington, would be involved in convoy escorts and anti-submarine patrols; in December ninety-four sorties were flown. During 1940 the crews began to convert to Beauforts, a slow, rather tedious business because of production delays. On 2nd April they made their first bombing attack with Ansons on a U-boat but without any conclusive results and in July claimed their first enemy aircraft – a Heinkel HS 59 floatplane. Like most of the Command's squadrons crews would be detached to other airfields, in their case to Carew Cheriton and Limavady.

In January nine de Havilland Hornet Moth biplanes formed No 6 Coastal Patrol Flight, its pilots operating in pairs on Scarecrows – patrols of coastal waters seeking enemy submarine activity. Six Flights operated around the coasts but only a couple of U-boats were sighted; the Flights were disbanded in May. Also during the early months of 1940 Sharks and Battles of No 2 AACU were detached from Roborough. The first 'heavies' appeared at St Eval – a detachment of Whitley IIIs of No 58 squadron 'on loan' from Bomber Command. Since October the squadron had been flying anti-submarine patrols from Boscombe Down and it would be transferred to Coastal Command in April 1942 at St Eval, whilst still operating Whitleys.

St Eval now took on the role of a fighter airfield and with the formation of No 10 Group became a Sector Station. On 18th June, twenty Spitfire Is of No 234 (Madras Presidency) squadron, under Squadron Leader R.E. Barnett, MBE, arrived from Church Fenton, where it had become operational early in May. The squadron's first success came on 8th July when a Junkers 88 was destroyed with two more claimed later in the month. But it suffered its first fatality when Pilot Officer Geoffey K. Gaunt was killed when his Spitfire crashed at Porthtowan on the 25th after a night patrol over Plymouth.

In early July a detachment of Blenheim Ifs and IVfs of No 236

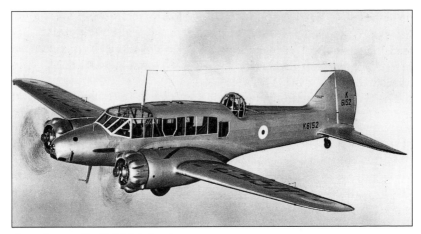

Avro Anson: the Faithful Annie.

Beauforts of No 217 squadron. (via R. Baker)

squadron arrived; it had transferred to Coastal Command in February 1940 to become a 'Fighter Reconnaissance' unit. Its first victory came on 11th July, followed by another in August when the whole squadron had moved in for a stay of about six months. On 1st August the squadron lost its Commander, Squadron Leader P.E. Drew, when he and his two man crew failed to return from an escort mission over Querqueville airfield. The Blenheim crews were engaged on a variety of tasks; patrols along the French coast from Brest to Ushant, known as Busts, escorting Sunderland flying boats and No 217's Beauforts on their bombing raids, as well as seeking Fw 200 Condors, which were already making their presence felt in the Bay of Biscay. In September Pilot Officer A.R. deL. Inniss claimed a Heinkel 111; as a Wing Commander he would later lead the squadron. The squadron would lose another Commander on 12th December when Squadron Leader G.W. Montagu went missing on a reconnaissance mission to Brest.

The Spitfire squadron remained at St Eval until mid-July when it moved to Middle Wallop, to exchange with No 238, a Hurricane squadron. It had experienced a torrid time at Middle Wallop, losing ten aircraft with eight pilots killed and two wounded in action. One was its CO, Squadron Leader H.A. Fenton, who had been shot down, and ditched in the Channel fortunately to be rescued by a Naval vessel. As a result Flight Lieutenant Minden V. 'Mindy' Blake arrived at St Eval on the 16th to temporarily take over command of the squadron as acting Squadron Leader until Fenton returned about three weeks later. This brilliant New Zealand airman, who had joined the RAF in 1937, would make quite an impact at St Eval in the coming months.

In August Gladiators of No 247 squadron at Roborough began to use the airfield. Throughout the winter there were a handful making regular night-patrols but with scant success; the pilots also flew night-training flights. On the 21st of the month the airfield suffered its first air raid when six Blenheims were destroyed and one of the hangars was heavily damaged; it would receive further attention from the Luftwaffe during October.

The Hurricanes moved back to Middle Wallop on 10th September and immediately became heavily engaged in the Battle of Britain, indeed the squadron lost seventeen pilots during the Battle, the second highest loss in Fighter Command. Their departure brought about the return of No 234's Spitfires, which had lost twelve aircraft and four pilots killed during its brief spell at Middle Wallop. Two were very experienced airmen – Flight Lieutenant P.C. Hughes, DFC and Squadron Leader J.S. O'Brien, DFC (its new CO) – both killed on 7th September when between them they had ten victories. The most successful pilot now was Pilot Officer Robert F.T. Doe, who had claimed his first victory on 14th August and his eleventh on 7th September, including three Me 110s in one day. Indeed, No 234 would become No 10 Group's highest scoring squadron in the Battle for the loss of five pilots. 'Mindy' Blake returned to St Eval on the 22nd to take command of the squadron. He would add two more victories to his name before the year ended, being awarded the DFC. Doe would also receive the DFC before moving to No 238 squadron.

Alongside all the fighter activity the Anson/Beaufort crews were increasingly involved in bombing raids, especially against invasion barges gathered in the French ports, and Brest was frequently targeted. It was not until December that the final Anson sortie was flown. In October Nos 829 and 812 FAA squadrons arrived for brief stays, equipped with Albacores and Swordfish respectively. They mounted bombing operations and laid mines; one Swordfish failed to return on 11/12th December after laying mines outside Brest harbour. In the following spring several other FAA squadrons, Nos 801, 809 and 816, would briefly use the airfield.

The first Spitfires of the Photographic Reconnaissance Unit (PRU) had already arrived at St Eval; Flight Lieutenant G.P. Christian flew the initial PR sortie on 5th July to photograph St Nazaire, and during August thirty PR sorties were flown over the Brittany ports. The PRU came under Coastal Command's control in June and 'B' Flight was based at St Eval. Its Spitfires had been specially modified to accept fixed cameras, also their armament and some equipment had been removed to increase their speed, and provision made for extra fuel capacity to enhance their operational range. Several colour schemes were experimented with to achieve the best camouflage, and ultimately PR Spitfires were painted overall in a sky-blue, officially known as 'PR Blue'.

On 25th January 1941 the airfield suffered a particularly heavy raid in which twenty-one personnel were killed. On 12th March another raid damaged a number of aircraft on the ground and two days later a rather antiquated Handley Page Harrow of No 271 squadron was destroyed; these aircraft were used to move airmen and equipment of fighter squadrons around various airfields. The Luftwaffe was quite determined to target the increasingly busy airfield and St Eval would be bombed on a number of occasions until mid-May with considerable damage being inflicted on buildings and aircraft.

With the formation of No 19 Group during January and its formal assumption of operational control on 5th February, St Eval was considered one of the major airfields in the new Group and as such its days as a fighter station were almost at a close. Nevertheless, in late February Whirlwinds of No 263 squadron flew in from Exeter before moving on to Portreath less than a month later; during its short stay a number of Whirlwinds were damaged in the several air raids. No 247 squadron arrived from Roborough on the 17th but before the month was out its Hurricanes returned to their original airfield. Towards the end of the month (24th) No 234's Spitfires left for Warmwell, and No 236 moved away to Carew Cheriton to be replaced by another Blenheim squadron, No 53, which in the autumn would exchange its Blenheims for Hudsons. When the Sector responsibilities passed to Portreath in May, St Eval became a Coastal Command station pure and simple.

However, before this happened St Eval would mount one of the most daring and courageous operations of the war so far. On 23rd March the Admiralty received information that the *Scharnhorst* and *Gneisenau* had entered Brest on the previous day for repairs. Since January these battleships had accounted for twenty-two Allied vessels, and Churchill ordered, 'If the presence of the enemy battle-cruisers in a Biscayean port is confirmed every effort by the Navy and the Air Force should be made to destroy them and for this purpose *serious risks and sacrifices must be made* ' [my italics]. Bomber Command launched three night operations but without any serious damage being inflicted. However, PR sorties on 5th April revealed that the *Gneisenau* had moved out of dry dock; an immediate low-level strike was ordered. The only squadron readily available was No 22 with its detachment of nine Beauforts at St Eval. The squadron's commander, Wing Commander F. J. St. G. Braithwaite, detailed six crews for the strike planned for 'morning twilight' on 6th April. One of the crews was captained by Flying Officer Kenneth Campbell, a twenty-two year old RAFVR airman, who had already completed twenty-two operations. His bravery on this operation has become legendary and in March 1942 Campbell was posthumously awarded the Victoria Cross; Sergeants J.P. Scott, R.W. Hillman and W.C. Mullins, who died with him were not decorated as only the VC could be awarded posthumously.

The official citation barely conveys the outstanding bravery and determination of Campbell:

'The aircraft did not return, but from experience which has since accumulated it is clear that a successful attack was carried out and serious underwater damage caused to the German battle cruiser. A similar attack was attempted half an hour later in full daylight but had to be abandoned when the aircraft had nearly reached its objective, owing to the fierce anti-aircraft barrage and a rising haze which hid the target.

The battle cruiser forming the target was secured alongside a wall on the north shore protected by a stone mole bending round to the west, and a system of nets round the ship herself. On rising ground behind stood protective batteries. Others clustered thickly all round two arms of land encircling the outer harbour, where, near the mole, were moored three heavily-armed ships guarding the battle

Flying Officer Kenneth Campbell, VC, RAFVR. (Imperial War Museum)

cruisers, making Brest with other defences one of the most strongly fortified harbours in the world as regards air attacks.

Judging by the experience of the second aircraft, Flying Officer Campbell must have run the gauntlet of all these guns, flying almost at sea level, and have flown past the anti-aircraft ships at mast height, in the very mouths of their guns. He would have then skimmed the mole and fired the torpedo at point-blank range. The damage caused was such that the battle cruiser returned to the dock from which she had but recently emerged.

By pressing his attack to a successful conclusion in the face of the most formidable anti-aircraft fire, Flying Officer Campbell displayed determination, skill and daring of a quite outstanding character.'

For the remainder of the year St Eval mounted a variety of operations by Beauforts, Hudsons and Blenheims, and even detachments of Blenheims of No 2 Group of Bomber Command used the airfield for coastal shipping strikes. In mid-April No 105 squadron from Swanton Morley in Norfolk attacked a 5,000 ton vessel scoring a direct hit, but one Blenheim was lost in the action and a second crash-landed at the airfield on return. In the autumn the first Beaufighters arrived at St Eval, a detachment of No 248 squadron, and at the end of the year No 502's Whitleys returned from Chivenor. The squadron had begun to receive Whitley VIIs equipped with ASV radar.

In early 1942 St Eval was predominantly a Beaufort station. Its major importance within Coastal Command can be gauged by the squadron complement of No 19 Group. Other than two flying boat squadrons at Mount Batten and Pembroke Dock, a Blenheim squadron at Carew Cheriton and a Wellington Flight at Chivenor, the rest of the Group's units were based at St Eval. No 86's Beauforts were in residence along with detachments of Nos 22 and 217's Beauforts. Hudsons of No 224 squadron returned to Limavady in February, although the squadron would return for a longer stay during 1943/4. The Whitleys of No 502 still operated from the airfield, as did the Hudsons and Spitfires of No 1404 (Met) Flight.

During February there was almost a reprise of the famous Beaufort attack on the German battleship of the previous April. On the 12th the *Scharnhorst*, *Gneisenau*, and *Prinz Eugen* made their famous 'Channel Dash'. The flotilla had virtually escaped when Beauforts from St Eval were ordered to make one final attack. Twelve Beauforts, six manned by No 86's crews and three each from Nos 22 and 217 squadrons, left for Thorney Island shortly before 1300 hours, led by Wing Commander Charles Flood of 86 squadron; his aircraft was the only one with ASV radar! After a briefing at Thorney Island, the crews left for Coltishall to rendezvous with two Beauforts of No 82 squadron and escorting Spitfires, neither of which materialised. One aircraft dropped out due to engine trouble, and the remaining crews headed for the Hook of Holland, the estimated position of the German force. In near darkness and quite atrocious weather the flotilla was located without the use of radar but the crews came under heavy anti-aircraft fire and fighter attacks. In the melee the Beaufort crews were dispersed and left to make individual attacks; this final strike was just as unsuccessful as all the rest.

Meanwhile No 502's Whitley VIIs were continuing their anti-submarine patrols, and in the spring were joined by the first Hampdens to operate in Coastal Command. A detachment of No 415 (RCAF) squadron, based at Thorney Island, mounted the first Hampden sortie from St Eval on 27th April. In the following month another Hampden squadron, No 489 (RNZAF) under Wing Commander J.A.S. Brown, operated from St Eval. Considering the number of torpedo bomber squadrons that had operated from the airfield, it would be appropriate to note that the Air Ministry calculated their crews had only a 17½% chance of surviving one operational tour and just 3% for two tours! This was by far the lowest survival rate in the three Commands; the *average* rate was 45% and 19% respectively.

On 14th July nine Lancaster Is of No 61 squadron of No 5 Group of Bomber Command arrived for a detachment of about six weeks. Air Chief Marshal Harris had reluctantly released some of his precious Lancasters to Coastal Command. Three days later a Lancaster captained by Flight Lieutenant P.R. Casement, destroyed *U-751*, returning with a photograph of its crew swimming away from the U-boat as positive evidence! Earlier in the day it had been damaged by a Whitley of No 502 squadron. Although further sightings were made by the Lancaster crews, they could not repeat their early success. Shortly before returning to their home airfield at Syerston the crews were engaged in attacking blockade runner, *Corunna*, a large oil tanker located in the Bay of Biscay. Despite several bombing runs the vessel survived and escaped to a French port; two Lancasters failed to return. During its brief time at St Eval over 90 sorties had been flown totalling some 878 hours.

The Lancasters had been joined at St Eval by sixteen Whitley Vs of No 10 OTU based at Abingdon in Berkshire. Its period of detachment would last almost twelve months. The Whitleys were crewed by

Armstrong Whitworth Whitleys operated anti-submarine patrols from St Eval. (RAF Museum)

instructors and trainee airmen in their final weeks of training, and the Unit was led by Wing Commander P. Charles Pickard, DSO Bar, DFC, one of the most famous and charismatic airmen of the war. He had gained early popular fame as the pilot of a Wellington, *F for Freddie* in the successful film *Target for Tonight*. Pickard then led the famous raid on Bruneval in February 1942. After leaving the OTU he commanded No 161 (SD) squadron, landing and picking up agents in occupied France. In February 1944, as a Group Captain, he was killed whilst leading a Mosquito Wing in the daring low-level raid on Amiens prison. During its time at St Eval the Unit lost a considerable number of aircraft, many due to enemy action but others as a result of flying accidents and engine problems. Over 16,400 hours were flown by the trainee crews and they made 55 attacks on U-boats, destroying two.

Another famous heavy bomber of the Second World War made an appearance at St Eval – the Boeing Flying Fortress. A detachment of No 206 squadron, under Wing Commander J.R.S. Romanes, DFC, based at Benbecula in the Hebrides, used the airfield during the year and Fortresses would return in 1943. To add to this impressive array of heavy bombers, eight B-24s of 409th squadron of the Eighth's 93rd

Bomb Group were seconded to Coastal Command in October. They merely proved to be the precursors of two USAAF antisubmarine squadrons transferred to England in November.

The Spitfires and Hudsons of the PR and Met. Flights were still flying their regular patrols and by the summer of 1942 the PRU had grown to eight flights, totalling over 70 aircraft flying from six airfields. In October it was decided to make up the Spitfire Flights into three squadrons, all formally based at Benson; a detachment of No 573 squadron operated from St Eval. In the following year (August) No 1404 Met. Flight would also be increased to squadron strength – No 517.

In November B-24s of two USAAF squadrons, Nos 1 and 2, of what became the 480th Antisubmarine Group, began to arrive at St Eval. The first USAAF operational mission was mounted on 16th November. The American airmen soon began to settle into their new surroundings, most billeted in guest houses in Newquay. Their Commander, Lieutenant-Colonel Jack Roberts, quickly established a good working relationship with Group Captain W.L. Dawson, the Station Commander, and although under the administrative control of the Eighth Air Force, the two squadrons operated under No 19 Group.

By mid-January 1943 both squadrons were fully operational and before the Group was transferred to Port Lyautey in French Morocco in March, over 210 missions had been made with twenty U-boat sightings and eight attacks. The only success claimed at St Eval – U-519, on 10th February – has since been amended, due to post-war research, to U-752 attacked with minor damage inflicted. Two aircraft were lost in action, another crashed into cliffs near Hartland Point and a fourth was involved in a runway collision at St Eval with a Whitley of No 10 OTU with a number of fatalities. The Group would have greater success from North Africa, sinking four U-boats. However, the ground had been well prepared for the next influx of USAAF airmen into St Eval during the summer.

1943 proved to be the most successful year for anti-submarine operations mounted from St Eval, when no fewer than fourteen U-boats were sunk. Without considerable study it is difficult to be conclusive on the matter, but St Eval was probably the most successful Coastal Command airfield in the U-boat offensive certainly during 1943 and probably throughout the war.

In January No 502 squadron began to be supplied with Handley Page Halifax IIs. Coastal Command had been continually petitioning the Air Ministry for either Lancasters or Halifaxes to improve its long-range operations, all their appeals being adamantly rejected. Then, on the direct orders of Churchill, fifty Halifaxes were initially allocated to the Command sufficient to equip two squadrons. The squadron's Halifaxes had their mid-upper turrets removed to provide space for extra fuel tanks, increasing their operational range to cover the outer limits of the Bay of Biscay as well as convoys in the Atlantic. The squadron had a brief spell away at Holmsley South in Hampshire but returned in March along with a detachment of Halifaxes of No 58 squadron, under the command of Wing Commander Wilfred E. Oulton, DFC, who was one of the Command's U-boat 'specialists'.

Over the next six months or so detachments of Wellington VIIIs, Fortress IIs and Liberator Vs of Nos 53, 59, 179, 206, 220 and 224 squadrons would operate from St Eval, most of them making U-boat 'kills'. Although the first U-boat to be destroyed in 1943 was claimed by a Whitley crew (Flight Sergeant J.A. Marsden) on 22nd March when U-665 was sunk off the coast of Ireland, this 'kill' was not credited to No 10 OTU until 1992. In the following month (29th) a Liberator of No 224 squadron captained by Flight Lieutenant A.R. Laughland destroyed U-332.

May was a most successful time for the crews of No 58 squadron. They destroyed four U-boats, U-528, U-266, U-463, U-563, two of which fell to Wing Commander Oulton and his crew and he was awarded the DSO. In June (14th) No 10 OTU made their second 'kill' when U-564 was sunk off Cape Ortegal; the boat's defensive fire brought down the Whitley, and Sergeant A.J. Benson and his crew spent three days and nights adrift before being rescued by a French fishing vessel and taken prisoners-of-war. The Unit completed its long spell of detachment in July; in under three months eleven Whitleys had been lost, some falling to Junkers 88s, which were taking quite a toll of the Command's aircraft. The Unit's move was ostensibly to make room for the USAAF's 479th Antisubmarine Group, which had already arrived at St Eval.

The crews of the 4th and 19th squadrons flew their B-24s over from Gander in Newfoundland, and considered the flights across the Atlantic as 'nothing more than gentle and easy hops . . . not as long as our ordinary routine patrols'! The Group's other squadrons, 6th and 22nd, followed in August. Colonel Howard Moore, the Group Commander, established a regime of a week's training on radio procedures, codes and signals and at least one long training flight, before each crew entered the fray; the first operation was mounted on 13th July. Although the crews operated from St Eval for less than one month, they shared in the destruction of three U-boats, *U-558*, *U-404*, and U-706, losing one aircraft on 20th July to U-boat flak. When they moved to Dunkeswell in August, they were replaced by the US Navy's VB-103 squadron flying PB4Y-1s, followed in September by VB-105 and 110 squadrons. Although the Naval squadrons began their operations from St Eval, by the end of October all had moved away to Dunkeswell.

During July and August another four U-boats were destroyed. *U-628* and *U-514* were sunk by Liberator crews of No 224 squadron; Squadron Leader Peter J. Cundy, DSO claimed the first on 3rd July and five days later the famous Squadron Leader T.M. 'Bull' Bulloch, DSO, DFC, made his third 'kill'; his previous successes had come when he was serving in No 120 squadron. Bulloch was flying a special Liberator provided with a Leigh Light and armed with eight depth charges, a Mk24 mine and four rocket projectiles on each side of the fuselage! On 5th July Flight Sergeant W. Anderson, RNZAF, captaining a Liberator of No 53 squadron despatched *U-535*. Towards the end of the month (30th) Flying Officer A. van Rossum's crew of No 502, along with five Naval vessels, shared the destruction of *U-462*.

The frantic pace of anti-submarine operations had taken their toll; No 58 squadron lost seven Halifaxes. Seven Liberators also went missing, including that of Flight Lieutenant G.A. Sawtell of No 58 squadron, who had shared with a B-24 of 19th AS squadron in the destruction of *U-558* on 24th July. By the autumn the U-boat offensive had eased somewhat, but on 23rd October Squadron Leader E.J. 'Billy' Wicht, a Flight Commander with No 224, shared in the destruction of *U-274* with HMS *Duncan* and *Vidette*. Wicht was a rather rare RAF officer, being a Swiss national. In November the squadron would be joined by two (LL) Wellington squadrons, Nos 407 and 612.

It was not only 'heavies' that used the airfield during the summer. A detachment of Beaufighter VICs of No 235 squadron were in evidence during June, and they were followed in August by Beaufighter XICs of No 143 squadron, an original member of the first Beaufighter Strike Wing; led by Squadron Leader R.A. Ullman they would provide air cover for the anti-submarine aircraft. On the 25th whilst on an Instep patrol six Beaufighters were attacked by a strong force of Fw 190s. Only two returned and Squadron Leader Ullman was one of the missing airmen. In the following month the squadron moved to Portreath.

Early in September (8th) four USAAF B-17s arrived to undertake long-range Met. patrols. They were commanded by Captain Alvin J. Podjowski, and in April 1944 it would be designated the 8th Recon.

Weather Squadron (Heavy). The B-17s were attached to No 517 squadron, although its aircraft moved to St Mawgan in late October. Even when the squadron moved out to St David's in November, the B-17s still used the Cornish airfields as staging posts for their flights to the Azores, coded Sharon, and to the south-west of Ireland, known as Allahs, despite the fact that the USAAF squadron was then based at Wattisham in Suffolk.

During the summer considerable construction work was underway at the airfield, new roads were laid, buildings erected and the runways extended. One important project was the installation of FIDO or Fog Investigation Dispersal Operation (in June 1945 renamed Fog, Intensive, Dispersal Of!). FIDO was a system whereby pipelines were laid along each side of a runway into which petrol was injected under pressure, then fired by burners set at certain intervals along the pipelines. The intense heat generated caused an updraught that dispersed fog in the vicinity of the runway. At St Eval additional lines of burners 75 yards outside the normal limits were installed to cope with the wet sea fogs so prevalent in the area. Graveley in Cambridgeshire had been the first of fifteen airfields to be provided with FIDO in February 1943. The first operational use of FIDO at St Eval came in April 1944 and the last a year later.

For most of 1944 St Eval was a major Liberator base; No 224 was joined on 3rd January by No 53 squadron, followed a week later by No 547 squadron. In March, No 206's Fortresses arrived to be exchanged for Liberator VIs; the latest mark. The VIs had first arrived in Britain for trials in December, with initial deliveries to Coastal Command in January. It was the first to feature a nose turret as well as dorsal and tail gun positions and by June the other three Liberator squadrons at St Eval had received a number of VIs.

Although January was a quiet month for U-boat sightings, No 224 managed to make several attacks; on the 3rd *U-373* was damaged and had to return to port for repairs (coincidentally *U-373* would be sunk by the squadron later in the year). No 53's crews made three attacks during the month, increasing to seven in the following month. In May, Flight Lieutenant Forbes of No 53 squadron remarkably made three U-boat attacks on successive patrols – a record.

By June the airfield was crowded with Liberators, some seventy on complement, of which over thirty were Mark VIs. It was Flight Lieutenant J.W. Carmichael's crew of 53 squadron that gained the first U-boat kill on the night of 6/7th destroying *U-629* (originally credited

Lt. Frank Perdue and his crew of B-24 Biscay Belle of 19th AS squadron,

479th Antisubmarine Group at St Eval. (National Archives & Records)

Liberator being loaded with depth charges. (Imperial War Museum)

to 224 squadron and not amended until 1997). On the following night Flying Officer K.O. Moore's crew of No 224 squadron destroyed two U-boats, *U-373* and *U-441*, to the west of Brest whilst on the same patrol – an unique performance which resulted in his award of the DSO. On 10th June Flight Lieutenant A.D.S. Dundas (another famous RAF 'family') of No 206 squadron sighted four Mosquitos attacking a U-boat to the west of Brest; *U-821* was finally sunk by a combination of depth charges and cannon fire. The final U-boat, *U-988*, destroyed in the month fell to Flight Lieutenant J.W. Barling's crew of No 224. Their Liberator, along with four Naval vessels, sank the U-boat in the English Channel to the west of Guernsey. Fifteen U-boats had been destroyed in the month with St Eval's squadrons claiming a third; on the debit side six Liberators were lost in action.

In July No 206 squadron moved away to Leuchars. During August just six U-boats were destroyed by anti-submarine squadrons and Naval vessels, of which two were credited to No 53 squadron. On the 10th Wing Commander R.T.F. Gates, AFC and his crew, assisted by HMS *Wren*, sank *U-608* to the north-west of La Rochelle. Five days later Flight Lieutenant G.G. Potier, along with HMS *Duckworth* and *Essington* sank *U-618* near Lorient. Unfortunately the squadron lost three aircraft during the month.

From September U-boat activity in the Bay of Biscay had virtually ceased, only four were destroyed up to the end of the year. No 53 squadron moved to Reykjavik in Iceland, No 547 to Leuchars and finally No 224 to Milltown. Warwicks of No 282 (A/S/R) squadron arrived from Davidstow Moor and remained until the squadron disbanded in July 1945. The airfield's days as a premier anti-submarine station appeared to have ended, but then in November No 179's Wellington XIVs arrived from Chivenor. The crews exchanged their Wellingtons for Warwick Vs to become the first to use these aircraft on anti-submarine operations. In January Wing Commander P.H. Allington, DFC, took over command of the squadron, and in February (24th) Flight Lieutenant A.G. Brownsill's crew destroyed *U-927* off the Lizard. The only U-boat sunk in the month by Coastal Command, and the only one by a Warwick squadron, it was the tenth and final U-boat destroyed by the squadron, although post-war research has reduced the total to nine.

In March No 304 (City of Silesia) squadron arrived from Benbecula with its Wellington XIVs, and it was left to the Polish crews to record the final U-boat 'kill' from the airfield. On 2nd April Warrant Officer R. Marczak's crew sank *U-321* off the south-west coast of Ireland; the

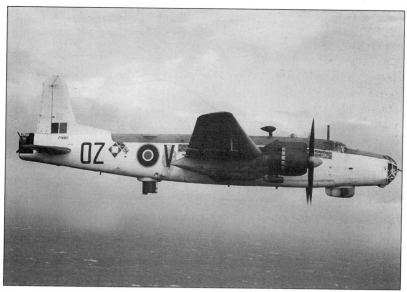

Warwick V of No 179 squadron. (RAF Museum)

The memorial window in the parish church of St Eval.

squadron's solitary victim in over 2,400 sorties and sixty attacks during which eighteen aircraft had been lost. The crews flew their last operational sorties on 30th May and moved to North Weald in July. No 224 squadron made a welcome return to St Eval, still operating Liberators. It had completed its war having destroyed twelve U-boats with another three damaged, which was the second highest squadron total in Coastal Command.

St Eval closed on 6th March 1959 and the parish church has become a remarkable and very fitting repository of the station's history. There is a Book of Remembrance recording the names of those airmen who lost their lives whilst serving there. Squadron plaques line the walls of the church, but perhaps the most emotive feature is the splendid stained glass memorial window in the Lady Chapel, which was dedicated on 1st October 1989 – the fiftieth anniversary of RAF St Eval.

15

ST MAWGAN

The old adage, 'Large streams from little fountains flow, tall oaks from little acorns grow', aptly describes St Mawgan in Cornwall. A small and rather basic landing ground at Trebelzue grew into a large modern airfield by the end of the war, and subsequently in post-war development. The history of St Mawgan can be traced back to August 1933 when Sir Alan Cobham brought his 'Air Circus' to a forty acre site known as 'The Big Field' at Trebelzue, about three miles north-east of Newquay; even then it was considered as 'Newquay's aerodrome'. His Air Circus would return during August for the next two years, although by then the aerodrome had been licensed and achieved a certain status as a recommended AA landing ground. In May 1939 Western Airways began to call there on its regular twice-daily services from Swansea and Manchester to Land's End. However, Trebelzue's commercial days proved to be short-lived because come September the airfield was duly requisitioned by the Air Ministry.

The Air Ministry's plan for Trebelzue was to develop the airfield to act as a satellite for Coastal Command's important station at St Eval, just a few miles further north. The construction work was put in hand during 1940/1, the existing road across the airfield was closed and two short but hard runways were laid down. In May 1941 the airfield, whilst still occupied by the building contractors, was heavily bombed; it is not really known whether the airfield was the Luftwaffe's target or rather the nearby Chain Home radar station at Carnanton. Fortunately little damage was sustained and in September RAF Trebelzue was formally opened.

The airfield was quickly utilised by various units operating from St Eval for the nightly dispersal of aircraft as a precaution should the Luftwaffe decide to return to St Eval. However, at the end of December Trebelzue was passed over to No 44 Group of Ferry Command, which had formed on 20th July under the command of Air Chief Marshal Sir Frederick Bowhill. The Command was a direct development of the Atlantic Ferry Organisation of the Ministry of Aircraft Production, which since late 1940 had been responsible for the transport of American aircraft across the Atlantic. The rapid increase in the numbers of American aircraft supplied to the RAF under the Lease-Lend agreement had necessitated the formation of the Command. It comprised two Groups, No 45 administered the transatlantic operations from Montreal, whereas No 44 controlled all ferry flights from the United Kingdom as well as mounting training courses for new ferry crews.

Personnel of the Overseas Aircraft Despatch Unit that had been detached to Portreath arrived at Trebelzue to set up the mechanics and organisation to arrange ferry flights from the airfield to the Middle East using Gibraltar as a staging post; the first such aircraft movements were made in February. However, it soon became very evident that the relatively small airfield did not really fit the bill for the Command. The runways were far too short, and prone to quite treacherous cross-winds, furthermore there was insufficient available land for the proper dispersal of aircraft. In April just fourteen aircraft left Trebelzue for the Middle East, at a time when the Command was committed to make in excess of 100 movements monthly; quite obviously Ferry Command was forced to review the long term future of the airfield.

In late April it was concluded that a minimum of three runways were essential for this type of traffic; they also required to be of greater length and better aligned in order to minimise the effects of the cross-winds. The decision was taken to effectively build a new airfield slightly further inland and to the east of the existing airfield, which could then be absorbed to provide increased aircraft storage and greater dispersal facilities. In July (10th) HRH The Duke of Kent visited the airfield and made a tour of inspection. The Duke, an Air Commodore, was attached to the staff of the Inspector-General of the RAF. Later in August (25th) the Duke would be killed when his Sunderland crashed in the north of Scotland whilst on a flight to Iceland.

Construction work on the new runways began towards the end of August 1942, which would only further inconvenience and impinge on

219

Hawker Henley towing a target drogue.

the operational use of Trebelzue in the meanwhile. Nevertheless, the small Hawker Henleys of No 1 Anti-aircraft Co-operation Unit from Cleave still managed to use the airfield, from whence they towed their target drogues over the Army ranges at Penhale and Cameron Camps. Nos 1602 and 1604 Henley Flights would also use Trebelzue for periods during the winter when Cleave's landing ground became waterlogged. In the autumn a number of C-47s of the USAAF were stored at Trebelzue pending their ultimate move to North Africa.

In December 1942 the first operational aircraft to fly from Trebelzue moved in from Portreath. They were a detachment of North American Mustang Is (P-51s) of No 400 (RCAF) squadron, then based at Middle Wallop. The squadron, originally No 110 (Auxiliary) RCAF, had arrived in the United Kingdom in February 1940, and was immediately allocated to army support duties and equipped with Lysanders. The squadron, renumbered in March 1941, was now commanded by Wing Commander R.C.A. Waddell, DSO, DFC. Its pilots had exchanged their Curtiss-Wright Tomahawks for Mustang Is in the previous July as indeed had most (AC) squadrons.

The Mustang, which was destined to have such a dramatic effect on the European air war, owed its very existence to the British Air Purchasing Commission in the United States. In April 1940 it had ordered more Tomahawks (P-40s) than Curtiss-Wright could deliver in time, so it was suggested that North American Aviation might build 'substitute P-40s'. The Company went one better and responded to the challenge with alacrity; in just 102 days North American produced a new fighter, although it did bear a certain resemblance to a P-40. The

Mustang I of No 400 (RCAF) squadron. (Canadian Aviation Museum)

new aircraft, after some modifications, first flew in September 1940 and was designated P-51. From the outset the aircraft looked an outright winner; it had clean fine lines, an ideal cockpit layout, good performance, was well-armed and had a long operational range. The Air Ministry was suitably impressed and immediately ordered 320; the first Mustang (originally named 'Apache') arrived in Britain in October 1941. RAF trials showed that the aircraft had a most impressive performance at low altitudes, but this tended to fall away at higher altitudes. It was considered not suitable for escort duties, so, like the Tomahawk, it was seconded to Army Co-operation squadrons. Of course, the aircraft's ultimate salvation came with the experiment of replacing its Allison engine with a Rolls-Royce Merlin, the P-51 then became one of the classic fighters of the Second World War. It is perhaps with some poetic justice that this aircraft, which would cause such havoc with the Luftwaffe day-fighter force, was designed by a German-born aviation engineer, Edgar Schmued, North American's chief designer!

The Mustang pilots were engaged on escort duties to aircraft en route to Gibraltar, as well as operating Insteps over the Bay of Biscay. The squadron lost one aircraft in January, shot down by a Typhoon, a sad case of mistaken identification for a Fw 190; later in the month the pilots returned to Middle Wallop. A detachment of Mosquito IIs of No 264 squadron from Colerne, used Trebelzue briefly in the New Year before moving down to Portreath in early February.

By early 1943 the new airfield had been completed, resplendent with three concrete runways – 3,000, 2,000 and 1,400 yards in length, although two would later be extended to 3,400 and 3,000 yards respectively; indeed construction work would continue until 1944 with the provision of a new control tower and increased hardstandings along with a myriad of concrete taxi tracks. On 23rd February it opened under a different name – St Mawgan – as it was situated in that parish, claimed to be 'one of the most beautiful in Cornwall'. However, it would be another four months before the first aircraft arrived to use the new runways – USAAF B-24s bound for North Africa, shortly followed by B-17s.

In June the 491st Base and Air Base Squadron of the USAAF's Air Transport Command moved into St Mawgan, although the station was still in RAF control with Group Captain R.P.P. Pope, DFC, AFC as Station Commander. The first of the new runways was ready by 1st July and by the summer St Mawgan had begun to get into its stride as a ferry airfield with a considerable number of movements to the Middle East, mainly by the USAAF aircraft. Certainly by the autumn it had become one of the most active airfields in Transport Command (as Ferry Command had been re-named on 28th March).

During the last few months of the year a number of aircraft used the airfield for Meteorological flights over the Western Approaches. Late in October (27th) four B-17s of the USAAF's Heavy Weather squadron arrived from St Eval and on 5th November they were joined by another Met. Flight of four B-17s. They expected to stay for three months but remained for less than three weeks, moving away to Bovingdon on the 23rd. In December a few RAF Fortress IIs of No 517, which had been formed a couple of months earlier at St Eval from No 1404 Met. Flight, made the squadron's first meteorological sorties from St Mawgan on the 15th. The rest of the squadron, recently converted to Halifax Vs, was then operating out of St David's.

Also in November St Mawgan became a recognised staging airfield for BOAC on its regular flights from its 'A' base at Whitchurch to Gibraltar and Algiers. At the onset of war the Secretary of State for Air assumed control of both Imperial Airways and British Airways, which on 1st April 1940 formally became British Overseas Airways Corporation; although since November 1939 they had been operating under unified control. During the war BOAC was placed entirely at the disposal of the Government, its routes – both land and sea – were prescribed for it, not by commercial consideration but purely for war needs. It carried almost exclusively Government passengers and

Former KLM DC-3, Zilverreiger (Silver Heron) operated with BOAC on its flights to Lisbon. (RAF Museum)

freight, as well as transporting RAF personnel and supplies to various far distant war stations, working closely with RAF Transport Command. Although ostensibly a civil organisation most of its personnel were drawn from the ranks of the RAF. It was claimed that throughout the war BOAC flew on average over 19 million miles each year, with both landplanes and flying boats. In 1944 a fulsome tribute was made in Parliament to its captains and crews: 'They are operating week in and week out, regardless of the weather, driving their aircraft along these routes, facing not only the very frequent hazards, but the inevitable risk of enemy interference. There has been a toll among the personnel from enemy action. They have died in the country's service.'

Sadly in December there were two tragic flying accidents from the airfield. On the 21st of the month four USAAF airmen were killed when a B-24 crashed near St Columb on a flight to Marrakesh. Just a week later a US Navy PB4-Y, which was returning to the United States with tour-expired airmen crashed immediately after take off. The thirteen airmen on board were all killed and another five were drowned whilst making a brave rescue attempt.

USAAF B-24 Liberator at St Mawgan in 1944. In the distance a number of C-47s. (National Archives & Records)

During 1944 aircraft movements into and out of St Mawgan reached a peak, over 16,100 separate flights in the year. One of the features was the number of aircraft arriving from the USA on a single day in February, when no fewer than 169 landed at St Mawgan. During the year BOAC and Transport Command made over 3,800 Atlantic crossings, indeed in December Captain W.L. Stewart of BOAC became the first British pilot to complete 100 transatlantic flights. These figures did not include the countless numbers of transatlantic flights by B-17s, B-24s and C-47s of the USAAF to equip its two large Air Forces – the Eighth and Ninth. During the year Transport Command also delivered over 3,330 aircraft to the Middle East and Africa. In March St Mawgan became involved in Transport Command's passenger flights. No 271 squadron, commanded by Wing Commander M. Booth, DFC, Bar, was especially engaged in carrying passengers, as was No 24, under Wing Commander H.B. Collings, MVO, DFC, which was almost solely devoted to transport of VIPs. The importance of the airfield's part in all these flights, can be seen by the number of aircraft movements at St Mawgan during the year – some 16,000.

However, in November 1944 BOAC left St Mawgan (and Whitchurch) when Hurn became the country's major international terminal for land based aircraft, although BOAC's flying boats continued to operate from Poole Harbour. In the following month

No 1529 (Radio Aids Training) Flight used Airspeed Oxfords.

Airspeed Oxfords of No 1529 (Radio Aids Training) Flight arrived to provide training for Transport Command crews in the use of the new Instrument Landing System (ILS), which had recently been installed at St Mawgan. This Flight was the only RAF unit to be permanently based at the airfield throughout the war. The AS.10 Oxford, or 'Ox-box' as it was more commonly known to RAF airman, was a rather remarkable aircraft, used for aircrew advanced training, radar calibration work, beam approach training, communications duties, towing targets, and as air ambulances. The aircraft had been developed by Airspeed from its successful small passenger airliner, the Envoy. It entered the Service in late 1937 as the first twin-engined monoplane for advanced flying training. Right up until 1954 Oxfords gave sterling service to the RAF, with over 8,580 being produced in four different Marks.

The new landing approach system was originally known as the American Signals Corps System 51 and had been conceived and developed in the USA since 1939 where it was in place at most USAAF airfields. It was considered far superior, safer and more accurate than the Standard Beam Approach system universally used at RAF and FAA airfields. Strenuous petitions by the USAAF's Eighth Air Force persuaded the Air Ministry to trial ILS. In August 1943 it had been briefly in place at Davidstow Moor and was moved to St Eval in

September. However, it was from Hinton-in-the-Hedges airfield in Northamptonshire that the new system would be rigorously tested.

In simple terms the system was based on two ground transmitters, which provided an approach path for the aircraft's exact alignment and also produced the correct glide-slope for the aircraft's final descent onto the runway. The two transmitted radio signals were visually represented by two intersecting needles at right angles and furthermore when they remained in that position, the approach and landing of the aircraft would be accurate. Without doubt the ILS showed a marked improvement over SBA, and it operated successfully in all weather conditions. However, it was not generally introduced into the RAF until after the war, but the first ILS receivers were fitted into aircraft of Transport Command. Of course, highly sophisticated Instrument Landing Systems are now in use at commercial airports and Service airfields throughout the world.

Perhaps as a natural progression a School of Air Traffic Control was established at St Mawgan in July 1945 to train 'airfield controllers', which had been a new RAF trade when introduced in July 1942. Many of the airfield controllers were tour-expired aircrew or airmen taken off operational flying because of injuries. Hitherto much of the training had been undertaken at Watchfield near Swindon, where the RAF's first School of Flying Control had been established.

With the end of war in Europe the airfield was utilised for flights to America and Canada. Between mid-May and early July 1945 over 2,110 B-17s of the USAAF left for the USA, and a large number of these departed from St Mawgan; the USAAF traffic controllers did not finally leave the airfield until August. During June over 160 Lancasters of No 6 (RCAF) Group of Bomber Command flew home to Canada. There were also many delivery flights out to India and the Far East, as well as aircraft returning from service in the Middle East. But by the end of the year aircraft movements had fallen quite dramatically.

In July 1946 St Mawgan was used by Lancasters of No 35, a famous Pathfinder squadron, based at Graveley in Cambridgeshire. The squadron, under the command of Wing Commander Alan J.L. Craig, DSO, DFC had been selected to undertake a goodwill tour of the United States with their sixteen Lancasters, which were painted in tropical livery – white on black – signifying they would form part of the Tiger Force for service in the Pacific. The Lancasters left St Mawgan for the States via the Azores, and whilst in America visited New York, St Louis, Los Angeles, San Antonio and Washington, as well as representing the

35 squadron led by Wing Commander A. J. L. Craig, DSO, DFC, on return from the U.S.A., August 1946.

RAF at the Army Air Forces Day before visiting Canada. The squadron and its Lancasters returned to St Mawgan in late August.

It seemed quite inconceivable that such a large, modern and splendidly equipped airfield should close, but on 1st July 1947 St Mawgan was placed on a Care and Maintenance basis. However, less than four years later – 1st April 1951 – the Air Ministry reopened the airfield as Coastal Command's School of Maritime Reconnaissance and it remains a major Service airfield. In the summer of 1959 Starways Ltd commenced a passenger service to Liverpool, and three years later Newquay Council managed to obtain Air Ministry permission to build a small passenger terminal on the north side near the village of Carloggas. In 1977 Brymon Airways took over the London service, and at the time of writing British Airways operate domestic and European services, as well as several transatlantic flights to various airports in the USA from 'Newquay Airport'.

16

ST MERRYN

This major Fleet Air Arm training station originated as a small aerodrome developed during 1937 under the aegis of St Merryn Aerodrome Ltd. The site, some fifty acres in extent, was situated about three miles to the south-west of Padstow adjacent to the villages of St Merryn and St Ervan. A famous name in Service aviation circles was involved in its early development – William H. Rhodes-Moorehouse – a member of the Auxiliary Air Force living close by at Constantine; William was the son of Second Lieutenant W. Rhodes-Moorehouse, VC, RFC, the first airman to be awarded the Victoria Cross in April 1915. Sadly, like his father, Rhodes-Moorehouse would be killed flying operationally. His Hurricane was shot down on 6th September 1940 whilst he was serving in No 601 squadron during the Battle of Britain. Although St Merryn was advertised as the 'first public airfield in Cornwall', there is little evidence to suggest much pre-war use, except that the odd RAF aircraft made the occasional appearance at the airfield.

In late 1939 the Admiralty duly requisitioned the airfield along with another 550 acres of surrounding farmland to develop an operational flying training station. Three months later the small landing ground at Treligga, to the north-west of Delabole, was also acquired. This rudimentary airfield had previously been used for gliding or 'sailplaning' as the sport was then more generally known. The site, along with some 250 acres of coast, was intended to be used as a bombing, gunnery and later rocket projectile range, and possibly, with

228

the addition of three rather rough landing runs some 2,200 feet long, to provide an emergency Relief Landing Ground for the main station at St Merryn.

Over the next seven months St Merryn airfield quickly took shape; four tarmac runways, the main one at 1,270 yards, two each 1,000 yards long and the fourth at 1,030 yards, had been laid and four hangars erected. The provision of accommodation blocks was slow, this part of the building programme having fallen behind schedule; the first Naval airmen were billeted in Padstow and local villages. Nevertheless, on 10th August 1940, St Merryn was commissioned as HMS *Vulture*, and gained the dubious honour of being the first wartime airfield to open in Cornwall. Treligga as befitting a satellite airfield was named *Vulture II*. The WRNS who occupied Treligga were initially out-housed at Port Isaac until suitable accommodation was erected. It had become general Admiralty practice to name all Royal Naval Air Service (RNAS) shore bases after birds.

Within five days of commissioning, the first training unit was formed, No 792 squadron, which was placed under the command of Lieutenant H.E.R. Torin, DSC, RN. The squadron operated as an Air Target Towing Unit and initially equipped with six Blackburn Rocs and Skuas. Just over a month later No 774 squadron arrived from Evanton near Inverness, under the command of Lieutenant Commander P.L. Mortimer, RN. It had been formed in November 1939 as an Armament Training Squadron for observers and telegraphist/air gunners. The squadron was also equipped with Rocs and Skuas, as well as a number of Swordfish. The Roc was the first FAA fighter to be provided with a turret – an electrically actuated Boulton Paul four gun – and was obviously used for turret firing practice.

The two squadrons, Nos 774 and 792, would remain at St Merryn for most of the war, and each would be equipped with a wide variety of aircraft during that time – Defiants, Sea Hurricanes, Sea Gladiators, Masters, Martinet TTs, Proctors, Lysanders, Albacores, Fulmars and Barracudas. Furthermore the airfield would house, at various times, most of the Fleet fighters that operated in the FAA. The first operational squadron to use St Merryn, No 829, arrived on 14th September with its Fairey Albacores. This biplane had been designed back in 1936/7 as the ultimate replacement torpedo bomber for the Swordfish, but because of engine development problems Albacores did not enter the FAA until March 1940. Although very similar in design to the Swordfish, it was sturdier and had added refinements, such as an enclosed cabin

Fairey Albacore with a Blackburn Roc in attendance.

provided with heating and a more powerful engine (Bristol Taurus XII) which gave a maximum speed of 160 mph. The Albacore also carried heavier armament, one .303 machine gun in the forward wing and twin Vickers 'K' guns in the rear cockpit. Some 800 were ultimately produced (compared with 2,300 Swordfish) and Albacores served operationally until 1944, but the Swordfish was still operating as a front-line aircraft over eighteen months later.

No 829 squadron had only been formed in June under Lieutenant Commander O.S. Stevinson, RN, and was now operating under Coastal Command's direction, with its crews engaged in mine laying and bombing French coastal targets. When No 829 moved to St Eval on 7th October, it was immediately replaced by No 826 squadron, which had been formed in March (15th) specifically to introduce the Albacore into the Service, but already its crews had seen action with their Albacores, over Dunkirk when operating from Detling with Coastal Command. About three weeks later a third Albacore squadron, No 828, arrived from HMS *Peregrine* (Ford in Sussex). When the Albacores finally left Cornwall for Scotland in November, Nos 826 and 829, took their aircraft to sea for the first time, on HMS *Formidable* for convoy escort duty to South Africa.

The Albacores were briefly replaced by Fairey Fulmar Is of No 807 squadron, yet another new Fleet fighter squadron that had only been

Publicity photograph captioned 'Gunnery Training in the FAA'. (via B. Woods)

formed in mid-September at HMS *Kestrel* (Worthy Down in Hampshire), where its crews had been busy on work-up trials on their new aircraft. No 807 was commanded by Lieutenant Commander J. Sholto Douglas, DSO, RN, a member of another famous Service family; Air Marshal (later Air Chief Marshal) Sir William Sholto Douglas, KCB, MC, DFC had recently been appointed the AOC-in-C of Fighter Command, and from January 1944 he would be in charge of Coastal Command.

The Fulmar had been designed to replace the Roc as a Fleet fighter, and it was supplied to No 808 squadron in June 1940 less than six months after the prototype first flew. Although much was expected of the Fulmar – it was even hailed as the 'FAA's Spitfire' – the aircraft was rather hampered by its bulk and from the Admiralty's insistence that it should be a two-seater, as it was felt that navigation at sea was a prime consideration. Although powered by a Rolls-Royce Merlin VIII engine it was relatively slow for a fighter with a maximum speed of about 280 mph; but, like the RAF's fighters, it was armed with eight .303 machine guns, but with a far greater endurance (five hours) or a range of some 800 miles. Many FAA pilots that had flown Hurricanes found the Fulmar comparatively heavy and far less manoeuvrable, although they

Fairey Fulmar: the FAA's equivalent to the Spitfire.

considered the aircraft had 'a good take-off, moderate rate of climb and plenty of endurance.' Only 602 Fulmars were produced in just two marks, and although they survived operationally until February 1945, they were by then far out-classed by other FAA fighters, although one is preserved in the Fleet Air Arm Museum at Yeovilton. The Fulmars of No 807 squadron left at the beginning of December for service on HMS *Pegasus*.

During the autumn of 1940 the various training activities at and around the airfield attracted the attention of the Luftwaffe who like the RAF, was committed to attacking training airfields in an attempt to disrupt flying training programmes. In October the airfield was bombed on three separate occasions and on 11th November a solitary Heinkel 111 made a low-level attack damaging two hangars. The Luftwaffe returned in the Spring and on 5th May six aircraft made a determined assault, damaging over twenty aircraft and injuring two personnel.

Like all training airfields St Merryn suffered its share of accidents, though they seemed far fewer than many others. In April and May, 1941 two Swordfish of No 774 squadron were lost. On 10th May Swordfish L2799 hit overhead electric cables near Tintagel and the four airmen were killed. Another Swordfish crashed close to the airfield on 1st August 1944 when it spun out of control on its landing approach killing the three crewmen.

Earlier in 1941 Skua IIs of No 801 squadron arrived from service on

HMS *Furious* to undertake dive-bombing trials and practice in preparation for a proposed strike against the German battleships in Brest. However, the trials were less than successful, and the squadron moved away to HMS *Landrail II* (Campletown) towards the end of March, after spending several days at St Eval. They were replaced by another Fleet fighter squadron, No 809, with its newly acquired Fulmars. The crews would stay at St Merryn for about 2½ months effectively becoming the precursor of numerous Fleet fighter squadrons that would use St Merryn's training facilities for short periods. Another Fulmar squadron, No 800, arrived in mid-June, stayed for about a fortnight, left and returned in September. During November and December Nos 882, 883 and 888, arrived and departed in strict rotation. This practice would continue throughout 1942 with ten fighter squadrons staying for a month or so, as St Merryn became increasingly devoted to fighter training. All these squadrons were operating the main Fleet fighters of the time – Fulmars, Martlets and Sea Hurricanes, with two, Nos 836 and 837, equipped with Swordfish.

During the summer of 1942 Fulmars of No 809 squadron arrived for training on army support duties pending its move to North Africa. On 1st October 'B' Flight of the squadron was formed into a new squadron, No 879 with just six Fulmars. Ten days later it moved to Charlton Horethorne in Somerset, another FAA training airfield, which in January would be commissioned as HMS *Heron II*. The new squadron would also be used on army co-operation duties until joining HMS *Attacker* in the Mediterranean.

On 15th April No 762 squadron arrived from HMS *Heron* (Yeovilton). It had formed there in late March as an Advanced Flying Training School, under the command of Lieutenant R. McD. Hall, RN; the squadron operated Fulmars, Martlets and Masters. However, in early September the School returned to Yeovilton. Later in the year, on 12th October, No 748 squadron was formed at the airfield as a Fighter Pool squadron, but it effectively provided refresher flying training courses on Martlets, Fulmars, Hurricanes and later Spitfires. The squadron had taken as its motto, 'We labour that others may learn', which was almost the same as that of No 792's motto, 'We suffer that others may learn'; echoing the sentiments of so many patient and persevering flying training instructors!

Considerable construction work was put in hand during 1943 to accommodate the increased flying training commitments and future expansion plans to house what was known as the School of Air Combat.

The Fleet fighter squadrons, although now fewer in number, still arrived and left with the same regularity until at least August. Supermarine Seafires, the Naval version of the Spitfire, made their first appearance at St Merryn. The first trial carrier landings by Spitfire VBs had been successfully accomplished in July 1941 and the green light was given to convert Mark Vs by the provision of arrestor hooks and catapult spools; they became known as Seafires. Purpose built Seafires entered the FAA in June 1942, and went into action during the Allied invasion of North Africa in November. In 1943 Mark IIIs went into production and over 1,200 were built up to July 1945. Their famous folding 'praying mantis' wings enabled the aircraft to be moved on aircraft carrier lifts and afforded easier deck handling. The Seafire proved to be a salvation for the FAA; surviving into the post-war era with one Seafire squadron operating in the Korean War in June 1950.

Major changes to the training organisation came about in 1943. On 24th February 'Z' Flight of No 787 squadron moved in from HMS *Daedalus* (Lee-on-Solent) with its Swordfish IIs, having been formed only a month earlier as a development unit for the operation of rocket projectiles on FAA aircraft. The Flight would undertake trials with their Swordfish and later Fulmars and Sea Hurricanes at the Treligga firing range, code-named Glow-worm. Later the Unit would also train front-line squadrons in the techniques of firing rocket projectiles. It was a Swordfish of No 819 squadron from HMS *Archer* that sank the first U-boat (*U-752*) with rocket projectiles on 23rd May 1943.

In March No 748 squadron became No 10 Naval Operational Training Unit, and in due course would receive its first Seafires. The squadron's 'B' Flight moved to Yeovilton in October, and as has been noted a detachment of Seafires served at Chivenor until February 1944. The whole Unit would transfer to HMS *Dipper* (Henstridge) on 4th February, before moving into Yeovilton about a month later. The squadron returned to St Merryn in August 1945.

On 3rd September the School of Air Combat – No 736 squadron – transferred in from Yeovilton, where it had been formed on 24th May, to take over the responsibilities for Naval pilots from the RAF's Fighter Leaders School. The squadron would inculcate the latest techniques of air combat to experienced FAA pilots. By 1945 the School also provided an Air Instruction course, as well as Torpedo bomber strike courses.

The School, along with the two training squadrons, Nos 774 and 792, continued with their heavy training commitments throughout 1944. No 774's biplanes, Albacores and Swordfish were being slowly phased out.

A fine formation of Supermarine Seafires of No 2 NAFS, 1943. (FAA Museum)

Another Fairey aircraft, the Barracuda, was now being used. Although this aircraft had first flown in December 1940, Barracudas did not enter the FAA until January 1943 but one year later there were no fewer than twelve squadrons, most built by either Blackburn or Boulton Paul as Fairey Aviation was fully engaged producing Seafires. At the end of the war the FAA would have more Barracudas on complement (534) than any other single aircraft. The other squadron was almost fully equipped with Defiant TTIs and Martinet TTIs, both specially produced target towers.

'Z' Flight of No 787 squadron, which in mid-January had returned to St Merryn after a short spell at HMS *Nightjar* (Inskip in Lancashire), remained at the airfield until 1st July when the Flight was disbanded. A couple of Seafire squadrons, Nos 885 and 808, served briefly at St Merryn during February to April. These two squadrons would become part of No 3 Naval Fighter Wing operating from Lee-on-Solent as the gunnery observation force for the Royal Navy, although under the control of the Second Tactical Air Force. No 816 Swordfish squadron, one of those on loan to Coastal Command for D-Day and beyond, based at Perranporth, also used St Merryn until it was disbanded on 1st August 1944.

As the training demands on the School of Air Combat steadily increased during the year, it was decided to form three additional training squadrons. The first, No 719, came into existence on 15th June to mount Naval Air Firing courses. No 715, formed on 17th August, was effectively an additional air combat unit, although largely engaged in training Fleet fighter leaders. The third squadron, No 709, followed a month later to concentrate on training and honing ground attack techniques. This squadron would operate with Seafire IIIs and Grumman Hellcat IIs and IIIs.

By now Chance Vought Corsairs were evident at St Merryn. This aircraft was universally acknowledged as the most outstanding carrier-based fighter of the Second World War. The first Corsair had been supplied to the US Navy at the end of 1942, and they saw action in the following February. With a maximum speed in excess of 440 mph, strongly armed with six .50 inch machine guns and carrying two 1,000 pound bombs or eight five inch rocket projectiles, it was a most formidable fighter. The first Corsairs entered the FAA in June 1943 with No 1830 squadron, having been acquired under the Lend-Lease agreement. By the end of the war there were 19 squadrons operating in the FAA, mostly with the East Indies and Pacific fleets. The enemy were always forewarned of attack due to the whistling noise caused by the aircraft's air intake; this became known by them as the 'Whistling Death'! The last Corsair of some 12,500 of this outstanding single-seat fighter was produced for the US Navy in December 1952.

In August 1944 Lieutenant Commander (later Commander) R.E. 'Jimmie' Gardner, DSC, RNVR, was given command of the renamed School of Naval Air Warfare. Gardner had joined the FAA in 1939, and was one of the FAA pilots to be loaned to Fighter Command during the Battle of Britain; he flew with No 242 Hurricane squadron under Squadron Leader Douglas Bader. After a brief sojourn flying Beaufighters in Coastal Command, Gardner joined No 807 squadron on HMS *Ark Royal* for service in the Mediterranean. He later commanded No 889 squadron, which operated Hurricanes from land bases in North Africa. When he returned to this country he was eventually posted to St Merryn with 8½ victories to his name. In June 1945 he was made an OBE and retired from the Navy in March 1946.

The School of Naval Air Warfare was now mainly engaged training pilots and crews for the Japanese war in the Far East and the Pacific. The Treligga range had been adapted to simulate the terrain and targets the Naval airmen would face overseas. On 2nd January 1945 No 792

Chance Vought Corsair: The outstanding carrier-based fighter of the war.

squadron was finally disbanded, as indeed was No 719; both squadrons were effectively absorbed into a reformed No 794 squadron, which had been disbanded in June 1944 after some four years as an Air Firing Unit. The squadron now comprised three Flights – Ground Attack, Air Combat and Photo-reconnaissance – and would remain at St Merryn until 9th August when it moved to Eglinton in Northern Ireland. A couple of days earlier No 725 squadron moved in as an Air Target Towing Unit, although by the end of the year it had effectively disappeared, being merged into No 736 squadron.

Thus St Merryn ended the war as it had begun as a major FAA training station. Its fortunes over the next decade would greatly fluctuate in the climate of post-war reorganisation. In June 1955 the airfield was placed under Care and Maintenance, and it finally closed down in January 1956. Flying is still conducted from what little remains of the airfield, and it is used by the Cornwall Parachute Centre.

17
UPOTTERY

S. Baring-Gould in his 1907 *Little Guide to Devonshire* described Upottery as 'a pleasantly situated village with a much restored church', but one discovers that the wartime airfield bearing its name was sited closer to another village, about half a mile to the south-west of Smeatharpe; it was frequently referred to as such rather than Upottery. The airfield site was allocated to the USAAF in November 1942 but construction work on the Class A Standard bomber airfield did not commence until the summer of 1943. When completed, in February 1944, Upottery became the third of a clutch of airfields in the Blackdown Hills with Dunkeswell and Church Stanton a short distance away.

The airfield, with its three standard concrete runways, fifty 'loop' hardstandings, two 'T2' hangars, and seven accommodation sites, was placed under the RAF's care until the USAAF was ready to move in. The Ninth Air Force unit destined to serve there, had not yet arrived in the country. On 26th April Upottery virtually became a spot of 'little America' in 'this hidden corner' of Devon, when the C-47s and C-53s of the 439th Troop Carrier Group roared in from Balderton in Nottinghamshire.

The Group, commanded by Colonel Charles H. Young, arrived from the States in early March, its crews having already undergone navigation training, as well as later taking part in training exercises with airborne troops and towing gliders with other USAAF Groups based in the east Midlands. The four squadrons, 91st to 94th, had each been given an identity code – L4, J8, 3B and D8 respectively – which had been painted on their aircraft. The airfield became officially known as 'Station 462'; all American air bases were so numbered and this number appeared on official reports and correspondence. The airmen serving there were actively encouraged to use the station number rather than its more local name – be it Upottery or Smeatharpe!

The Douglas C-47s were the 'work horses' of the USAAF, operating as transports, troop carriers, glider towers, air ambulances and passenger aircraft. It was the company's military version of their successful twin-engined DC-3 civil airliner, which had first flown in January 1935. This passenger aircraft was then far in advance of its time, built to a simple but robust design offering speed and comfort to its passengers. The military model was ordered by the US Army Air Corps in 1940 and entered the Service a year later and never looked back. It was not until 1942 that the C-47s began to come off the Douglas production lines in any great number; the company had built a new plant at Long Beach, California to cope with USAAF's demands.

The C-47 was powered by two Pratt & Whitney Twin Wasp engines, giving a top speed of 230 mph but it cruised at some 185 mph. It became a most dependable transport aircraft, able to carry up to two tons of supplies and stores, which could be handled quite easily with its double roller tracks on the floor of the fuselage. Its most important wartime

C-47 of 91st squadron of 439th TCG with a glider in tow. (USAF via B. Hodge)

role was as a troop carrier with both the USAAF and the RAF, not only in Europe but notably in Burma. Besides its full complement of twenty-eight airborne troops, the aircraft could also carry five to six 'pararacks' of supplies under its wings. However, the C-47 did have a rather limited operational range. It was unarmed and lacked armour plating for its crews, while the fuel tanks were not self-sealing; all factors that made the aircraft and its crews vulnerable to both flak and fighters, as shown by the losses suffered during D-Day and in Operation Market in September. At the end of the war the RAF had 1,490 Dakotas in service. In the post-war years the C-47 or Dakota was operated by many commercial airlines and cargo freight companies throughout the world. Over sixty years later the Dakota is still flying, and considering that some 20,000 Dakotas, over half as C-47s, were built, it is one of the most remarkable and prolific aircraft ever produced.

The C-53 or 'Skytrooper' was really another version of the C-47, but it had a smaller door and a lighter flooring. The aircraft only saw limited production, compared with the C-47. Upottery would also house the Allies' two main assault gliders – the American Waco CG-4A and British Airspeed AS. 51 Horsa. The Waco glider had come into service in 1941, and when operating with the RAF it was called the Hadrian. This glider was often described as 'an ugly blunt-nosed dragonfly'! It could accommodate thirteen troops or a jeep or a 75mm howitzer with its crew. The Horsa carried twenty-five men into battle. Both made their operational debut during the invasion of Sicily in July 1943. Over 13,900 Waco CG-4As were built compared with some 3,650 Horsas.

The Group's task on D-Day was to deliver troops of the US 101st Airborne Division to dropping zones (DZ) near Ste Mère Église, situated directly behind the US beach-head Utah. The troops gathered at Upottery a few days before 6th June and were accommodated in the two hangars and confined to base for security reasons. In the early hours of D-Day eighty-one aircraft in two separate 'serials' took off from Upottery, led by Colonel Young in his personal C-43 - *The Argonia*. The aircraft flew in tight 'V' formations across the Channel in a strictly prescribed ten mile corridor at about 500 feet, with their navigation and cabin lights switched off. Their planned approach to the DZs was to cross the French coast to the west of the Contentin peninsula in order to avoid the heavy concentrations of flak batteries known to be protecting the beach-heads. By then they should have climbed to about 1,000/1,500 feet, but as they neared the DZs the pilots reduced speed to 110 mph and came down to 500/700 feet – the jumping altitude.

The forecast of a clear moonlit night had not materialised. The crews encountered a heavy blanket of cloud, which obliterated the ground and some of the pathfinder beacon markers, and the resultant parachute drop was rather scattered. The subsequent harsh and costly battle for Ste Mère Église has passed into the legends of the US Army. The Group lost three aircraft; on the following day fifty C47s towed thirty Horsas and twenty CG-4As with reinforcements for the beach heads, and one aircraft was lost. For these two operations the Group was awarded a Distinguished Unit Citation.

The 439th continued to make supply flights into Normandy, returning with wounded personnel. In July three squadrons, some fifty aircraft and crews, were detached to Orbetello in Italy and in August they were engaged in the invasion of Southern France transporting men and equipment of the 517th Parachute Infantry Regiment. The remaining squadron, 93rd, operated from both Ramsbury and Membury supplying forward troops in Normandy with arms and ammunition. The four squadrons were reunited at Upottery on 25th August, although on 8th September the Group became one of the first to move to France, initially to Juvincourt, later Louray. The 439th was fully involved in Operation Market dropping troops of the US 81st Airborne Division, but from their original airfield – Balderton.

The airfield was now relatively deserted, although it had been handed back to the RAF. On 7th November US Navy *PB4-Ys* from Dunkeswell began to use the airfield for their anti-submarine missions, whilst remedial work was being carried out on the main runway at Dunkeswell. Later in the month (18th) Avengers of No 820 (FAA) squadron, commanded by Lieutenant Commander S. P. Luke, RN, flew in from St Eval. They stayed for three days, leaving for HMS *Indefatigable*.

C-47s of 439th TCG lined up at Upottery, September 1944. (USAF via B. Hodge)

In January 1945 two US Navy Patrol Bomber squadrons, 107th and 112th, arrived to make the airfield their home for the duration of the war. The squadrons operated PB4Y-1s and were engaged in anti-submarine operations. Both had operated from airfields in North Africa patrolling the South Atlantic, VB-107 had been particularly successful destroying no fewer than six U-boats from July 1943 up to the end of September 1944. During their stay at Upottery only a couple of sightings were made with just a single attack without any result. Shortly after the end of the war the RAF resumed control of the airfield. It was then used, by Maintenance Command, for the storage of surplus material and equipment until November 1948.

The airfield quickly returned to agricultural use, but remarkably there is still evidence of its wartime history – the odd hut, sections of the runways in a rather ruined state and the empty shell of the control tower standing forlorn in the centre. Parts of the airfield are still used by a flying club and occasionally by stock-cars when racing takes place at what is now known as 'Smeatharpe Stadium'!

PB4Y-1 of the US Navy on patrol. (National Archives & Records)

18
WINKLEIGH

Winkleigh was a prime example of a wartime airfield that not only had a long period of gestation, but when it did finally materialise appeared to be almost surplus to requirements, and as such was severely under-utilised, at least in operational terms. Indeed with the benefit of hindsight, the total cost, possibly in the region of £1 million, proved to be a poor investment.

The airfield had originally been planned in 1939 when a site about 1½ miles to the north-west of Winkleigh in Devon was ear-marked for development. Work started on the site in 1940 with the intention of providing a satellite for Chivenor, some 16 miles to the north. The B3220 road from Winkleigh to Torrington, which bisected the airfield site, was closed. Much of the lengthy delay was caused by the nature of the subsoil. The land was very wet with poor drainage, and thousands of tons of ballast and hardcore were required to provide a relatively firm foundation for the two planned runways to be laid down in a crossbow configuration.

Finally, on 1st January 1943, the airfield was handed over to the RAF, although it could hardly be described as habitable as it was covered in acres of mud – a not uncommon occurrence with wartime airfields! Nevertheless, the contractors had erected a single 'T2' hangar and eight Blister hangars. A concrete perimeter track linked the two runways, as well as giving access to the numerous hardstandings. The airfield was allocated to No 10 Group of Fighter Command, as Coastal Command had expressed the view that it had no operational use for it. This seems

243

rather a strange decision especially as 1943 became probably the busiest year for all of the Command's existing airfields in No 19 Group. At the end of February a handful of RAF airmen arrived to formally take over the airfield, but very little happened until the autumn. Indeed, on 20th August the airfield was placed on a Care and Maintenance basis; to my knowledge this is one of only two wartime airfields to be put 'on hold' *before* any aircraft or units had used its facilities. The other airfield, Birch in Essex, actually never housed any permanent flying units.

However, early in October the airfield was temporarily handed over to the USAAF's Ninth Air Force and over 700 American airmen moved in. For the next two months USAAF Spitfires, Martin B-26s (Marauders) and Fairchild UC-61As (Forwarders) used the airfield, mostly employed in a number of pre-invasion US Army exercises and trial beach landings along the North Devon coast. In February aircraft of the USAAF were again in evidence, especially during the 22nd to 24th when numerous C-47s, under the direction of 74th Service Group of the Ninth Air Force, brought a division of US land troops into the area. This was of course the time of a massive build-up of troops, vehicles and supplies prior to Operation Overlord. By the end of the month the 'Gooney birds', as the C-47s were called by GIs, had flown away and Winkleigh returned once again to its quiet and almost somnolent state.

Winkleigh's brief spell of operational action was ushered in on 14th April when Beaufighter VIFs of No 406 (RCAF) landed after a short flight from Exeter, where the squadron had served since the previous November. No 406 was commanded by the RCAF's premier night-fighter pilot – Wing Commander Robert C. Fumerton, DFC, Bar – known to his airmen as 'Moose'! He had joined the RCAF in December 1939 and after a spell with No 1 (RCAF) fighter squadron, he was posted to No 406 at Acklington in June 1941. On 1st September he and his navigator/radar operator, Sergeant (later Flying Officer) L.P.S. Bing, shot down a Junkers 88 over Newcastle, the first night-victory for the RCAF. Fumerton went on to serve with distinction in the Middle East and Malta, steadily adding to his tally of victories. By the time he left the squadron in July to return to Canada, he had 14 night-victories to his name, the highest number for a Canadian pilot.

The Beaufighter, as a night-fighter, had all but disappeared out of Fighter Command by this time. In fact No 406 would be the only squadron still operating them in June 1944, although the crews would soon begin to convert to Mosquito NFXIIs. Nevertheless, since the dark days of September 1940 the Beaufighter had given admirable service to

Fighter Command. The Mk. VIFs were beginning to show their age, having entered the Command in early 1942. They were the first to be fitted with a .303 Vickers 'K' gas-operated machine gun in the observer's position, and also supplied with AI Mk VIII radar enclosed in the so-called 'thimble' nose. This impressive fighter gained the grim nickname of 'Whispering Death', when Mark VIs first served in India and the Pacific against the Japanese!

However dated the Beaufighters might be, the Canadian crews quickly demonstrated they were still most formidable night-fighters. On 23rd/24th April when the Luftwaffe directed over 100 aircraft to bomb Bristol, four Junkers 88s were shot down. One fell near Start Point to one of the squadron's Beaufighters crewed by Warrant Officer G.F. MacEwan and Flight Sergeant C.S. Headley. Six nights later when a force of Dornier 217Rs attacked Plymouth Harbour with glider bombs, Squadron Leader D.J. Williams, DFC and Flying Officer Kirkpatrick destroyed two; they were flying a Mosquito NFXII on the squadron's first Mosquito night-patrols.

It is rather strange to think that by this time even the Mosquito NFXII was a little out-dated! Although this Mark had only entered the Service in February 1943, with a similar 'thimble' nose, it had been largely replaced by the NFXIII, which had now become Fighter Command's principal night-fighter. However, such was the speedy development of the Mosquito that even this later Mark would soon be superseded by the NFXXXs. These were powered by high-altitude engines (Rolls-Royce Merlin 72 or 76s) and could accommodate both British and American AI radar. The Mosquito NFXXX became the final and ultimate night-fighter variant to be used during the war. The Canadian crews would receive their first XXXs in late July.

There could have been no greater contrast between 'these beautiful, graceful, little grey machines' as the Mosquitos had been famously described, and the rather lumbering biplanes that appeared at the airfield on 8th May. Just eight Albacores of another Canadian squadron, No 415, arrived from Bircham Newton and Manston under the command of Wing Commander C.G. Ruttan, DSO. This squadron had entered Coastal Command in August 1941 as a torpedo bomber squadron, its badge, a Swordfish, and its motto, *Ad Metam* or 'To the Mark,' had been chosen to illustrate its anti-shipping role. As has already been noted the squadron operated its Hampden Is from both St Eval and Predannack. In September 1943 it was taken off operations and was now a 'hybrid' unit equipped with about 15 ex-FAA Albacore

Mosquito NFXII with AI Mk.VIII radar in the nose.

Is (received in October 1943) and eleven Wellington XIIIs, both tasked with seeking out German surface vessels and especially the dreaded E-boats. The equipment and use of this Canadian squadron had deeply concerned Air Marshal Breadner of the RCAF, he felt that both types of aircraft were decidedly obsolete and that his crews should be better utilised. The Air Marshal had been continually petitioning the Air Ministry to convert No 415 into a full bomber squadron to take its place in No 6 (RCAF) Group of Bomber Command. A compromise was finally agreed – after 1st April only RAF crews would be posted to No 415, and in July the squadron would be equipped with Halifaxes; No 415 went on to complete 104 bombing raids from East Moor in No 6 Group, losing 13 aircraft in action.

The Albacores continued to operate from Winkleigh until 12th July, when they left for Manston, where the aircraft were transferred to another Coastal Command squadron, No 119, a week later. The Albacore crews worked closely with the Wellington XIIIs of No 254 squadron then operating from Davidstow Moor. During May some Defiants, Hurricanes and Oxfords of No 286 (Anti-aircraft Co-operation) squadron also used the airfield, whilst the squadron was based at Colerne.

Fairey Albacore I: No 415 (RCAF) squadron operated these aircraft from Winkleigh during 1944.

The night of 14/15th May proved to be most successful for No 406's crews. The Luftwaffe returned with a small force of Dornier 217s and Junkers 88s to bomb Bristol again; eleven enemy aircraft were destroyed and the squadron claimed four of them with three probables and one damaged, its best night-operation of the war. Wing Commander Fumerton destroyed a Junkers 88, his fourteenth and final victory. In early June the squadron had six Mosquito XIIs and 18 Beaufighter VIFs on complement; No 406's crews were in action early on D-Day. In fact the first Beaufighter left Winkleigh at 22.40 hours on the 5th followed five minutes later by another Beaufighter; two more would take off during the early hours of D-Day. The crews were part of Operation Outmatch, regular nightly patrols over Allied shipping in the English Channel and over the beach-heads; the flights were of a duration of about 3½ hours and all passed without any serious incidents. Also on the night of the 5/6th, Flight Lieutenant H.D. McNabb and Flight Sergeant P.F. Tindall left on a Ranger over Morlaix and Lannion airfields in Brittany and although their aircraft received a direct hit from flak the crew managed to return safely. On the following night two Mosquito crews were sent on another Ranger to the same airfields, and succeeded in destroying a Dornier 217R. Four Beaufighter crews had left Winkleigh on Operation Bigot, night patrols of the English Channel, and all four had returned safely by 0500 hours on 7th June.

During July the crews were taken off their regular nightly patrols to concentrate on conversion to Mosquitos. They were also given the task of providing night-air protection of the Naval vessels operating off the Brest Peninsula, which was still occupied by enemy forces. On the 21st of the month the crews were in action against a number of Dornier 217s that were attacking four Naval destroyers off the coast of Brittany. Squadron Leader Williams and Flying Officer Kirkpatrick shot down two enemy aircraft all in the space of about ten minutes. By the middle of the month the Albacores had left, although the occasional black Lysander of No 161 (Special Duties) squadron from Tempsford, used Winkleigh as an advance airfield to pick up agents of the SOE (Special Operations Executive) operating in occupied France. By now the squadron was mostly using Hudsons for these operations, and they finally ceased in September, after over three years of brave, clandestine 'moonlight' operations (see *Hertfordshire and Bedfordshire Airfields in the Second World War*).

The last Beaufighter operational sorties were mounted on 9th August, when two Beaufighters piloted by American airmen, 1/Lieutenants J. M. Purdy and S.W. Fikosky, both of the USAAF, patrolled at night over Naval destroyers off the Brest Peninsula. This was a historic occasion; since mid-September 1940 these doughty night-fighters had given admirable service in the night skies over Britain. The Beaufighters left Winkleigh on 27th August and by the end of the month No 406 was completely equipped with Mosquito NFXXXs. On 17th September the squadron, now commanded by Wing Commander D.J. 'Blackie' Williams, DFC, previously a Flight Commander, left for Colerne en route for Manston, where the crews would be engaged on night Rangers over enemy airfields. However, as has already been noted, the Canadian squadron would complete its wartime service at Predannack.

The airfield was, for the second time, placed on Care and Maintenance though not for long, because in November it was transferred into No 23 Group of Flying Training Command and used as a flying training school for Norwegian airmen prior to the re-establishment of the Royal Norwegian Air Force. The School would be commanded by Commander Torstein Diesen, and initially equipped with North American Harvards. The Harvard was the most universally used military training aircraft of all time, and had first flown back in December 1938. It was the first all-metal advanced trainer and used in great numbers by both the RAF and the USAAF. Many pilots and instructors considered that it was an inferior trainer compared with the British-built Miles Master II, the wooden constructed advanced trainer.

The Norwegian Flying Training School was equipped with North American Harvards.

Although the Harvard was said to be 'noisy and unpleasant to fly', over 17,000 were built and they remained in service until 1955. Later a number of Fairchild Cornells used by the Norwegian flying training school in Toronto, arrived from Canada. The Cornell was yet another American-built primary trainer, which had first flown in 1940; they were predominantly used by the numerous flying training schools in the various Commonwealth countries under the Empire (later British Commonwealth) Air Training Scheme. Many of the Cornell IIs or PT-26s had been produced in Canada under licence.

In November 1945 the Norwegian training school was removed to Gardermoen in Oslo and this heralded the demise of flying at Winkleigh, although the airfield was not finally sold until December 1958. The Torridge District Council erected a stone memorial on the site of the airfield, which was unveiled on 12th May 1995. Adjacent to the memorial is an excellent information plaque, showing the plan of the airfield with an accompanying text of its wartime operations; both can be found close to the industrial estate just off the B3320 road to Torrington.

The Memorial Stone at Winkleigh.

19

OTHER AIRFIELDS

There were several other airfields in the two counties, which although they may not warrant a separate chapter, are nevertheless deserving of notice.

Falmouth

Thirty stations for marine aircraft had been created during the First World War, mostly in existing harbours, but by September 1939 just seven were left. The Air Ministry's Aerodromes Board was also enjoined to survey potential locations for flying boat stations; in theory Falmouth's fine natural harbour appeared to be an ideal situation, especially considering its position in Cornwall so far west. In the late 1930s moorings in the outer harbour between Trefusis Point and Flushing village had been used by detachments of flying boats, notably in late 1938 by the Saro Londons of No 201 squadron, then permanently based at Calshot.

On 20th September 1939 three Londons of No 240 squadron from Invergordon moved into Falmouth to commence convoy patrols. However, their stay was rather short as they moved back to Scotland on 4th October. A couple of days earlier three Supermarine Stranraers of No 209 squadron had landed from Oban to take over the convoy escort duties.

Stranraers of No 209 squadron operated at Falmouth in late 1939.

The Stranraer, the last of three biplane flying boats (the others were the Southampton and Scapa) produced by Supermarine for the RAF during the inter-war years, had first appeared in 1935. It was originally known as the Southampton V. Its two Bristol Pegasus X engines gave the aircraft a cruising speed just in excess of 100 mph. It was armed with three .303 Lewis guns, with the rear gun position as an open cockpit. Stranraers entered the Service with No 228 squadron in December 1936, and No 209 received their new flying boats in November 1938. The Stranraers had a relatively short operational life, most would be replaced by either Sunderlands or Saro Lerwicks by the summer of 1940.

Before the Stranraers left in early November, one was lost on the 3rd when it crashed off Falmouth. The two remaining Stranraers returned to Oban where in the following month No 209 would be the first squadron to be equipped with Lerwicks. During the winter of 1940/1 Falmouth was used occasionally by Sunderlands of No 204 squadron based at Mount Batten. In March N9021 was damaged when it went aground in the estuary during bad weather. Mainly because of a lack of facilities and the unsuitability of the mooring places when conditions were inclement, Falmouth was placed on Care and Maintenance under the control of RAF Mount Batten, but by the end of 1942 it was closed down.

Haldon

This small pre-war Devon aerodrome dates from September 1929 when Haldon Airport Ltd was formed by a local Teignmouth businessman. It was situated some 760 feet high on heathland to the north-west of Teignmouth and adjacent to the golf course. During the 1930s a number of Air Services used Haldon (or Teignmouth as it was more generally known) as a stopping point on regular flights to and from Plymouth. Flying instruction was also provided and perhaps its main claim to fame was that Whitney W. Straight (later Air Commodore) was taught to fly there. In January 1937 his Corporation took over the management of the aerodrome, but needless to say in September 1939 Haldon was closed to flying and promptly requisitioned by the Air Ministry.

After very irregular use by a number of small aircraft from the Aeroplane & Armament Experimental Establishment at Boscombe Down, which used the airfield for its bombing range in Lyme Bay, Haldon was handed over to the Admiralty. In August 1941 it became a satellite for Yeovilton and commissioned as *Heron II*. The airfield was expanded to both the north and the south to extend the landing run, even some of the golf course was acquired. In the following year some hardstandings would be laid down, along with Sommerfeld tracking in an attempt to alleviate the problems of surface water.

Detachments of just three FAA squadrons from Yeovilton used Haldon – Nos 759, 761 and 794 – with a mixture of Fairey Fulmars and Swordfish, Blackburn Rocs and Skuas, Miles Masters, Sea Hurricanes

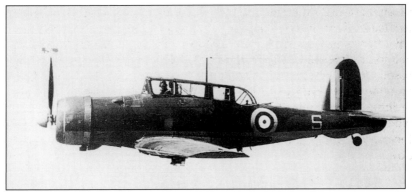

Blackburn Skuas of the FAA flew from Haldon during 1942.

and Boulton Paul Defiants. Nos 759 and 761 were Advanced Flying Training Units, the latter having only been formed at Yeovilton on 1st August 1941 under Lieutenant C.P. Campbell-Horsfall, RN. Both units would use Haldon for air firing practice. No 794 was an Air Target Towing Unit, which would ultimately reform at St Merryn in January 1945.

The airfield's location and poor drainage made flying conditions there less than ideal; it was frequently buffeted by high winds and during quieter spells of weather the airfield suffered from hill fog. Thus it was perhaps not too surprising that in early January 1943 the airfield was de-commissioned in favour of Charlton Horethorne in Somerset, which now became *Heron II*; in the following May Haldon was placed on a Care and Maintenance basis. Other than for the occasional emergency use flying had ceased. Today very little remains of the airfield, except that a car park close to the golf course has been named *Aerodrome Car Park* by Teignbridge District Council.

Land's End

This small aerodrome situated on the B3306 road between Sennen and St Just and about two miles to the north-east of Land's End, owes its existence to Captain Gordon P. Olley of Olley Air Services. In May 1936 he formed a new company, Channel Air Services, with the intention of providing a regular service to St Mary's on the Isles of Scilly, from what was originally known as St Just's aerodrome. This roughly triangular field gave a maximum landing run of 2,100 feet and was provided with a single hangar, a booking office and fuelling facilities. The aerodrome was completed in June 1937 and on 15th September Channel Air Services started their daily services to St Mary's under the slogan '20 minutes and you're over.' Less than a year later, on 25th June, one of the company's de Havilland D.H. 84 Dragon aircraft crashed shortly after taking off, killing the pilot and his six passengers.

In December 1938 Great Western & Southern Air Lines Ltd took over the service, but from May 1939 Western Airways also operated a service to Swansea via Newquay and Barnstaple from the airfield. At the outbreak of war all internal air services were cancelled whilst the National Air Communications (noted under Exeter) considered which of the services should be continued. The few that were retained mostly

Land's End Aerodrome in 1999.

served islands off the mainland: the Isle of Man, the Shetlands, the Orkneys, the Hebrides, the Channel Islands and, last, the Isles of Scilly. Thus on 25th September Great Western & Southern were authorised to resume their services. Their three de Havilland aircraft were camouflaged, the cabin windows were painted over for security reasons and the landing lights were masked. The aircraft would also be used for army co-operation exercises when not being used on the regular flights. In addition RAF Lysanders would use the airfield during 1939/40.

From 27th July 1940 all surviving small airline companies were under the management of the Associated Airways Joint Committee, which had its headquarters at Speke airfield near Liverpool. The overall controller of the internal air services was Wing Commander A.H. Measures with Captain Gordon Olley as his deputy. In the Committee's first complete year of operations, despite the Battle of Britain and all other Luftwaffe activity, its airline companies had flown over 1½ million miles carrying over 46,000 passengers without a serious incident – quite an achievement!

Although it was only 28 miles from Land's End to St Mary's the flights were not without risk, either from enemy or indeed friendly aircraft, and it is quite surprising that there was only one fatal casualty. On 3rd June 1941 a Dragon, G-ACPY, disappeared shortly after leaving St Mary's with the loss of Captain W.D. Anderson and his five passengers. The service was suspended whilst an Inquiry was set up, which concluded that the aircraft had been shot down by an enemy aircraft. Normal services were resumed on 27th October but eight days later the Air Ministry suspended flights and the ban was not lifted until January 12th 1942.

In June 1945 scheduled services recommenced and by February 1947 Great Western & Southern Air Services had been taken over by British European Airways. At the time of writing Land's End Aerodrome, as it is still described in publicity leaflets, is still operating very regular Skybus services to St Mary's – flight duration 15 minutes. In fact the small airfield remains little changed over the years.

Okehampton

About 1½ miles to the north-west of Okehampton in Devon and along the A386 road was a grassed landing ground known as Folly Gate. During the summer months of the 1930s this rudimentary field was used by various detachments of Army Co-operation units engaged with the Army artillery practice camps situated on nearby Dartmoor.

With the advent of war very little changed; although in the summer of 1940 RAF aircraft – a detachment of Lysander IIs of No 16 squadron – arrived from Teversham (better known as Cambridge). The Lysanders operated from Okehampton from 9th August until late September, when they moved away to Roborough, under which chapter the squadron has been fully noted. They were replaced by another Lysander squadron, No 225, which had also used Roborough. No 225, under the command of Wing Commander R.J. Burrough, would remain at Okehampton until late November.

In May 1941 the small airfield became a satellite for Weston Zoyland near Bridgewater, which since the previous September had become an important airfield for army co-operation squadrons, operating closely with the Army's Western Command. Okehampton was used by a number of aircraft involved in the various Army exercises in the area. However, in March 1942 No 73 Maintenance Unit was formed at the airfield, under No 43 Group of Maintenance Command, which had come into being in April 1938. Most MUs were provided with airfield facilities for the receipt of new aircraft from the manufacturers which the Unit would inspect and test before delivery to squadrons. However, the Units' main task was the storage and supply of aircraft spares, as well as the installation of special equipment not fitted at the factories.

No 73 MU would service most of the airfields in the South-West, although there was another in the area – No 67 at Taunton. By December 1944 No 73 MU was under the control of No 57 Wing (Southern) based at Milton, and known as an 'Equipment Park'. In the following July the MU was closed down, although it would be another three months before the site was finally vacated.

St Mary's

The first 'aerodrome', if it could be so described, at St Mary's on the Isles of Scilly was sited on the golf course, and it was here that the first Channel Air Ferries service arrived on 15th September 1937. By July 1939 a 'proper' airfield had been fashioned on a sloping site at High Cross about a mile or so to the east of Hugh Town. The new airfield was officially opened on 16th August 1939 and became the terminal for Great Western & Southern Airlines service from Land's End.

It must have surprised the local residents when six black Hurricane Is of No 87 (United Provinces) squadron landed at the small airfield in the early evening of 19th May 1941. This Hurricane squadron had fought during the Battle of Britain mainly from Exeter and Bibury, but had latterly been engaged on night-operations from Charmy Down near Bath. Indeed, before the Flight had been detached to St Mary's its pilots had practised landings on a prescribed landing strip at their home airfield – the main grassed landing run at St Mary's was no longer than 1,350 feet! Since December the squadron had been commanded by Squadron Leader Ian R. 'Widge' Gleed, DFC, who had served with No 87 since its days in France back in May 1940. Also serving with the Flight was Flying Officer Roland P. Beaumont, an 'exceptional fighter pilot' who would later command a Tempest Wing and destroy at least 26 V1 rockets.

The facilities at the airfield were very basic, the ground crews lived in tents at the south side where the Hurricanes were dispersed, whereas the pilots were billeted out at Hugh Town. Within an hour or so of their arrival two Hurricanes, one flown by the CO and the other by Pilot Officer I.J. Badger, were scrambled to intercept an enemy aircraft; a Arado Ar 196 floatplane was located and shot down by Pilot Officer Badger. Five days later Squadron Leader Gleed and his wingman accounted for a Dornier 18 flying boat and a Junkers 88 was probably

257

destroyed by the CO on the 28th of the month. At the end of May the Hurricanes returned to Charmy Down where the squadron began to be equipped with Hurricane IICs.

In the middle of June (16th) the detachment of Hurricanes returned to St Mary's but it would not be until 18th July that the pilots added to their score – a Heinkel 111. Two Junkers 88s were destroyed in August, and on 21st October a Me 110 was shot down. The Luftwaffe's activity tailed off during the winter and the pilots were employed on army co-operation exercises. Their Hurricanes had now been fitted with long-range fuel tanks, which greatly extended the pilots' patrol area. Both Gleed and Beaumont had left the squadron by the end of November; sadly Gleed, as a Wing Commander, went missing in action in April 1943 whilst serving in Tunisia.

Although the squadron, now commanded by Squadron Leader Dennis S. Smallwood, was based at Colerne, the Hurricane detachment remained at St Mary's until 14th March 1943 when it was formed into No 1449 Flight. Now that the detachment had been placed on a more permanent footing, improvements were made to the airfield, such as the construction of a wooden control tower and the erection of a Blister hangar along with a number of Nissen huts. The main landing run was extended and steel meshing laid down.

The Flight continued regular patrols of the seas around the Isles, but

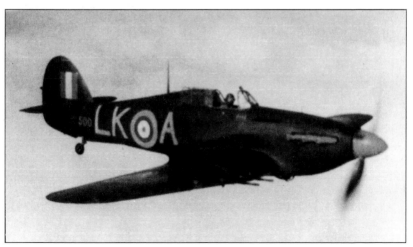

Squadron Leader Dennis Smallwood, CO of No 87 squadron in his Hurricane II, May 1942. (RAF Museum)

often they found themselves acting as escorts to air-sea rescue aircraft, especially the slow and lumbering Walruses, as well as shepherding the occasional damaged bomber back to the mainland. In February (23rd) a Liberator of No 247 squadron from St Eval had been heavily damaged in action and its pilot, Flying Officer T.G. Dixon attempted a crash-landing on the small airfield. Tragically he was killed but his crew of seven, along with a passenger, survived.

As D-Day approached the Flight had ten Hurricanes on complement though only seven pilots, and it was commanded by Flight Lieutenant C.E.O. Hamilton-Williams. Most of the Hurricanes were Mark IIs but two were Canadian-built designated Mark XIIs and one surviving but rather old Mark I. During the evening of 5th June six aircraft in pairs patrolled the coast from Land's End around to Dartmouth, and on D-Day all the pilots were patrolling from 1125 hours to 2100 hours with some urgent scrambles thrown in but on each occasion the aircraft were 'friendly'. Two pilots were called upon to give air support to a flotilla of Naval destroyers. Only one aircraft was lost throughout June, and that was to a flying accident on the 19th.

By August much of the action had moved further east and the *raison d'être* for the Flight no longer existed; the final sorties were flown from St Mary's on 29th August and on 17th September No 1449 Flight was disbanded. The modernised airport at St Mary's still continues its daily services to the mainland, both to Land's End and Newquay.

20

CIVILIANS AT WAR

September 3rd 1939 – a bright and sunny Sunday morning but millions of people were indoors and clustered around their wireless sets to await with some trepidation what the BBC described as 'an announcement of national importance'. Few that heard the inevitable but nevertheless dread news that 'consequently this country is at war with Germany', would have expected, or even believed, that five years later the conflict would be still raging, death from the skies remaining a constant fear, and that countless and irksome wartime restrictions would be still in force. Indeed when an official statement was released on 10th September that the Government was preparing for a war lasting 'three years or more', most people dismissed it as 'official scaremongering', convinced that the war would be over in less than a year.

The 'People's War', as it became known, touched the lives of every person in the country irrespective of their age or where they lived. Early in 1939 every household in the country had been issued with the National Service Handbook, which gave people details of what they could contribute in a crisis – demolition parties, decontamination squads, driving ambulances, nursing help, fire watching or even helping in the provision of food and drinks. During that last peacetime summer the public was made aware that the country was inexorably being placed on a war footing. Air Raid Precautions had been put in place, sirens erected, public air raid shelters appeared in streets and parks, ARP warden and First Aid posts along with static water tanks had been placed in suburban streets, the universally detested gas masks had been issued and the ubiquitous sandbag barricades emerged around buildings. In late August the passing of the Emergency Powers (Defence) Act, which gave the Government wide and almost draconian powers over the country and its people, along with the mobilisation of the Armed Forces, presaged that war was very imminent.

But perhaps the most ominous sign of the impending conflict was the mass evacuation of mothers and children from London and other major cities, which was set in motion on 1st September. The sight of thousands upon thousands of children with name tags and carrying their gas masks and few treasured possessions in bags, produced some of the most poignant images of the war. Most towns and villages in Cornwall and Devon received their share of evacuees, which for many of the children from poorer city areas was their first experience of the countryside. By the end of September over 82,000 had arrived in Devon, mostly privately rather than officially, whereas Cornwall had received only 3% of the numbers it had been told to expect at that time. However, many more would move into the area during the summer of 1940, when it was estimated that some 20,000 had arrived in Cornwall. The evacuation would have a considerable effect on the two counties; Dartmouth's population suddenly increased by almost 16%. A number of private schools moved *en bloc* into the area, as did several companies based in London, notably the Prudential Assurance Co Ltd to Torquay and Gaumont British News to Crediton.

In late September the National Register was established, which enabled the Government to issue National Identity Cards to every person (including children) – buff coloured with a personal number of six or seven digits. The Card had to be carried at all times and produced on demand to anybody 'in authority'. These would be closely followed by ration books, the two documents becoming the most important in wartime Britain. Petrol rationing was introduced, though in fact this affected only 10% of the population – such was the low level of car ownership in 1939. The infamous blackout regulations were strictly enforced, at times by over-zealous ARP wardens on their regular nightly 'lights patrols'; 'Put that light out' became an early wartime catch phrase! There were many instances of fines of £2 being imposed on those people who deliberately flouted or ignored the regulations. It was reported that the Chief Constable of Plymouth flew over the city in a RAF Sunderland to judge how effective the blackout was! In the first month of operation there was a 100% increase in road accidents compared with the previous year, and the majority of people considered blackout restrictions to be the most annoying wartime measure, worse even than food rationing.

The first War Budget was presented on 27th September. It brought an 'unprecedented level' of income tax at 7s 6d in £1 with increases in the duties on beer, wine, spirits, tobacco and sugar along with a special excess profits tax of 60%. This was merely the start of quite exorbitant levels of wartime taxation, which were endured rather stoically because 'After all this war must be paid for'!

However, relatively quickly the civilian population had 'slipped very easily into war habits', at least according to one wartime diarist. This almost imperturbable acceptance of a vastly changed world was helped by what had become known as the 'Phoney' or 'Bore' war; the forecasted heavy aerial attacks had not materialised and there appeared an almost total lack of military action. Places of entertainment that had closed immediately on the outbreak of war now reopened, and cinemas especially would be well-attended throughout the war years despite the air raids.

The winter of 1939/40 would test the resolve and fortitude of the civilian population to the full. It proved to be the most severe since 1881 with week upon week of hard frosts and heavy snowfalls. Coal was in very short supply due to the weather conditions and food rationing, which had been first introduced in November, was greatly extended in early January. Furthermore a whole range of everyday goods had suddenly become scarce and endless queuing had become a normal and necessary feature of daily life; the cynics would say 'if you see a queue join it'! The uncertainty of what the future held for families and loved ones only added to the strain and misery suffered during the harsh winter; most wanted 'the war to begin and get it over with'. In retrospect many claimed that this first wartime winter was the worst period of the war.

Largely because of the extreme weather, the blackout and severely restricted bus and train services, the BBC became the country's chief solace during the long and dark winter nights; three households in four possessed a wireless set. The BBC's news bulletins had quickly become essential and compulsive listening, as they would throughout the war, with the newsreaders – Alvar Lidell, Frank Phillips, Stuart Hibberd *et al* becoming familiar and well-loved voices. However, it was the comedy shows such as *Hi, Gang!*, *Band Waggon*, and *It's That Man Again* (later *ITMA*) that became the nation's favourites; they brought humour into the drab and dreary wartime years. In 1942 16 million listened to

ITMA's fifth series; one of the most popular members of the cast was Jack Train, who had been born in Plymouth, with his famous characters *Funf the spy* and *Colonel Chinstrap*. It was said that '*ITMA* sparkled through the life of the country like bubbles through soda water.'

In late January (30th) the people of Plymouth turned out in great numbers to welcome back HMS *Ajax* from the South Atlantic after the successful battle with the German battlecruiser *Admiral Graf Spee* in the previous December – the first victory of the war to bring a modicum of cheer in an otherwise dismal and bleak time. Sixteen days later another vessel of the victorious Naval squadron, the battered HMS *Exeter*, arrived at Plymouth to an equally royal welcome and its crew was given a civic reception. Winston Churchill, in his official capacity as First Lord of the Admiralty, was part of the welcoming committee, the first of his several wartime visits to Plymouth.

When Easter came at the end of March, people flocked to the coastal resorts almost as if they had a premonition that this would be their last real holiday break of the war. Visitors returned once again to Devon and Cornwall almost as if there was no war, 'Cornish Riviera tours' were advertised as were 'Daily Marine excursions'; indeed even as late as September the Grand Hotel at Torquay was being recommended as a 'Sanctuary Hotel' where 'the drone of an aero engine is rare and sirens even more infrequent', and the Queen's Hotel, Penzance was the place for 'a sense of security that cannot be beaten'! One wartime diarist recalled a holiday spent at Babbacombe during the height of the London blitz. She 'arrived complete with tin hat and gas mask and I felt so stupid because there it was all so peaceful and beautiful . . . It was another world . . .' However, all too soon the peace and tranquillity of this corner of England would change with a vengeance.

The invasion of Belgium and Holland on 10th May brought the 'Strange War', as Neville Chamberlain, the Prime Minister called it, to an abrupt end. The threat of invasion was now a very real and sombre probability. As a result of the ill-fated Norwegian campaign Chamberlain lost a vote of confidence in the House of Commons and was forced to resign. He was terminally ill and died in November. The formation of an all-party National Government under Winston Churchill only further stressed the perilous and vulnerable state of the country. The arrival at the helm of this inspiring and charismatic war leader proved to be a matter of 'the hour had brought forth the man'. Churchill had the innate ability to greatly inspire the British people whatever their political persuasion. His stirring and unforgettable words during the darkest days and greatest danger seemed to express the indomitable spirit and deep feelings of the British people. Wherever he travelled he was universally feted and cheered. Throughout the coming years no less than 78% of the public approved his conduct of the war. One lady later recalled, 'It was Churchill who dragged us through. That voice of his. Still gives me a thrill all those years later when I hear it. He held us together and bluffed our way through.'

The deep concern felt in the country was fuelled by the issue to every household of *Rules for Civilians in Case of Invasion*. The pamphlet gave instructions to 'stay indoors . . . hide maps, food, petrol and bicycles . . .' Road signposts in country areas disappeared, as did the names on railway stations, and maps and guides were removed from shops. Strange constructions began to appear in the countryside and towns, anti-tank traps, pill boxes, and concrete road blocks, with the coasts designated as Defence Areas with a variety of defensive measures put in place, such as 'dragon's teeth', barbed wire and girder obstacles, and access to these areas and beaches was severely restricted. From June church bells were silenced and would only be rung again as a signal of an enemy invasion. Each town and village appointed its own Invasion Committee and established a designated 'inner keep' where soldiers and the Home Guard would make a last stand. Also reserve stocks of food – tea, corned beef, tinned soup, sugar, margarine, and biscuits – were collected, to be used only in a grave emergency; mostly they were stored in the church or vicarage. These Invasion Committees were not finally disbanded until 1944.

The extreme gravity of the country's situation was heightened by the broadcast on the evening of May 14th by Antony Eden, the newly appointed Secretary of State for War, asking for 'large numbers of men in Great Britain who are British subjects between the ages of fifteen and sixty-five, to come forward and offer their services.' Their principal task would be to oppose the enemy's airborne troops as they landed. They would not be paid, but they would receive a uniform and arms (eventually!) and they would be required to serve a minimum of ten hours a week. The Government hoped to raise a force of 150,000 men, but within a fortnight 400,000 had enrolled; at Tavistock 135 men had enlisted including a 79 year old Boer War veteran. Within six weeks the number of volunteers that had come forward was close to one million. The force was originally known as the Local Defence Volunteers, and at first they received little more than their LDV armbands – the initials were jokingly said to be short for 'Look, Duck and Vanish'! It was not

Bampton Home Guard on the march. (via Joyce Weston)

until late July that they were given their more familiar name – The Home Guard – which Churchill had suggested back in October 1939.

Almost every town and village would have either its own battalion or platoon. By October 1944 there were 25 battalions in Devon, four of them in and around Plymouth. The Home Guard took their duties very seriously. They manned road-blocks, patrolled their territory and inspected identity cards of persons moving during the hours of darkness. Contrary to the comic images created by *Dad's Army*, the Home Guard became quite a professional force, with many manning anti-aircraft batteries as well as undertaking regular army duties later in the war. During 1943 there were ceremonial parades held throughout the country to commemorate its third anniversary, at Barnstaple over 1,300 men paraded. One of the reasons for these celebrations was that a lowering of morale within the Home Guard was causing some official concern. During this year 'women auxiliaries', as they were known, were allowed to join the Home Guard. They were not armed or given uniforms but were provided with an identification badge. Although by April 1944 they numbered only 28,000 most had already been working unofficially with the Home Guard. In a fascinating book *Britain's Home Guard* by John Brophy published in 1946, there are a number of paintings of Guardsmen by Eric Kennington, the famous war artist; one portrays 'Sergeant Bluett, Cornwall Home Guard' with St Michael's

Mount in the background. Looking at the various portraits one can believe the American lady, who famously declared, 'The Home Guard has dignity.'

The fall of France in June 1940 effectively brought Devon and Cornwall well and truly into the 'War Zone'. From the capture of Paris on the 15th of the month the ports and harbours along the South-West coast became congested with vessels of all types and sizes bringing the remnants of the British Expeditionary Force back from ports in northern France. Plymouth, Newlyn, Brixham and Falmouth were particularly congested with vessels where, it was reported 'the exhausted troops were packed like herrings on their decks.' One resident of Falmouth recalled that 'from the shore you could not see the horizon, so many boats were parked in the bay; a sight that will probably never be seen again.' Also the large number of civilians seeking refuge in England was increased by those fleeing from the Channel Islands. Soon the whole area would be made aware that it was very much in the frontline

Exhausted troops arriving at Falmouth, June 1940. (RCPS via Peter Gilson)

within easy reach of the Luftwaffe's bases, which were now just across the English Channel.

On 5th July the Ministry of Home Security reported that there was 'spasmodic bombing over Devon and Cornwall'. Thus commenced the aerial bombardment of the two counties, which would continue for almost another four years. During this period relatively few places in the area escaped the Luftwaffe's attention and it is impossible to record all of the raids; on some 240 days/nights there were bombing incidents in the two counties. Plymouth and Exeter would suffer grievously with the heaviest damage and the greatest number of fatalities, but other towns such as Torquay, Falmouth, Teignmouth, Dartmouth, Camborne, Truro, Brixham, Exmouth, Salcombe, and Newlyn would also suffer night and day raids to a greater or lesser degree. Even Land's End was bombed in June 1941 – the most westerly bombing incident and fatality of the war; and Averton Gifford, a small village on the Avon, sustained considerable damage on 26th January 1943.

These air raids brought into action the full legions of Civil Defence workers – ARP wardens, rescue and demolition teams, auxiliary firemen, special policemen, first aid parties, nursing auxiliaries, ambulance drivers, fire watchers, telephonists, boy messengers etc, and of course the numerous volunteer services such as the WVS, the Red Cross and St John Ambulance. The majority of these Civil Defence workers would, after their night duties, return the following morning to their daytime work in factories, offices, shops, schools and canteens frequently without the benefit of much rest. During 1941 especially it was maintained that 'sleep became elevated to a position of national importance.'

During 1940 the ports of Falmouth and Plymouth especially attracted the Luftwaffe's attention. Indeed, for a short period Falmouth was considered to be the most bombed town in Britain. Its first raid came on 5th July followed ten days later by an attack on the docks when several vessels were heavily damaged and one was sunk. At this time it was reported that 'there is not a single public air raid shelter in the county [Cornwall]'! Plymouth's horrendous ordeal commenced on 6th July when the first civilian fatalities were recorded. On 29th December it suffered its heaviest raid so far with eleven people killed. However, the city's greatest trial was yet to come.

On 20th March 1941 HM The King and Queen Elizabeth visited Plymouth to inspect the heavy bomb damage and to talk to people who had been bombed out. Shortly after they had left the city the Luftwaffe struck with ferocity on successive nights. In these two nights 68,000

Civil Defence personnel at Barton Hall, Torquay. (via Mary Boon)

tons of incendiaries and over 580 tons of high explosive bombs were dropped. The centre of Plymouth was almost flattened and had become virtually 'a desert of dusty rubble'; the BBC News announced that 'Plymouth had been "Coventrated".' The cost in civilian lives amounted to 336 with 18,000 houses destroyed and some 30,000 made homeless. Five heavy raids in late April brought further devastation and loss of life, with Devonport being almost wiped out. A Mass-Observation team reported, 'The civil and domestic devastation exceeds anything seen elsewhere, both as regards concentration throughout the heart of the town, and as regards the random shattering of houses all over. The dislocation of everyday life also exceeds anything seen elsewhere, and an enormous burden is being placed on the spirits of the people.' On 2nd May Winston Churchill visited the stricken city and as he drove through the ruins he kept repeating, 'I've never seen the like.' He praised the fortitude of the people, saying, 'your houses are down, but your spirits are high.' Little did they know at the time but the worst of their nightmare was over. However, in 59 raids 1,172 civilians were killed in addition to the many servicemen and women also killed during the blitz.

The North Hill district of Plymouth: a scene of devastation. (via A. Brook)

Without doubt 1941 was the lowest ebb of the nation's fortunes. By the end of the year over 43,000 civilians had been killed (72% of the total wartime figure) with another 51,000 seriously injured. The 'Home Front', as the Government liked to call wartime Britain, was bearing the full brunt of the war so far. Food rationing had become more severe, eggs had all but disappeared to be replaced by powdered egg substitute and milk was rationed for the first time. Although bread was never rationed the white loaf was no more and in its place appeared the National Wheatmeal Loaf, which was universally detested and described as 'nasty, dirty, dank and coarse.' Income tax had risen to 10s in £1 and purchase tax (the forerunner of VAT) was introduced. Towards the end of the year a 'points system' was introduced for canned goods, and clothing and footwear could only be purchased with coupons. With such abject shortages of goods the black market flourished where scarce consumer goods, petrol and clothing coupons, sweets, cigarettes, and spirits could all be obtained but 'at a price'.

As the year came to a close, conscription for unmarried women between the ages of 20 and 30 years was introduced. The conscripts were given the choice of serving in any of the three female auxiliary armed services, civil defence or industry. Already thousands of women, both married and single, were filling jobs vacated by men serving in the forces, and by mid-1943 the number of women engaged in war work of some kind was in excess of three million. Most were engaged in the aircraft and munitions factories, others on trains and buses, many delivering post and milk, some were employed in shipyards and others as labourers in the construction of airfields. Perhaps the mass employment and independence of women can be seen as one of the most significant social changes brought about by the war years.

Since the outbreak of war women had taken up voluntary work and perhaps most notably in the Women's Voluntary Service. The WVS had been formed in 1938 by the Dowager Marchioness of Reading with the intention of encouraging women into the Civil Defence. These 'women in green', as they were more generally known from their grey-green tweed suits, made an immense and magnificent contribution to the Home Front throughout the war, often working in most trying circumstances. They assisted in the evacuation of children and families in 1939, aided victims of the air raids, ran the Queen's Messenger Convoy mobile canteens in bombed towns, operated reception and rest centres for servicemen, organised the distribution of clothing and other items to bombed families, and were engaged in the collection of salvage items. No task seemed beyond the capabilities of the 'women in green'.

For two such heavily agricultural counties as Devon and Cornwall perhaps the most conspicuous female war workers were the girls of the Women's Land Army with their distinctive uniform. The WLA had been revived by Lady Gertrude Denman in June 1939, who hitherto was best known to the public through her assocation with the Women's Institutes. By the outbreak of the war 17,000 women had volunteered, 1,000 of whom were ready to be employed but at the end of 1939 only 29 were employed on farms in Devon, although their number would increase greatly in the following years. One of the Training Centres in Devon was at Seale Hayne near Newton Abbot; in Cornwall, Bosahan, the home of Lord and Lady Seaton near Helford was used as a Training Centre, where they would receive about a month's training before being allocated to a farm.

The girls were drawn from all walks of life but mainly from industrial towns, having been enticed by the visions of 'a healthy and happy job' in some rural arcadia, as portrayed in all the publicity posters for the WLA. The reality was very different; the work was long, hard, exhausting and undertaken in all weathers. The wages were low and accommodation often inadequate; furthermore they had to earn the respect of a largely suspicious and deeply sceptical farming community, where there still existed a considerable amount of mutual distrust and ignorance between the town and the country. The WLA, at its peak in 1943, numbered over 87,000, some working in the Women's Timber Corps engaged in forestry work. The Land Army girls became an essential part of the wartime farming scene and made a most

WLA girls at harvesting time at a farm near Mount Barton, Devon.
(via M. Smith)

valuable contribution to the war effort. The WLA survived well after the war and was not disbanded until October 1950.

The grim austerity of the wartime years was reflected in regular salvage drives of books, rags, bones, jam jars, rubber, old aluminium pots and pans, glass, newspapers and scrap metal; 'Waste Not Want Not' and 'Make Do and Mend' became the guiding principles. Even kitchen waste was dutifully saved and ultimately fed to pigs. The various salvage drives were organised from street level upwards with schoolchildren being actively engaged on the collections. Perhaps the most famous salvage collection was the compulsory removal of iron railings from parks, public buildings and private houses to be melted down into scrap metal. Although this campaign engendered considerable debate and complaint, one writer remarked that 'the heart of Exmouth has been converted from a commonplace, ugly, town centre into one of distinctive attraction'!

One of the greatest success stories of the war on the 'Home Front' was the National Savings Movement, started back in November 1939 as the War Savings Scheme, which aimed to collect £475 million in a year. The National Savings Movement, which was run for the Government by Sir Robert Kindersley, went from strength to strength and proved to be an outright winner with National Savings groups established in every street, office, factory and school; such was its importance to the war effort that the BBC News reported the total weekly contributions. Despite the heavy and penal rates of taxation it was estimated that at least 25% of the average weekly income was given up to savings compared with just 5% before the war. Perhaps this was helped by the relatively high wages paid in the aircraft and munitions factories and the sad lack of consumer goods available for purchase in the shops. Although the National Savings campaign spent greater sums on advertising than the Ministry of Food!

The most dramatic and outstanding successes of the Savings Movement came with the special drives organised on a national basis throughout the war. From the Spitfire Fund in the summer of 1940 through War Weapons Week, Warship Week, Wings for Victory, Salute the Soldier and Thanksgiving Week. Every city, town and village took part in these drives with an agreed target figure based on the size of the population. The various Savings Weeks were usually accompanied by sports events, fancy dress competitions, fairs, concerts and military parades, which did help to brighten wartime life. The inevitable large barometers were located at some prominent position in the towns and villages to record the progress of the money collected towards the target. For instance the residents of Truro collected £1,335,000 in the five special weeks! Whereas Plymouth collected over £1½ million for Wings for Victory Week in 1943 and over £7 million in total. To try to put these figures into some context, Torrington collected £90,000 in Wings for Victory Week, sufficient for two Spitfires and two Lancasters! It was later reported that in one year alone (1944–5) the war cost the country £4.8 billion, which just illustrates how important the National Savings Movement was.

Since the outbreak of war the civilian population had been constantly exhorted to 'Dig for Victory', and to turn their gardens over to the production of vegetables. Furthermore all available land was acquired for allotments; the number increasing from 815,000 in 1939 to 1½ million in 1943. The poor beleaguered housewives were daily targeted in the press, on the radio and by posters and leaflets on 'Food Facts' and 'Food Hints' offering advice on eking out the food rations and how to improve their families' diets. They were told that they were 'fighting on the Kitchen Front'! All this advice flowed from the Ministry of Food with its nationwide network of local offices, under the command of its ebullient and enthusiastic Minister, Lord Woolton; the second most popular wartime politician after Winston Churchill, he even had a pie named after him!

The farming community was also under constant and continual pressure to increase food production. Financial incentives were offered to farmers to clear and drain land which hitherto had been unproductive. So successful was this policy that by 1944 more than 25% more land was being farmed in Devon and Cornwall than had been under the plough in 1939. Most market gardeners and flower growers in the area were restricted to a small quota of flowers, but by 1943 a complete ban was imposed on flower growing and they were compelled to turn their land over to the cultivation of potatoes and other vegetables.

In an attempt to ensure that all families had the opportunity of at least one cooked and nourishing main meal a day, the Government encouraged the establishment of Community Feeding Centres or 'British Restaurants' as they were called at Winston Churchill's insistence. They were non-profit making and run by local authorities, whereby good, wholesome and hot food could be obtained. Breakfast cost 4d and a three course mid-day meal 1s, a cup of tea cost an extra 1d! By 1943 there were British Restaurants in most towns – over 2,000 in number serving over 600,000 mid-day meals each day. By the end of the year Lord Woolton could proudly boast that the diet of the country was now better than it had ever been despite food rationing.

In 1942 it was Exeter that suffered severely at the hands of the Luftwaffe. The city was the first, on 23rd April, to be bombed in the 'Baedeker Raids', the enemy's reprisal bombing for the RAF's raids on Lubeck and Rostock. On two successive nights, 23rd/24th and 24th/25th April, Exeter was heavily bombed, and there was a short respite until 3rd/4th May when the city was again severely attacked. In just 1½

Exeter High Street after the Baedeker raids 1942. (via T. Verity)

hours 10,000 incendiaries and 75 tons of high explosives rained down. The devastation was complete, 30 acres of built-area was flattened, much of the medieval city was razed to the ground; 400 shops and 1,500 houses had been totally destroyed with another 18,000 damaged and 164 people killed.

During the year daylight raids were made mainly on coastal towns – Teignmouth, Exmouth, Brixham, Dartmouth, Salcombe, and Torquay. The latter town suffered 19 raids during the year and on 4th September 31 people were killed. In Cornwall, Falmouth, Bodmin, Helston, Camborne and Truro were bombed. Truro received its most severe raid on 6th August when the Royal Cornwall Infirmary suffered a direct hit and 14 people were killed. During the following year the so-called 'Tip and Run' raids by Fw 190s caused considerable alarm, damage and loss of life. On 10th January 18 people died at Teignmouth in one such attack, and Torquay suffered particularly on a sunny and warm Sunday afternoon, 30th May. In this sudden attack 45 died including 21 children and 3 teachers attending a Sunday school at a local church.

By the end of 1942 most of the population felt that 'we have turned the corner at long last'. According to the BBC News, Bomber Command was inflicting heavy damage on German targets nightly, and the first real success by land forces had been celebrated – El Alamein, the

Focke-Wulf 190: 'Tip and Run' raids by FW 190s caused damage and loss of life in coastal towns.

famous desert victory. The church bells had rung again in November to mark the victory but Churchill was cautious in his praise: 'This is not the end. It is not even the beginning of the end. But it is perhaps, the end of the beginning.' The country was now in its fourth year of war and it seemed like an eternity but quite possibly, at long last, there was a light at the end of very long tunnel; after all the 'Yanks' had arrived on the scene!

American servicemen first began to appear in the area during 1942, mostly airmen serving first at St Eval then Dunkeswell, Davidstow Moor, St Mawgan, Winkleigh, and later at Upottery and Exeter. However, it would be in the summer of the following year that the two counties would begin to resemble 'the 49th State of the Union' with a massive influx of American army and navy personnel. Their camps sited throughout the two counties were effectively 'Little Americas' where the American way of life had been transferred to the West Country – movies, hot dogs, doughnuts, baseball, candy bars, chewing gum *et al* – and many goods and foods that had long since disappeared from the shops began to filter out from these camps. The narrow lanes soon became congested with American staff cars, lorries and jeeps; no Americans ever seemed to walk any distance, nor indeed did they drive slowly! Most towns and villages in the area echoed to the sound of

American Naval airmen making friends at Dunkeswell.

(National Archives & Records)

American accents, in fact in Salcombe the residents were outnumbered by American servicemen. Ports and areas of coastline had virtually been taken over by the American forces. Perhaps the most famous example was the complete evacuation of 25 square miles of land at Slapton in Devon, which became the American Battle Training Area. The WVS undertook their biggest single task of the war in moving and rehousing some 3,000 local residents from the six parishes by 20th December 1943.

The two counties became a large training and preparation area for the coming invasion, with the US 29th Infantry Division based in Cornwall and 4th Infantry Division (known as the 'Ivy' boys from 'IV') largely in Devon. As D-Day approached the numbers seemed to increase if that were possible; it was estimated that over 217,000 moved into Cornwall alone in April 1944. The local pubs became favourite places of recreation for GIs and it was here that the clash of the two different cultures was most noticeable. Perhaps one contentious issue was the quantity of beer they consumed, which being in short supply led to a certain amount of friction, although the GIs would gladly turn to local cider, dubbing it 'Invasion juice'! There were few reported incidents with the locals, the most problems occurred between American white and coloured GIs – one in Truro in September 1943 resulted in a pitched battle with shots being fired and finally ending with court martials. However, the humour, politeness and generosity of most American servicemen melted any antipathy and resentment felt by the local people. The Americans' quite boundless benevolence to children and local hospitals became legendary and gained them immense respect especially over the Christmas of 1943. When thousands of GIs left from the ports along the southern coast, a huge vacuum was left and the area returned to some semblance of normality. Nevertheless there was still a large contingent of US servicemen remaining in the area, and it was not until 10th July 1945 that Major D.H. Black wrote to Viscount Astor, 'For nearly two years the City of Plymouth has been a gracious host to the US Army . . . Now however, we are shortly due to leave. The American Army will be with you no longer.'

The massive build-up of troops, vehicles, equipment and vessels in the West Country had raised fears amongst the local people that the area would suffer renewed attacks from the Luftwaffe. These fears proved largely unfounded as there were relatively few air raids during the period, although Plymouth suffered its final raid when on 30th April 27 people were killed. Torquay was bombed on 28/29th May and

Falmouth received its final raid the following night, when a petrol store and two hotels along the sea front were hit and a US serviceman was killed. This attack brought to an end the area's long ordeal of aerial bombardment.

During the autumn of 1944 life on the Home Front was becoming a little easier and gradually returning to some normality. Much to everybody's relief the infamous blackout restrictions were being partially lifted and goods slowly reappearing in shops. However, food rationing was still very present and would remain so well into the post-war years. On 1st November the Home Guard was stood down; it now numbered over 1.7 million. There was considerable dismay at this decision and one volunteer complained rather bitterly to *The Times* that 'we were to fade away, leaving no trace of our existence'. Final stand down parades were made throughout the country and in early December King George VI in a radio broadcast paid fulsome tribute to the Home Guard: 'You have given your service without thought of reward. You have earned in full measure your country's gratitude.' I am not aware of specific memorials to the Home Guard except one to Falmouth's 7th Battalion on Pennance Head to the south of Swanpool. But its lasting affectionate memorial is, of course, the BBC's *Dad's Army*.

Christmas 1944 was a time for modest celebration – extra food and sweet rations were allowed and poultry was in greater supply. The final victory in Europe seemed a long time in coming, but on Tuesday 8th May 1945 every street, hamlet, village, and town in the country celebrated VE Day. Once again, as they had done all those years ago the people crowded around their wireless sets to hear Winston Churchill broadcast to the Nation. Later in the evening HM The King addressed the Nation, as he had done on the first day of the war: 'let us remember those who have not come back . . . Then let us salute in proud gratitude the great host of the living who have brought us to victory. Armed or unarmed, men and women, you have fought, striven and endured to your utmost. Today we give thanks for our great deliverance.'

The 'People's War' had thus come to an end but at a devastating cost. Over 60,500 civilians killed, another 86,100 seriously injured, and well over 2 million people made homeless. The scars of this long conflict and ordeal were only too plain to see, especially in the battered ruins of towns and cities like Plymouth and Exeter. Since the dark days of the Second World War those visible scars have healed but the memories remain with those people who lived through it – sharp and vivid still despite the passage of more than half a century. It seems most

The Royal Air Force International Air Monument unveiled on Plymouth Hoe on Sunday 3rd September 1989.

appropriate that the people of the City of Plymouth who suffered so harshly from the war in the air, should have erected a splendid memorial – the Royal Air Force International Air Monument – dedicated to all the men and women who served in the Royal Air Force, the Commonwealth and Allied Air Forces. This fine Monument stands on The Hoe and was unveiled on 3rd September 1989 – the fiftieth anniversary of the outbreak of the Second World War.

BIBLIOGRAPHY

During my research I consulted various books, the more relevant are listed below with my grateful thanks to the authors.

Air Ministry, *The Battle of Britain*, H.M.S.O. 1941.

Ashworth, Chris, *Action Stations: No 5 Military Airfields of the South West*, PSL, 1982.

Ashworth, Chris, *RAF Coastal Command: 1936–1969*, PSL, 1992.

Bannerman, Kenneth P., *A Towering Control: The Story of British Airfields*, ISE, 1958.

Bowyer, Michael J.F., *Aircraft for the Many*, PSL, 1995.

Calder, Angus, *The People's War: Britain 1939–1945*, Pimlico, 1992.

Franks, Norman L. R., *Fighter Command, 1936–1968*, Patrick Stephens, 1992.

Franks, Norman L. R., *Conflict over the Bay*, Grub Street, 1999.

Hamlin, John F., *Peaceful Fields: Vol 1 – The South*, GMS Enterprises, 1996.

Hendrie, Andrew, *Short Sunderland in World War II*, Airlife, 1990.

H.M.S.O., *Coastal Command*, 1943.

H.M.S.O., *Fleet Air Arm*, 1943.

H.M.S.O., *Merchant Airmen*, 1946.

Jarrett, M.J.M and Stevens, B., *U.S. Navy Fleet Air Wing 7 and 479th Antisubmarine Group, USAAF. Dunkeswell 1943–1945*. Dunkeswell Memorial Museum, 1998.

London, Peter, *Aviation in Cornwall*, Air Britain Ltd., 1997.

Longmate, Norman, *How We Lived Then: A History of Everyday Life during WWII*, Hutchinson, 1971.

Munson, Kenneth, *Flying Boats & Seaplanes since 1910*. Blandford Press, 1971

Nesbit, Roy Conyers, *The Strike Wings: Special anti-shipping squadrons 1942–45*, H.M.S.O., 1995.

Niestle, Axel, *German U-boat losses during World War II*, Greenhill Books, 1998.

Ramsey, W. G. (Ed), *The Battle of Britain: Then and Now*, Battle of Britain Prints, 1980.

Rawlings, John, *Fighter Squadrons of the RAF and their Aircraft*, Crecy Books, 1993.

Rawlings, John, *Coastal Support & Special Squadrons of the RAF*, Jane's Publishing, 1982.

Richards, Denis & Sanders, H., *The Royal Air Force, 1939–45*, H.M.S.O., 1953.

Saunders, Keith A., *RAF St Mawgan*, Alan Sutton Publishing, 1995.

Schoenfeld, Max, *Stalking the U-Boat: USAAF Offensive Antisubmarine Operations in WWII*, Smithsonian Institution Press, 1995.

Smith, David J., *Britain's Military Airfields, 1939–45*, P.S.L., 1989.

Sturtivant, Roy & Ballance, Theo, *The Squadrons of the Fleet Air Arm*, Air Britain Pubs., 1994.

Teague, Dennis C., *Mount Batten: Flying Boat Base Plymouth 1913–1986*. Westway Publications, 1986.

Terraine, John., *The Right of the Line*, Hodder & Stoughton, 1985.

Turner, John Frayn, *VCs of the Air*, Harrap, 1986.

Wasley, Gerald, *Devon at War, 1939–45*, Devon Books, 1994.

Watkins, David, *RAF Chivenor*, Alan Sutton Publishing, 1995.

Whiting, Charles, *Britain under Fire: The Bombing of British Cities, 1940–45*, Pen & Sword Books, 1999.

Wynn, Kenneth G., *Men of the Battle of Britain*, Gliddon Books, 1989

Zamoyski, Adam, *The Forgotten Few: The Polish Air Force in the Second World War*, John Murray, 1995.

INDEX

SQUADRONS

771   45
774   229, 232, 234
787   234, 235
792   229, 234, 236
794   237, 253, 254
800   42, 233
801   190, 202, 232
803   42, 43
804   43, 44
807   230–232
808   43, 231, 235
809   202, 233
810   190
812   202
814   42, 190, 191
815   44, 191
816   121, 159, 161, 202, 235
819   44, 47, 191, 234
820   241
824   45
825   46, 121
826   230
828   230
829   202, 229, 230
834   121, 131
836   233
837   233
838   133, 134
841   121
849   159, 160
850   159, 160
879   233
882   233
883   233
885   235
888   233

UNITS, GROUPS ETC

1 AACU   81, 84, 220
2 AACU   84, 138, 191, 195, 196, 199
1 ADRU   142
3 APG   197
16 FU   110
6 Coastal Patrol Flight   199
1404 (Met) Flight   205, 208
1417 Flight   70
1449 Flight   258–259
1457 (Turbinlite) Flight   178
1529 (Radio Aids Training) Flight   225
1602 Flight   86, 220
1603 Flight   86
1604 Flight   86, 220
1618 Flight   86
1623 Flight   196
1697 Flight ADLS   134, 157
GRU   113
3 GTS   124, 125
73 MU   256–257
Norwegian FTS   248–249
1 OADU   167, 175, 219
3 OTU   68–69
5 OTU   69, 74
10 OTU   90, 206, 208, 209
PRU   202, 208

USAAF & US NAVY

479th Antisubmarine Gp   99, 100, 209, 212
480th Antisubmarine Gp   98, 208
44th BG   87, 88, 90, 170
92nd BG   168, 170
93rd BG   87, 88, 90, 169, 170, 208
97th BG   180
381st BG   181
389th BG   170
360th FG   88
4th FS   101
6th FS   100
19th FS   101
22nd FS   101
336th Pursuit Sq   63
8th Recon. Weather Sq   211, 222
439th TCG   238–241
440th TCG   123–124
VB-103   102–104, 110, 210
VB-105   102, 210
VB-107   242
VB-110   102, 103, 106, 107, 210
VB-112   242
VB-114   107